BALTIMORE
& THE CHESAPEAKE BAY
ALIVE!

Barbara Radcliffe Rogers
& Stillman Rogers

HUNTER

Hunter Publishing, Inc.
130 Campus Drive
Edison, NJ 08818-7816
☎ 732-225-1900 / 800-255-0343 / Fax 732-417-1744
Web site: www.hunterpublishing.com
E-mail: hunterp@bellsouth.net

IN CANADA
Ulysses Travel Publications
4176 Saint-Denis
Montreal, Québec H2W 2M5 Canada
☎ 514-843-9882, Ext. 2232 / Fax 514-843-9448

IN THE UK
Windsor Books International
The Boundary, Wheatley Road
Garsington, Oxford OX44 9EJ England
☎ 01865-361122 / Fax 01865-361133

ISBN 1-58843-120-7

Index by Elite Indexing Services

4 3 2 1

About the Authors

Stillman (Tim) and Barbara Rogers have lived and played in various parts of the Chesapeake Bay area and never tire of the contrasts between Baltimore, Annapolis and the Eastern Shore. In addition to *Baltimore & The Chesapeake Bay Alive*, they are the authors of more than two dozen other travel books. These range from *The Adventure Guide to Canada's Atlantic Provinces* to *Signpost Portugal* and *Exploring Europe by Boat,* as well as *The Adventure Guide to the Chesapeake Bay*. When they're not traveling or writing, you're likely to find them paddling their kayaks in a tidal estuary.

About the Alive Guides

Reliable, detailed and personally researched by knowledgeable authors, the *Alive!* series was founded by Harriet and Arnold Greenberg.

This accomplished travel-writing team also operates a renowned bookstore, **The Complete Traveller**, at 199 Madison Avenue in New York City.

We Love to Get Mail

This book has been carefully researched to bring you current, accurate information. But no place is unchanging. We welcome your comments for future editions. Please write us at: *Alive Guides*, c/o Hunter Publishing, 130 Campus Drive, Edison, NJ 08818, or e-mail your comments to hunterp@bellsouth.net. Due to the volume of mail we receive, we regret that we cannot personally reply to each letter or message, but your comments are greatly appreciated and will be read.

Acknowledgments

For their help and encouragement in writing this book, we thank all the patient people throughout the cities and the Eastern Shore who took time to answer our persistent questions and sent us off with directions to their favorite places. We especially thank Connie Yingling, Anne Mannix and Mindy Bianca, whose company always makes our travels more fun and whose detailed knowledge of the area invariably leads us to places we'd never have found without them. Our appreciation also to Nancy Hinds, Larry Noto, Julie Horner, Sandy Turner, Kathy MacGruder, Bethany Lantham, Terry Nyquist, Anedra Wiseman and Beth Rhoades for smoothing the road before us.

For their help with the actual writing, a big thank-you to food-writer Juliette Rogers for many of the Baltimore restaurant reviews and to Lura Rogers for the inside scoop on the city's shopping and nightlife. Both also added their perspectives on the city's many offbeat museums.

We also appreciate the advice and help of our family, which spreads all over the Baltimore-Annapolis area: Shirley and Charles Radcliffe, Suzanne and Jeff Wilhoit, Carol Derbis, Debbie and Aiden Derbis, Janelle and Jay Derbis.

Finally, our appreciation to our long-suffering editor, Lissa Dailey, who has been flexible in the face of computer failures and patient with our occasional crankiness, has saved us from our inability to read our own scribbled travel notes correctly, and has shuffled our words about in such a way as to make us sound literate.

www.hunterpublishing.com

Hunter's full range of travel guides to all corners of the globe is featured on our exciting Web site. You'll find guidebooks to suit every type of traveler, no matter what their budget, lifestyle, or idea of fun. Full descriptions are given for each book, along with reviewers' comments and a cover image. Books may be purchased on-line using a credit card via our secure transaction system. All online orders receive a 20% discount.

Alive! guides featured include: *Antigua, Barbuda, St. Kitts & Nevis; Aruba, Bonaire & Curaçao; Bermuda; Jamaica; Buenos Aires & The Best of Argentina; Venezuela; The Cayman Islands; Cancún & Cozumel; St. Martin & St. Barts; Nassau & The Best of The Bahamas*; *Martinique, Guadeloupe, Dominica & St. Lucia; The Catskills*; *Dallas & Fort Worth*; *Miami & The Florida Keys*; and *Atlanta*.

Check out our *Adventure Guides*, a series aimed at the independent traveler who enjoys outdoor activities (rafting, hiking, biking, skiing, canoeing, etc.). All books in this signature series cover places to stay and eat, sightseeing, in-town attractions, transportation and more!

Hunter's *Romantic Weekends* series offers myriad things to do for couples of all ages and lifestyles. Quaint places to stay and restaurants where the ambiance will take your breath away are included, along with fun activities that you and your partner will remember forever.

Contents

Maps

Dedication

To Dierdre and Tom, and to Cameron, who protects us from monsters, wherever we travel.

Introduction

B*altimore Alive!* While we did not choose the title for this book – it's part of a series that the publisher has named – it would be hard to find an adjective that more accurately describes Baltimore and neighboring Annapolis. Each revolves around its harbor, and each of these waterfronts throbs with activity and life. There's an excitement in the air that almost equals the lively atmosphere that must have characterized them at the pinnacle of the Golden Age of Sail. Their docks and piers have a level of electricity that still makes little boys (and some very big ones, too) want to run away to sea.

Tall masts of historic ships and working vessels sway in the tide. Little boats bob and putt between the larger ones – water taxis, dinghies, Sunfish, even kayaks and paddleboats add to the bright, moving kaleidoscope on the water. Many of the historic boats are open for tours, and you can almost hear the whispers of the ghosts that inhabit them – slaves rescued from the dank holds of slaveships by the USS *Constellation*, and World War II sailors writing their sweethearts from cramped bunks on the *Torsk*.

These are cities of the sea, and the sea influenced trade, commerce, social life and populations. Annapolis was settled by those seeking religious freedom from the narrow confines of Virginia's established church, and its early connection with the sea and with the US Naval Academy have made it a favorite place for people connected with the US Navy to live.

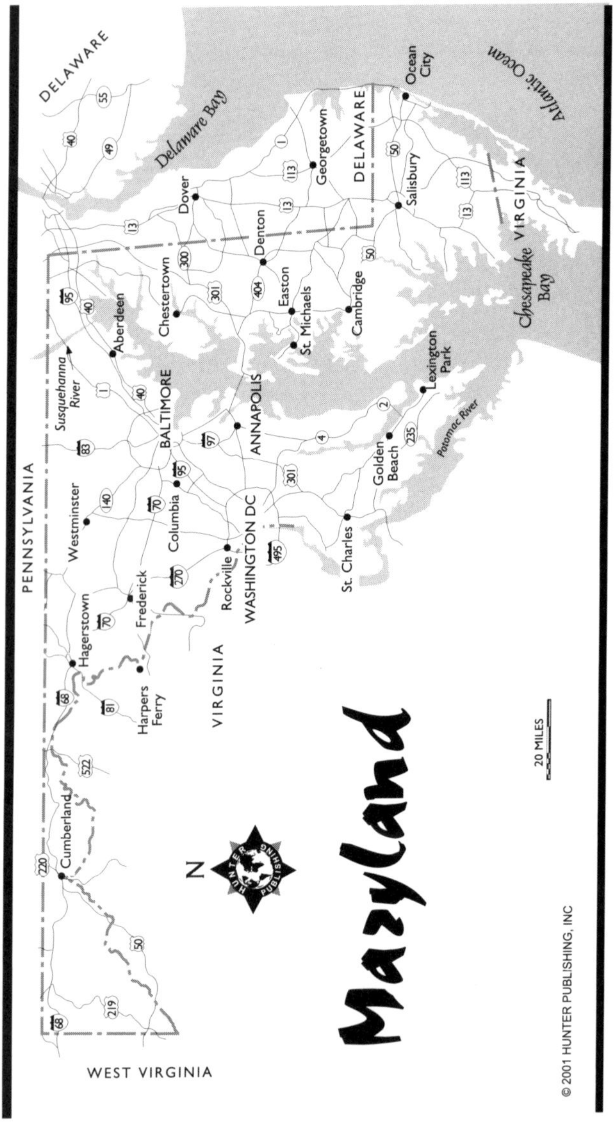
Maryland
PENNSYLVANIA
DELAWARE
WEST VIRGINIA
VIRGINIA
Delaware Bay
Atlantic Ocean
Chesapeake Bay
Susquehanna River
Potomac River
Cumberland
Hagerstown
Harpers Ferry
Frederick
Westminster
Rockville
Columbia
WASHINGTON DC
BALTIMORE
ANNAPOLIS
Aberdeen
Chestertown
Dover
Denton
Easton
St. Michaels
Cambridge
Georgetown
Salisbury
Ocean City
Lexington Park
Golden Beach
St. Charles
20 MILES
© 2001 HUNTER PUBLISHING, INC

Those combined influences of Old Liners and *Anchors Aweigh* still influence the city.

History

You can't escape it here no matter how hard you try. Great names and events in Colonial America, the War of 1812, the Civil War, the Industrial Revolution, the Civil Rights movement, and other landmark events just keep popping up. It's not that Baltimoreans are name-droppers, it's just that when a local lawyer who was stuck on an enemy war ship during the bombardment of his hometown writes about seeing his flag still flying at dawn, and the nation adopts his words as its national anthem, someone is bound to mention it.

Annapolis is like that, too. John Paul Jones lies beneath the chapel at the Naval Academy, and all Maryland's signers of the Declaration of Independence were local boys. George Washington gave up his commission in the Army to enter politics at the State House, which is the oldest still in use in the United States.

Things happened here and you're bound to hear about them. Maryland was one of the original 13 colonies, settled in the 1600s. The first settlers came on board two ships, the *Ark* and the *Dove*, which sailed up the Potomac River. They established the first capital at St. Mary's City, now under excavation and reconstruction. You can see how they lived by visiting the living history village that grows on the site as the work continues to rebuild the first capital.

Annapolis was settled by dissidents who felt hemmed in by Virginia's strict adherence to the Church of England, and it was an important early port. But it was Baltimore, with its well-protected harbor, that was destined to become the colony's – and later the state's – principal city and trade port. As long ago as the early 1700s, when nearly all transport was by ship, Baltimore Clippers sailed all over the world, and Baltimore grew into the bay's most important commercial and transportation hub. It became established as a distribution port for grain, tobacco and other goods grown and produced all over the region.

The Jones Falls River provided enough drop as it entered the city to power mills, and soon the grain was ground into flour in Baltimore before it was shipped. By 1729, Baltimore had become a customs port. Merchants built fine homes close to their workplaces in the busy harbor, and mill-owners, shipbuilders and tradesmen soon followed.

The Spoils of War

After the colonies declared independence, Baltimore ships were granted "letters of marque," licensing them as privateers who could seize British ships. Not only did this cut supplies to British forces, but captured cargoes could be sold at a profit. It was a useful and lucrative business for both the new country and its ship owners, and Baltimore was in the thick of it.

Baltimore was a prime target of the British during the War of 1812 because the British navy was still stinging from the attacks and seizures of so many of their ships by Baltimore privateers. At the battle at Fort McHenry, the British failed to take the city and the local lawyer who had been sent to negotiate the release of some prisoners watched the battle from the British ship on which he was detained. You can see his original copy of the poem, *The Star Spangled Banner*, in the Maryland Historical Society and you can visit the Baltimore house that was the shop of the seamstress who sewed the giant flag. Fort McHenry still stands on Locust Point, at the entrance to the Harbor.

THE OLD LINE STATE

Although no battles of the Revolution were fought in Maryland, its forces, under General Smallwood, fought with such bravery to hold their line in order to cover the retreat of George Washington and his troops after the Battle of Long Island that they earned the state its title of the Old Line State.

Gateway to the West

After the Revolution, Baltimore's forward-thinking leaders saw that shipping was only half the transportation picture. With settlement opening to the west, overland routes would become important, so they made Baltimore the terminus for the railroad that opened the west, tying the overland rail trade routes to the sea trade routes at the city's busy waterfront.

The B&O line connected the city to Chicago by the 1870s, and its trains headed west with imported goods and east with the products of the interior coal mines. From the port of Baltimore, ships carried coal to New England to power the mills of the Blackstone Valley and the growing Industrial Revolution.

Its position as a distribution center and the demand for food, clothing and supplies for the Civil War put Baltimore in the lead as America became industriallized. With a constant stream of immigrants as its labor force, the city prospered and grew into a major manufacturing center. Meanwhile, the Eastern Shore tilled its low, level fields and grew food to feed the region and to ship elsewhere. Its produce arrived by ship from across the bay and was shipped out fresh or preserved in the canneries of Canton.

Armies needed safe food, which led Baltimore to develop safe canning processes. By the end of the war canned food was cost-effective to manufacture, and people had begun to think of it as safe. More than 100 canneries soon lined the wharves of Canton, and beside them grew the factories to make cans and print labels.

BALTIMORE FIRSTS

Two Baltimore "firsts" illustrate its importance in the printing and food container industries: in 1883 the first **typesetting machine** in the world was used here, and in 1892 the first **bottle caps** were manufactured.

The Civil War saw Maryland in a unique position. It was a slave holding state, but it refused to secede with the Confederacy. Although it remained with the Union, Southern sympathy ran high and many men, especially those from Southern Maryland, where most of the plantations were based on slave labor, went to Virginia to enlist in the Confederate Army. Maryland was a battleground in the war – in the streets of Frederick and on the battlefields at Antietam and Monacacy. You can visit these, along with the Civil War sites at Harper's Ferry, just over the river in West Virginia.

The Roots of Ethnic Baltimore

Immigration boomed in the 1800s, and because Baltimore was second to New York as a port of entry, the city had a ready workforce of new arrivals. Their influence is still clear in this city of strong ethnic identity. In 1904 the Great Fire destroyed much of the downtown commercial district, but the city quickly rebuilt, modernizing as it went.

Both the Great Depression in the 1930s and the prosperity that followed World War II worked against Baltimore. The first left it without jobs, its low-paid immigrant workforce bearing the heaviest brunt of the hard times. Instead of recovering in the postwar boom, Baltimore neighborhoods emptied as their residents were once again employed and left the inner city for spacious modern homes in the suburbs. Downtown businesses had no more shoppers in the 1960s than they had in the middle of the Depression.

Re-creating Baltimore

But just as the vision of its prominent citizens had made possible Baltimore's 19th-century prosperity as a transportation hub, a far-sighted mayor and city government brought Baltimore back to life in the 1970s. It continues to thrive and grow, capitalizing on its history, its magnificent buildings (which had not been replaced with new ones because there was no money to do so) and its beautiful harbor.

The harbor was the first target for rehabilitation. Abandoned and run-down buildings were restored or replaced, deteriorating wharves gave way to a bright new waterfront. Buildings with architectural significance – including such workaday structures as pumping and power stations – became venues for museums, shopping and entertainment centers. Major architects designed the new buildings that would complete the waterfront, which was then turned into a floating museum of historic vessels. The new Baltimore they created is used as a prototype and model for revitalizing harbor cities all over the world.

Smaller Annapolis, meanwhile, without the problems of a large city, and with the state government and Naval Academy as its employment core, continued to enjoy modest success and growth. Like Baltimore, it retained its fine buildings, most from the Colonial era, which now provide its physical core and a great part of its attraction to visitors.

Climate

We've always considered charts of average temperatures to be largely useless. It serves the prospective traveler very little to read that the temperature averages 67° in May. No day may actually have been 67°, a figure which was arrived at by adding the highs (which might have reached 90° on a late May afternoon) to the lows (a chilly 39° with soaking rain) and dividing by the total number to get at a figure that represents neither. So we'll spare you the averages.

The climate of the Chesapeake Bay is generally mild and, as you can expect from any maritime area, fairly humid and interspersed with rain. It gets hot in the summer – highs of more than 100° have been recorded from June through September – but that doesn't prevent temperatures from dropping as low as -7° in January. But is either of these extremes common? No.

In general, December through March sees daytime highs in the 40s and 50s and nighttime lows in the high 20s and low 30s. From June through September you can expect daytime highs to average between 78° and 86°. Spring and fall daytime temperatures hover in the 60s and 70s, dropping to the 40s and 50s at night.

Rainfall, which is often of more concern to travelers (especially those with cameras) than the temperature, is pretty constant throughout the year, generally from three to four inches a month. That figure rises a little more in July and August, but the usual number of rainy days each month changes very little throughout the year, usually about 11, dropping to eight in September and October.

Planning Your Trip

The temperature outside is certainly one consideration in planning your visit to the region. Especially for those who live in the north, summers here can be brutal. Even close to the water, the intensity of a summer heatwave sometimes doesn't even break at night. Hotels, restaurants and just about all other buildings are air conditioned, but if your purpose is to enjoy the ambiance of the waterfront, you won't be spending much time indoors. And the museum ships are not air conditioned – which, of course, gives you a far more realistic view of what life was like on board.

The Changing Seasons

Winter can be cold and blustery, but not nearly so bitter as New York's or Boston's. Baltimore's waterfront on a crystal winter day is a simply stunning sight, with bright flags flying and the gold decoration on the *Constellation* glimmering in the sun and her hull reflected in the water. Skaters fill the rink across the harbor and snow sometimes blankets Fort McHenry's ramparts. Music, theater and entertainment seasons are in full swing, replacing the spontaneous outdoor concerts of summer evenings. Neighborhoods seem to cluster tighter, with more local events, and people linger longer over fine dinners in the local restaurants. Museums are less crowded, and special programs highlight their collections. Annapolis seems somehow more Colonial, especially at the Christmas season, when its historic homes and streets are beautifully decorated.

Spring and fall are ideal – the weather is nice, often quite warm, and water activities are usually still in full swing. These are colorful times of year, with flowering trees in bloom or fall foliage painting the neighborhood streets. They are good seasons for visiting the gardens and other outdoor activities that summer heat and winter chill discourage.

While life goes on year-round in these busy, vibrant cities, each season has its own attractions – and disadvantages. More is happening on the water in the summer, and since each is a water-born city that revolves around its docks, you would miss some of the charm and action if you came at another season.

What to Wear

Whenever you choose to travel in the area, you will find the people you meet there dressed casually, comfortably and sensibly. You will, of course, want to bring dressier clothes if you plan to eat in the top restaurants in Baltimore, although you will be perfectly welcome at most of them if you are dressed in casual clothes. In the summer, people visiting the Inner Harbor attractions usually wear shorts and comfortable walking shoes. Whatever time of year, it's a good idea to pack a small folding umbrella, and even in summer you will want a sweater or light jacket for breezy evenings or places that get a little over-enthusiastic with their air conditioning.

Choosing a Place to Stay

Despite the building boom in hotels around the harbor, lodging is still not plentiful in Baltimore. It pays to reserve well ahead, especially during prime travel seasons. The big hotels surround the harbor, and for good reason. That's where the action is and where the best views are, too.

Along with the big chain hotels, Baltimore has several smaller hotels and inns, as well as a few in-town B&Bs. The latter are mostly in Fells Point and Bolton Hill. Most lower-cost motels and hotels are close to the interstate highways and at the airport.

In Annapolis, lodgings also gather near the harbor, with several downtown hotels. Most of the B&Bs – and Annapolis has a number of these delightful places to stay – are in the historic neighborhood between the harbor and the Naval Academy, just where you want to be.

Accommodations Price Scale

Every book has its own way of avoiding the use of exact prices. Why? Because those may vary from week to week, let alone month to month. The cost of rooms may vary widely within a single hotel or inn. Deluxe rooms are more expensive, all rooms increase in cost during the busiest seasons. What we look at is the range where the bulk of the accommodations fall. We've kept the numbers round and easy to remember, so you won't have to keep flipping back to check. Prices reflect the cost of a standard double room for two people.

ACCOMMODATIONS PRICE SCALE	
Inexpensive	under $100
Moderate	$100-$200
Expensive	$201-$300
Deluxe	more than $300

Dining

As you might guess from the giant sections of the book devoted to restaurants, food tops our list on what makes travel – and life – worthwhile. We are happy to report that whatever you may have heard about dining in Baltimore, it has made vast improvements in the past few years. Some first-rate chefs have opened their own restaurants, and have quickly replaced the somewhat tired "old favorite" restaurants among people who love fine food.

Dining Price Scale

Prices vary widely in the Baltimore area, although in general dining here is not as expensive as it is in Washington, Boston or New York. As we did for lodging, we have used a range scale to indicate what you can expect to pay for an average entrée. In this day of computer-printed menus, a chef can take advantage of the market and change a menu's contents and prices nightly if she chooses. But the overall range of a restaurant's prices will remain consistent, and it is the range that we indicate.

Please bear in mind that a few entrées will always fall outside this range – lobster, filet mignon or other luxury dishes may be more expensive, just as pasta primavera may be less. We are looking at the vast majority of entrées offered on a typical menu. When some unusual circumstance warrants it – such as a tasting menu with several courses included in one price – we'll mention specific prices. Here's how we sort them:

DINING PRICE SCALE	
Inexpensive	Entrées are $10 or less
Moderate	Entrées are $11-$20
Expensive	Entrées are $21-$30

We Get Letters

One of the reasons people travel is to see new sights and enjoy new experiences that are different from those everyday activities at home. Change is the essence of travel, and is implicit in it. Which is a roundabout way of saying "don't blame us" if things aren't as they were when we were last there. Maybe the chef quit, or the owner moved and sold the cute B&B to someone who didn't care as much. Or, more likely, we missed a great place you really liked. We want to hear from you, especially if that great place is a restaurant or ice cream stand or bakery that serves something absolutely irresistible. We don't want to miss it again.

You can reach us via internet or real mail, through Hunter Publishing, at the address on the back of the title page.

What to Expect

Take a good attitude with you and you can expect to have a very good time in Baltimore and Annapolis (take a bad attitude and you can expect a bad time anywhere). The people are friendly, open, interesting and lively. They will answer your questions patiently and send you off in the right direction cheerfully. They will tell you where their favorite place for crab cakes is and they will tell you how to get there. Women will call you "Hon" whatever your age or sex. And if they were born there, they will probably call their city "Balmer."

Safety

Baltimore and Annapolis are much like cities their size anywhere else in the United States and Canada. Wise travelers treat all cities with respect and use common sense while visiting them.

Baltimore's Inner Harbor and the other neighborhoods where you will be going for sightseeing, restaurants and the arts are well lighted, busy and safe. Annapolis is smaller and its downtown area is also busy and quite safe in the evening.

Baltimore has some neighborhoods you probably won't ever see, and which you certainly don't want to be wandering around in at night. One of these is a few blocks north of Inner Harbor, which houses the weary remains of the city's once roaring burlesque and strip-joint area. Likewise, you might not want to walk beyond Little Italy on East Pratt Street, through the abandoned area of vacant and crumbling former public housing.

The same precautions apply here as anywhere: If you are carrying the crown jewels with you, put them in the hotel safe when you leave your room. Don't wander in dark streets at night where there are few other people. Take taxis at night to neighborhoods you don't know. Ask at your hotel if the place you are going is within safe walking distance before heading there after dark. Have a restaurant call you a taxi for the trip home if you are in doubt. Don't carry large amounts of cash. We all know the rules; remember them and you will have no trouble.

Getting Here

By Air

Between Baltimore and Washington DC, but much closer to Baltimore is **Baltimore-Washington International Airport**, coded BWI (☎ 410-859-7100), just 10 miles south of the Inner Harbor. It is served by most major airlines and is a hub for Southwest Airlines.

Airport Ground Transportation

Both **Amtrak** (☎ 800-872-7245) and **Maryland Area Rail Commuter**, commonly called **MARC** (☎ 800-325-RAIL), connect the airport with Baltimore's Penn Station, 20-minute ride. But it runs only on weekdays. A free shuttle bus connects the main terminal and the airport rail station.

Mass Transit Administration (MTA) bus #17 (☎ 410-539-5000) also connects downtown Baltimore and the airport. More expensive, but also more convenient if you are carrying much luggage, **BWI Airport Shuttle** (☎ 800-258-3826) and **Baltimore**

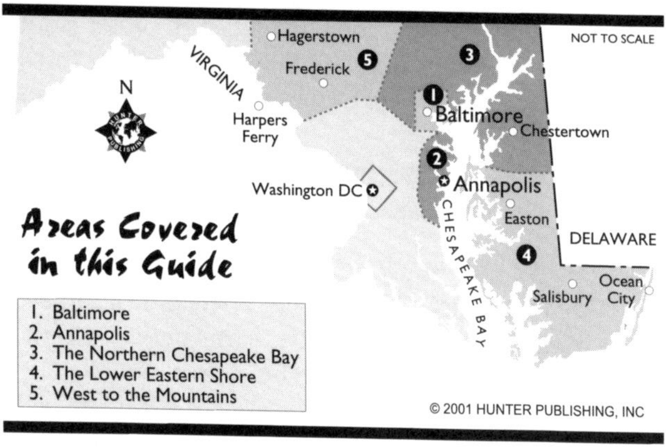

Airport Shuttle (☎ 410-821-5837) run between the Inner Harbor hotels and the airport.

See pages 39-40 for complete information on Baltimore's public transportation network.

By Car

Reach the Baltimore area by car from the north or south by **I-95**, which passes through the city to the east of its center. **I-83** enters the city from the north, **I-97** from the south and **I-70** from the west. The **Baltimore Beltway**, **I-695**, surrounds the city, with roads and avenues leading downtown from all directions, like spokes on a wheel. **Route 2** leads from Baltimore almost perfectly straight to Annapolis. **Route 295**, the Baltimore-Washington Parkway, connects the Baltimore Beltway with Washington's **Capital Beltway (I-495)**.

Prepare for some traffic backup at the Bay Bridge, eastbound on Friday evenings and westbound on Sunday evenings in the summer.

To reach the Eastern Shore from Baltimore, follow Route 2 to Annapolis and cross the curving **Bay Bridge**. It leads to Kent Island and on to the choice of Route 301 to the northern Eastern Shore or Route 50 south to Easton and St. Michaels and on to the Atlantic-side beaches of Ocean City and Assateague.

By Train

Amtrak (☎ 800-872-7245) connects Baltimore and BWI Airport to both New York and Washington DC, while **MARC** (☎ 800-325-RAIL) runs between Baltimore and Washington, a one-hour trip.

Festivals & Events

In Baltimore

January

Late in the month is the **Annual Harborplace Ice Carving Competition**, Harborplace Amphitheater; ☎ 800-HARBOR-1.

April

The **Baltimore Waterfront Festival**, featuring foods, boat rides, entertainment and other activities around the Inner Harbor, is held at the end of the month; ☎ 888-BALTIMORE.

July

The **July Fourth holiday** brings several days of events and activities, including a huge fireworks display at the Inner Harbor.

August

Early in the month, **AFRAM**, an African-American expo, is held in several places. In mid-month, the **Hispanic Festival** is held at Market Place, off Pratt Street, and the **German Festival** takes place at Carroll Park near the end of the month. Information on these three ethnic events can be obtained from the Baltimore Area Visitors Center, ☎ 410-837-4636; www.baltimore.org.

September

Early September brings the **Star Spangled Banner Weekend** at Fort McHenry, culminating in Saturday night fireworks; ☎ 410-962-4290.

In mid-month, enjoy the **Caribbean Festival**, held at Park Circle. In late September, the **Ukrainian Festival** is held at Patterson Park. For more information and exact dates for both of these events, contact the Baltimore Area Visitors Center, ☎ 410-837-4636; www.baltimore.org.

October

The **Fells Point Fun Festival** kicks off October with a giant block party featuring crafts, music and food; ☎ 410-675-6756.

November

The **Thanksgiving parade** features marching bands, floats, clowns and Santa Claus; ☎ 410-837-4636.

December

Early in the month brings **A Monumental Occasion**, the lighting of the Washington Monument, with street music and refreshments; ☎ 410-837-4636.

Also at the beginning of December, **Christmas with Choral Arts**, a program of music and readings, is held at the Basilica of the Assumption; ☎ 410-523-7070.

Mid-month offers **Merry Tuba Christmas**, with 200 tubas and euphoniums playing Christmas music at the Harborplace Amphitheater, ☎ 800-HARBOR-1; and the **Union Square Christmas Cookie Tour**, a neighborhood open house of two dozen decorated homes, ☎ 410-945-1497.

During the entire month, Baltimore is filled with holiday celebrations and displays, including a **Lighted Boat Parade** (☎ 800-HARBOR-1). The Baltimore Zoo has special holiday illuminations, called **Zoo Lights**, ☎ 410-837-4636. And at **Brookside**

Gardens, in Wheaton (see page 96), lighting displays fill the gardens.

In Annapolis

April

The **Annapolis Spring Boat Show** features sailboats and powerboats and boat-related activities, including fishing and water skiing; ☎ 410-268-8828, www.usboat.com.

May

The **Waterfront Arts Festival** highlights crafts, emphasizing maritime arts; ☎ 410-268-8828, www.usboat.com.

July

July 4th brings a parade, concert by the Naval Academy band, and fireworks on the waterfront; ☎ 410-263-1183.

August

The world's largest **crab feast**, with heaping trays of steamed crabs and crab cakes, is held at Memorial Stadium; ☎ 410-841-2841.

Running through October, the **Maryland Renaissance Festival** (☎ 410-266-7304 or 800-296-7304) fills the fairgrounds in Crownsville on weekends from late August through October with an entire town in medieval and Renaissance style. Continuous entertainment is offered on the streets and open-air stages, with everything from jousting and Shakespeare to medieval magic and human chess games. The atmosphere is that of an Old English market fair, with shops and booths selling handmade replicas of medieval and Renaissance crafts as well as an assortment of foods representing four centuries (see page 191 for more information).

September

Through November, **Naval Academy football games**; ☎ 800-US4-NAVY for tickets.

October

The **United States Sailboat Show** and the **United States Powerboat Show** are both held this month, offering two consecutive weekends of boatitude. Lodging is tight – actually, almost unavailable then, so book far in advance; ☎ 410-268-8828, www.usboat.com.

November

Christmas in Annapolis offers decorated homes and historic sites, a parade of lighted boats, house tours, and concerts; ☎ 410-268-8828.

December

On the second Sunday, **London Town and Gardens Holiday Tea and Greens Sale**; ☎ 410-222-1919.

On December 31, **First Night**, with hundreds of performers, concerts, theater and midnight fireworks; ☎ 410-280-0700.

On the Eastern Shore

May

The **Salisbury Festival** is held during the first weekend, when the entire town is abloom in dogwood and azalea; several of each are often featured in every dooryard.

Mid-May brings the **Maritime Arts Festival** at Chesapeake Bay Maritime Museum, St. Michaels, featuring decoys, ship models, maritime music, crafts, food; ☎ 410-745-2916.

September

During Labor Day weekend, the **Hard Crab Derby** is featured in Crisfield. Eat crabs in every form and style or bet on them as they race – well, in a manner of speaking; ☎ 410-968-2500, 800-782-3913.

November & December

Early November brings **Oysterfest** at the Chesapeake Bay Maritime Museum in St. Michaels, with cooking contests, kids' activities, boat rides and music; ☎ 410-745-2916.

Mid-month, the **Waterfowl Festival** happens in Easton; it's the premier wildlife art show in the US; ☎ 410-822-0065, http://eastonmd.org.

Throughout November and December, the **Ocean City Festival of Lights** features animated lighted figures that are viewed from a miniature train in Northside Park.

In the Western Region

February

During the last weekend of the month, **Linganore Winecellars** (see page 360) in Mount Airy lets visitors use their vines to make wreaths; ☎ 301-831-5889.

April

An **18th-century Market** on the last weekend of the month brings 100 top traders and craftsmen and an encampment of 1,300 people to Fort Frederick; ☎ 301-842-2155 (Fort Frederick State Park information and events).

May

The **Annual Frederick Craft Fair**, operated by National Crafts, Ltd., is held Monday-Wednesday during the third full week of May at Frederick Fairgrounds; ☎ 717-369-4810.

Re-enactors of the French and Indian War gather for the **Fort Frederick Muster** on the last weekend of the month; ☎ 301-842-2155.

June

In early June, Hagerstown is host to the **Western Maryland Blues Fest**, a Friday-through-Sunday event on the first weekend after Memorial Day. This annual event features some of the best Blues artists in the country. Venues are located throughout the city; some, including the Sunday "Blues Picnic," are free. For tickets and information call the Washington County Arts Council, ☎ 301-797-8782, or contact the Public Information Officer in Hagerstown, at ☎ 301-739-8577, ext. 116, www.blues-fest.com.

Also on the first weekend of the month is the **Frederick Festival of the Arts**, held in Carroll Creek Linear Park. The event includes art exhibits, hands-on programs and watersports for kids; ☎ 301-663-8687 or 800-999-3613.

July

Military Field Days are held in Fort Frederick in mid-month; ☎ 301-842-2155.

On the Fourth of July, the **Maryland Symphony Orchestra** plays at the Antietam National Battlefield. This is a free, "bring-a-picnic-and-blanket" event; it starts at 7:30 and is followed by fireworks (this event is of 15 years duration, and it draws a big crowd). Call the Washington County Arts Council, ☎ 301-791-3132, 41 South Potomac Street, Hagerstown, www.washcoartscouncil.org; or the Maryland Symphony Orchestra, ☎ 301-797-4000.

August

Hagerstown's German heritage is celebrated at the city's **Augustoberfest**, sponsored by the Maryland Symphony Orchestra and the Washington County Arts Council. There is German food, beer, and dancing along with the music. Ticket prices are $15 for the Friday concert, $10 for Saturday events, or $20 for both days; children under 12 are free. Contact the MSO, 13 South Potomac Street, Hagerstown, ☎ 301-797-4000, fax 301-797-2314; or the Washington County Arts Council.

October

The first weekend of the month brings the **In The Street Festival** to Frederick. The festival features a parade, street-corner concerts, games, kayaking demonstrations for kids, and other activities that fill several blocks of downtown Frederick; there is also a dance on the top floor of the city parking deck. ☎ 301-663-8687 or 800-999-3613.

Also held during the first weekend of the month is the **Maryland Mountain Festival** at Lynfield Farm, eight miles north of Frederick on US-15. A showcase for the work of professional Maryland artists and craftsmen, this show and sale features fine quality crafts and traditional and contemporary works of art, all juried. The Mountain Festival is open Saturday, 10-6, and Sunday, 10-5, ☎ 301-898-5466. Admission is $5; parking is free.

The **Catoctin Colorfest** is held on the second weekend of October in Thurmont. Venues include Thurmont Community Park, the Guardian Hose Company Activities Grounds and the Thurmont Middle School. Admission is free. Look for signs directing you to parking for the shuttle rides. More than 350 juried artists and craftspeople – some of the state's best craftspersons – exhibit in the three venues throughout the town. Crafts include every medium: pottery, ceramics, wooden furniture, knitting and crocheting, jewelry, children's clothing, dried flowers, weaving and spinning, wooden toys and Christmas ornaments. Along with crafts are all types of visual arts: oil paintings, watercolors, prints, photography, pen and ink drawings, sculpture and wood carving. The Catoctin Colorfest inspires the entire community to present arts-related events to coincide with the official festival.

In Westminster, also on the second weekend of October, the **Festival of Carving** is held at the Carroll County Agricultural Center, Agricultural Center Drive (next to the Farm Museum). At this event, Carroll carvers hold their annual show and sale, where some of the best examples of local wood carving, both folk and contemporary styles, are seen. The Carving Festival is open Saturday, 10-5, and Sunday, 10-4.

November & December

A **Christkindelsmarkt** (Christmas Market) is held the last weekend in November at the Schifferstadt Architectural Museum, 1110 Rosemont Avenue, Frederick. Decorations, ornaments, gifts and food are offered for sale at this traditional German Christmas market on Friday and Saturday, 10-4; and Sunday, noon-4. ☎ 301-663-3885.

The annual **Dickens Open House** is held at Elk Run Vineyards (15713 Liberty Road, Mount Airy, ☎ 301-834-2513, www.elkrun.com) on the last weekend of November. The event includes a tour of the 1750s home, with music and Dickens programs in the parlor.

On the last weekend of November and the first weekend of December, the **Maryland Christmas Show** is held at the Maryland Fairgrounds in Frederick. Hours are Friday and Saturday, 10-6; Sunday until 6; ☎ 301-898-5466.

Information Sources

Baltimore Area Visitors Center, on the Inner Harbor opposite Constellation Pier; ☎ 410-837-INFO (4636) or (800) 282-6632, www.baltimore.org. This small office is open daily and gets very crowded during the summer. The mailing address of the executive offices is 100 Light Street, Baltimore 21202.

Maryland Office of Tourism Development, Department of Business and Economic Development,

217 East Redwood Street, Baltimore, MD 21201; ☎ 410-767-6270.

Annapolis and Anne Arundel County Conference and Visitors Bureau, 26 West St, Annapolis 21401, ☎ 410-280-0445, is just off Church Circle. Parking (first hour free) is in the lot behind the building; open daily, 9 am-5 pm. An information booth is also on the City Dock.

The Top 10 Sights

You can't ask for a more subjective list, and we know that our top 10 may not be yours. But these are the things we think you should make a special point to see or do while you are traveling in Baltimore, Annapolis and the Chesapeake Bay area.

- **USS *Constellation*** – The last all-sail warship built by the US Navy, the ship has been completely restored. Excellent interpretive signage explains its long and fascinating history (page 46).
- **The National Aquarium** – You don't have to like fish to appreciate the displays here, which range from a rain forest filled with tropical birds to dolphin shows (page 50).
- **The Baltimore Museum of Art** – French Impressionist paintings are the highlight of the collections, which also include Old Masters, Asian arts and African tribal art (page 85).
- **The Walters Art Museum** – Five thousand years of art from all over the world

is shown in changing exhibits that may feature Faberge eggs, medieval illumination or Asian pottery (page 75).

- **Evergreen House** – The house, its décor and its flamboyant owners vie for attention with the art collections that hang there (page 88).
- **Maryland Historical Society** – Changing exhibits focus on facets of the city's unique history, while special collections (maritime, children's toys, American silver) offer insights into American history as well (page 76).
- **Walking Tour of Old Annapolis** – Beautifully restored and maintained homes, some of which are open for tours, line the brick streets leading from the docks (page 180).
- **Sailing trips on the Chesapeake Bay** – From Baltimore, Annapolis, St. Michaels or Cambridge, you can enjoy the bay at its best from a slanting deck under sail.
- **Brookside Gardens** – Acre after acre of show gardens, woodland, flowering trees, herbs, formal beds, rare trees and water gardens offer something to see year-round (page 96).
- **The Hammond-Harwood House** – One of the finest Georgian homes in America, this Annapolis mansion is filled with outstanding examples of Colonial cabinetmaking (page 184).

Baltimore

Although it's the Chesapeake Bay's major port, Baltimore is not actually on the Chesapeake Bay itself. It is on the Patapsco River, which widens out into the beautifully protected Inner Harbor and provides other dock areas along its shores for some distance before it enters the bay.

A Brief History

Baltimore was second only to New York as a port of entry for immigrants. Many of them were bound for the California gold fields, but got only as far as Baltimore. Today Baltimore retains more of the rich color and fabric of its ethnic neighborhoods than any other city we know.

As the major port of transport for manufactured and agricultural goods, Baltimore was the terminus of the railway that opened the west – the B&O. Close to the supply lines in both directions, it became a major manufacturing and processing city, with canneries (and the factories that made the cans and the printeries that created the labels), shipbuilding, and fabric mills. Clothing was manufactured here for the Civil War soldiers, and the abundant products of Eastern Shore farms were canned for their rations.

The city's role as a manufacturing and transport hub made it a banking and commercial center as well, and all of these factors joined to give it the architectural heritage we see today. Serious and stur-

Baltimore Area

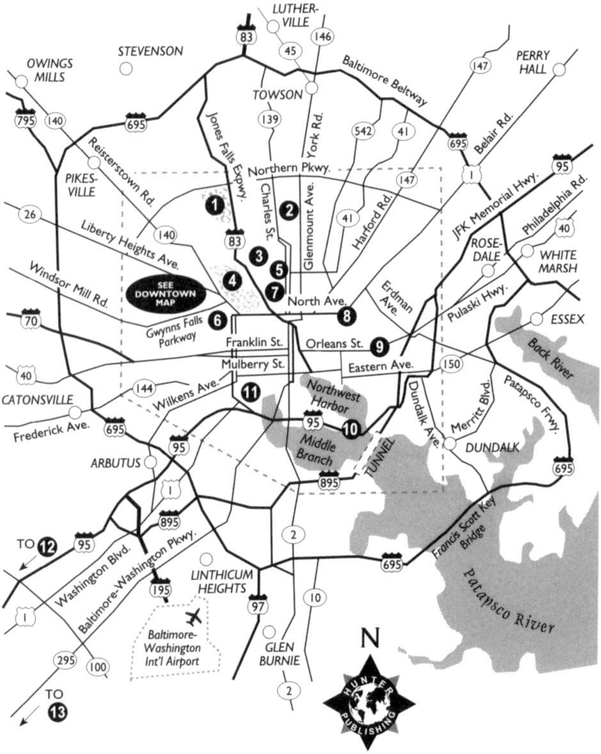

1. Cylburn Park & Arboretum
2. Sherwood Gardens
3. Johns Hopkins University; Evergreen House; Homewood House
4. Druid Hill Park; Zoo
5. Baltimore Museum of Art
6. Baltimore City Conservatory
7. Baltimore Streetcar Museum
8. Great Blacks in Wax Museum
9. Patterson Park
10. Fort McHenry National Monument
11. Mount Clare Museum House
12. Brookside Gardens
13. Six Flags America & Fort Meade Cryptologic Museum

dy brick factories and warehouses blend into ornate and elegant banking halls, row on row of substantial homes, and a skyline pierced by the tall spires and golden domes of churches representing all the various immigrant groups.

It is in the neighborhoods that these various groups – descendants of the colonists who formed the elite and the immigrants – gravitated toward, that you will find the most endearing of Baltimore's many charms. Each is quite different, and although the populations have spread and mingled, and the streets have lost some of their distinctly ethnic icons, the neighborhoods still have very different characteristics. You would never mistake Mount Vernon for Fells Point or Bolton Hill for Little Italy. Most of these residential neighborhoods have maintained their commercial cores, with shops and restaurants and churches.

The Neighborhoods

Inner Harbor

While it is not and never was a residential/commercial enclave in the way that the other neighborhoods were, the area known as the Inner Harbor is the core of present day Baltimore. Refurbished buildings now house shops and eateries, and cleaned up docks provide access to museum ships and to sparkling new museums and attractions.

Little Italy

Close to the Inner Harbor, a block to its east, is Little Italy, a residential and dining enclave of distinctly Italian character. Religious festivals of its two parish churches fill its streets with color and, if you look upward, you will see the roof gardens created by families of immigrants from the sunny slopes of southern Italy. The neighborhood's origins are from the era when the Port of Baltimore was second only to Ellis Island in the number of immigrants it admitted. To reach Little Italy, walk east on Pratt Street, crossing the wide President Street, where you'll see a painted brick wall welcoming you to Little Italy.

Fells Point

South of Little Italy (to the right from Inner Harbor) is Fells Point, one of the few remaining original maritime quarters in any American city. Homes of the merchants, shipwrights, carpenters and others whose livelihood depended on the maritime trade were built close to the docks. Fells Point is lively, especially on weekend evenings when students seem to take it over en masse. Two city markets, antiques stores, specialty shops, pubs and restaurants line waterfront Thames Street and Broadway, and the adjacent streets. Take the water taxi from Inner Harbor or walk south from Little Italy on Caroline Street.

Canton

East of Fells Point is Canton, named for the Chinese port where the land's first European owner made his fortune. During the Civil War and later, it was the center of Baltimore's oyster and vegetable canning industry, processing shellfish and produce from the Eastern Shore farms. The old Canton factories that made cans and printed labels now house a bookstore, café and chic restaurants.

The easternmost stop for the Water Taxi is at the dock in Canton.

Federal Hill

Federal Hill has been designated a National Historic District for its fine row houses, some of which date from the 1700s. It stands above Inner Harbor, on the opposite side from the World Trade Center and Constellation Pier. Its row houses have been restored as homes and its main commercial streets are lined with funky antiques shops and restaurants. Cross Street Market, at its center, is a busy and noisy mix of produce and meat stalls, lunch counters of every ethnic stripe and a bar. At the foot of Federal Hill, on the Inner Harbor side, are two major museums, and another lies along side it.

Camden Yards

Although it is not a neighborhood in the sense of community, the part of town around Camden Yards is of interest to sports fans and to railroad buffs. Here lie the two major professional sports stadiums and the B&O Railroad Museum, in the beautifully restored roundhouse. This area lies west of Inner Harbor, past the Convention Center.

Mount Vernon

While the immigrants lived close to the racy, raucous docks, The Four Hundred (the exclusive social set) chose to remove themselves to the higher ground of Mount Vernon. It is still a prestigious in-town address, as well as the center for art, music and culture. Along Charles Street is "Restaurant Row" and a good number of chic shops and galleries; several museums are also in the neighborhood. It centers around the gracious park square where Charles Street crosses Mount Vernon Place, with the Washington Monument at its center.

Bolton Hill

Northwest of Mount Vernon is quiet Bolton Hill, its streets lined with proper brownstone and brick townhouses. Other than the shops of Antiques Row and a couple of restaurants, only a few businesses have made incursions into the quarter, along with cafés frequented by ticket holders at the nearby Meyerhoff Symphony Hall.

Hampden

Hampden, north of Bolton Hill, is beyond the area where most tourists venture, but it's well worth seeking out if you are interested in what really makes Baltimore tick. Funky, quirky and very seventies, Hampden marches – or saunters – to its own beat. It's not unaware of its "image," and treasures its reputation as home to the classic Baltimore "Hon" – big hair, cat-eye glasses, hot pink sweater, chewing gum and all. You really can get your hair done in a beehive here.

TIP

During the Christmas season, be sure to see the decorated homes on 34th Street, between Keswick Road and Chestnut Avenue in Hampden. They are a real hoot, and get better every year.

Other Areas

Other neighborhoods lie farther afield, but those we have mentioned are the principal ones that have the most attractions. Not so much a neighborhood in the sense of the others, the area surrounding Johns Hopkins University also has a number of places you will want to visit. This part of town is north of the Mount Vernon and Bolton Hill areas, and is usually referred to as "Uptown."

Getting Around

Water Taxi

Although Baltimore is stretched out over a large area, its sights cluster into its neighborhoods, which seem like little cities of their own. To get between some of these – the Inner Harbor, Federal Hill, Fells Point, Canton – and even Fort McHenry – the best way is by water taxi. This convenient little fleet makes a steady shuttle circuit, and the staff is used to giving good directions and telling people which dock is the closest to where they're going. Their handy map with all the stops marked is also helpful.

Ed Kane's Water Taxi Guide, *free at the Visitors Center or on the boats, has a good map of the harbor area and its attractions.*

Ed Kane's Water Taxi (☎ 410-563-3901 or 800-658-8947), is a year-round service with 17 stops near major sights around the Inner and Outer Harbors. All-day passes are about $5 and include multiple re-boarding, plus trolley connections to Fort McHenry and discounts to attractions. They run daily, 11-6, from November through March; 11-9 in April, September and October (until midnight on Friday and Saturday); and 10 am-11 pm from May through the first week in September (until midnight on Friday and Saturday). In the summer, boats arrive at each landing 15-20 minutes apart.

> **TIP**
>
> With your Water Taxi ticket, you get a Letter of Marque, giving you discounts at a long list of dining, shopping and sightseeing options, such as the science and maritime museums and a tall ship cruise.

The **Harbor Shuttle** connects the Inner Harbor, Fells Point and Canton, and also runs connecting shuttles to Fort McHenry and Little Italy. They operate year-round, although less frequently in the winter; ☎ 410-675-2900.

Public Transportation

Many of the major attractions – museum ships, the aquarium, science center, Port Discovery and even Little Italy, Camden Yards and Mount Vernon – are within walking distance of the Inner Harbor. **Tourist trolleys** or **MTA** bus and rail services (☎ 410-539-5000) do reach other neighborhoods, but since the latter are designed for commuters, not tourists, they don't tend to connect the areas of tourist interest very conveniently, and they may involve several transfers. To make it even less convenient, the closest Metro stations are about three blocks from the Inner Harbor.

To help out-of-towners, the Maryland Mass Transit Administration (MTA), ☎ 800-543-9809 or 410-539-5000, www.mtamaryland.com, publishes an excellent map of bus, Metro subway, Light Rail and commuter train lines (MARC), which lists major attractions and hotels, and suggests their best connections. It also includes some useful details on using the lines, including the fact that you must have exact change and that you push the yellow stripe on the wall to signal the next stop.

> **TIP**
>
> If you plan to use the bus, Light Rail or Metro more than twice in a day, the $3 day pass is the best buy. We use it just to avoid having to fish for change.

Information Sources

Visitors Center

Baltimore Area Visitors Center, on the Inner Harbor opposite Constellation Pier; ☎ 410-837-INFO (4636) or (800) 282-6632, www.baltimore.org. This small office gets very crowded during the summer. The mailing address of the executive offices is 100 Light Street, Baltimore 21202.

Recommended Reading

We especially like two books on Baltimore. ***Wish You Were Here*** by Carolyn Males, Carol Barbier Rolnic and Pam Makowski Goresh, published by Woodholme House in Baltimore, is a detailed guide to the city's neighborhoods, well-written and filled with anecdotes and history that will make you feel like an instant insider.

If, like us, you delight in the graceful lines and period decoration of old buildings, ***A Guide to Baltimore Architecture***, by John Dorsey and James D. Dilts (Tidewater Publishers), is a must. Photographs show the city's significant buildings, with interesting details on the architecture, history and the architects. This book will lead you to places that are not necessarily tourist attractions, most of them everyday working buildings. They range from Mount Clare, a mansion built in the mid 1700s, to the new aquarium and the pentagonal I.M. Pei World Trade Center, the art deco former Kresge's store, cast-iron building fronts, elegant churches and many more. It's well-written and has a good glossary of architectural terms.

Although these books are hard to find outside Baltimore, you can get them both at **Hometown Girl**, 1000 West 36th Street, Hampden, ☎ 410-662-4438; or at their sister shop, **Celebrate Baltimore**, on the second level of the Light Street Pavilion, 301 Light Street, Inner Harbor area, ☎ 410-752-3838.

Sunup to Sundown

Recommended Sights & Activities

Happily, most of the attractions you'll want to see in Baltimore lie within these old neighborhoods, so you can enjoy their ambiance as you visit museums and historic sites. The exceptions to this are Canton, which has no "attractions" other than its restaurants and shopping, and the area around Johns Hopkins University, which has several places you'll want to visit, but less sense of neighborhood than the old in-town enclaves.

Tours

Visitors to the city of Baltimore itself could keep very busy for a full week and still not see everything of interest. We suggest beginning with a pair of tours, one by land, one by sea, to get your bearings and to learn a little about the history. First, sign on for Fran Zeller's **Harbor City Tour** (see page 101) and use it as a way to get from place to place, getting off to explore Fells Point and Mount Vernon, and reboarding for the rest of the circuit on a later bus.

The next day, take a water tour (see page 102) that includes Fort McHenry, and return to Fells Point to visit the new Maritime Museum.

Museums

Based on your own interests, plan to spend some time visiting the outstanding museums. You could spend a whole day in **Mount Vernon**, visiting **The Walters Art Museum** or the **Maryland Historical Society**, with a leisurely lunch on Charles Street and short visits to **Edgar Allan Poe's grave**, the library of the Peabody Conservatory, and a stroll around the streets of Mount Vernon.

Or choose one of the other special interest museums, covering subjects from dentistry to the B&O Railway. For a close look at Baltimore's workaday and industrial past, we would choose the fascinating **Museum of Industry** for at least half a day, combining it with a stroll through nearby Federal Hill's fine old homes and lunch at the Joy America Café in the **Visionary Arts Museum**.

If you are up to another day of museums, for art choose the outstanding **Baltimore Museum of Art** or, for history (as well as art), tour the two nearby mansions, **Evergreen** and **Homewood**. In either case, relax over a long lunch at Gertrude's, in the museum.

Plan to spend one day at the **Inner Harbor**, visiting the ships – especially the ***Constellation*** – and the **National Aquarium**. Those with a special interest in Science will want to continue around the harbor to the **Maryland Science Center**.

Shopping

You could spend a whole day browsing in antiques shops, dividing your time between **Antiques Row** in Mount Vernon and the shops of **Fells Point** or **Federal Hill**.

Exploring

You'll want to spend some time just wandering around in Baltimore's neighborhoods, for two reasons. First, they are among its most unique features, still retaining their distinct ethnic and historical flavors, along with their commercial and residential cores and often their traditional churches. The second reason is that they are where you'll find the attractions that brought you here – the museums, character-full restaurants, unique shops and colorful city markets.

Inner Harbor

While not a neighborhood in the traditional sense, this area along the waterfront where ships once loaded and unloaded the merchandise that made Baltimore a busy commercial city, is again the hub of activity. Along with a virtual flotilla of ships to tour and cruise on, the Inner Harbor has shopping, restaurants, hotels, concerts, street entertainers, even a skating rink in the winter. You can identify it from a distance by the pentagonal **World Trade Center**, designed by I.M. Pei, or by the unusual roof line of the brick **Powerhouse Building**.

Almost encircling Inner Harbor is the **Waterfront Promenade**, which, on completion, will connect the seven-mile shoreline with a brick-paved walkway. On its way around the harbor from the Visionary Arts Museum it will pass most of the major sights as it leads you around the piers, close to Little Italy and on to Fells Point and eventually Canton. With luck, it may be completed by the time you read this. It's for pedestrians only, no bicycles, and you'll find benches here and there along the way. If you tire partway through the trip, you're never very far from a water taxi stop.

As you tour the piers, you may wonder about the round building you glimpse occasionally, almost hidden behind the Pier 5 Hotel. **Seven-Foot Knoll Lighthouse** is Maryland's oldest screwpile lighthouse. You can get a full view of it from the end of the pier behind the Aquarium.

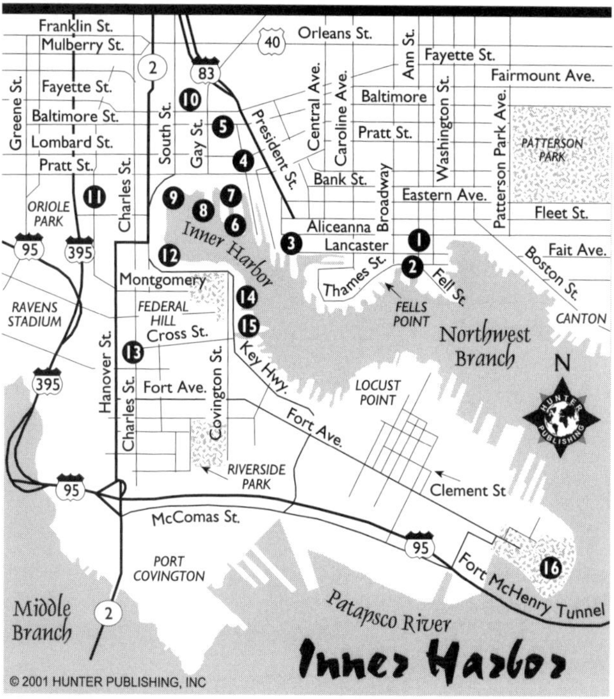

1. Robert Long House
2. Fells Point Maritime Museum
3. Baltimore Civil War Museum
4. Flag House & 1812 Museum
5. Port Discovery
6. National Aquarium
7. Baltimore Maritime Museum
8. World Trade Center
9. Harborplace & The Gallery
10. City Hall
11. Convention Center
12. Maryland Science Center
13. Cross Street Market
14. American Visionary Art Museum
15. Museum of Industry
16. Fort McHenry National Monument

TOP OF THE WORLD OBSERVATION LEVEL
World Trade Center
401 East Pratt Street
☎ 410-837-VIEW
Admission: $3, adults; $2, seniors and children

The first stop for many visitors who like to get their bearings with an overview of the city is the top of the world's tallest pentagonal building, I.M. Pei's 423-

foot **World Trade Center**. Along with the view, you'll get a quick introduction to Baltimore history in the displays. Open Monday-Saturday, 10-5; Sunday, noon-5. From 8-10 pm on the last Saturday of each month, from May through September, live jazz performances accompany the sunset and city lights views.

> **★ TIP**
>
> To get some interesting water-level views of the historic boats and the harbor, you can rent paddleboats at the **Paddle Boat Dock** at Harborplace; ☎ 410-563-3901.

USS *CONSTELLATION*
Pier I, 301 East Pratt Street
☎ 410-539-1797
www.constellation.org
Admission: $6, adults; $4.75, seniors; $3.50 ages six-14; under six, free

A complete overhaul and restoration of this sailing vessel in 1999 turned up new information on the ship, which had been confused with a frigate of the same name launched earlier in Baltimore. Subsequent refittings had hidden much of the ship' original construction, so naval historians were surprised to learn that this was not the sister ship to the USS *Constitution*, as previously believed. But the new information didn't lessen the ship's interest or historic significance in the least. In fact, it makes it unique as the last sailing vessel ever commissioned by the US Navy as a ship of war. The ship, built in 1854, was responsible for the capture of three slave-traders off Africa, rescuing and returning their unwilling passengers. Later, the vessel carried precious American art works to the Paris Exposition of 1878 and brought vital food on a relief mission to Ireland during the potato famine.

> **TIP**
>
> We rate the *Constellation* as the city's number one sight.

A tour of the ship is self-guided, following numbered stations, each with excellent panels describing the activity of that part of the ship, as well as historic events in which the ship was involved. The background material is well presented, so these events are tied into their times and other events. Even those well informed on naval history will learn something here. Taken along with the other museum ships nearby, it's a fascinating tour through much of America's history at sea. The *Constellation* is open daily, 10-6, from May through mid-October; 10-4 in the off-season. In summer it may also be open evening hours.

BALTIMORE MARITIME MUSEUM
Pier III, East Pratt Street
☎ 410-396-3453
Admission: $5.50, adults; $4.50, seniors; $3 ages five-12; buy tickets at the kiosk on Pier 3, by the Aquarium.

Photographic exhibits at the museum are brought to life by recorded accounts of men who served on the Taney.

The three other historic ships moored near the USS *Constellation* continue the story of the United States at sea. The US Coast Guard cutter *Taney* is the only ship still afloat to have survived the Japanese attack on Pearl Harbor in 1941. Having arrived there in December of 1940, it was scheduled for complete overhaul at the shipyards there, when the attack came. Within four minutes, all stations were manned and the *Taney* was engaged with subsequent groups of attacking Japanese aircraft. Later in the war, the ship engaged in anti-submarine action in the Pacific and escorted convoys in the Atlantic. You can read the battle report of the *Taney* following the Pearl Harbor attack. Before the war, in 1937, the cutter took part in the search for Amelia Earhart and saw later action in the Korean and Vietnam wars. In Vietnam, the ship patrolled the coast and inland waterways to catch arms and ammunition supply ships, which were disguised as fishing boats and trawlers. Its design as a Coast Guard cutter was perfect for navigating coastal waters and for boarding and inspection procedures.

The US submarine *Torsk* completed a record number of dives (11,884) in its long career, and holds the distinction of sinking two Japanese frigates in 1945, making it the last warship to sink an enemy vessel in World War II. The submarine also took part in the 1962 blockade of Cuba. Touring the cramped quarters of the submarine, where every inch of space is precious, dramatizes the life of the men who served (and continue to serve) as submariners. On summer weekends, and occasionally at other times, you might meet World War II veterans of the submarine service, who will answer questions or describe more fully the operation of these specialized vessels.

The Lightship *Chesapeake*, the third of the Maritime Museum ships you can tour, was commissioned in 1939, serving as a floating lighthouse in several parts of the Chesapeake Bay.

The museum is generally open daily, 10-6; they may have longer summer hours and be open only weekends in the winter; call ahead.

> **★ TIP**
>
> The ships and some other attractions around the harbor offer a combined pass with water transportation. National Historic Seaport of Baltimore combines the Maritime Museum ships, the USS *Constellation*, Museum of Industry and Fort McHenry. Buy passes at the kiosk on Pier 3; ☎ 410-396-3453.

PRIDE OF BALTIMORE II
Inner Harbor
☎ 410-539-1151

Not an original clipper, this is a faithful and authentic replica of the famous Baltimore clipper, a style of topsail schooner that was built here from the Revolution until the middle of the 19th century. The ship is Maryland's goodwill ambassador, and when it is not representing the state elsewhere, it is berthed here. The *Pride of Baltimore II* is open for free tours when it is in port.

NATIONAL AQUARIUM IN BALTIMORE

Pier 3, 561 East Pratt Street
☎ 410-576-3800
www.aqua.org
Admission: $14, adults; $10.50, seniors; $7.50, ages three-11

The aquarium's rainforest and jungle environment exactly simulates the rising and falling of the water level in the original habitat.

Education about sea creatures and their habitat is the mission of this outstanding aquarium, which is a combination of marine science center and biological park. Conservation and environmental issues involving the sea are explored in depth (sorry!), as visitors watch more than 10,000 creatures. Fish are only the beginning; birds, reptiles, amphibians and marine mammals share habitats that are as close as possible to their native wilds, separated from visitors by viewing windows.

The most remarkable of these explores the habitat of rain forest waters and the jungle that grows above them, in a long corridor of inter-connected tanks where you can see both above and below the waterline.

TIP

Tickets are timed and you can expect midday tickets to be sold out on summer days, holidays and weekends in spring or fall. Buy advance tickets at the aquarium kiosk when you arrive in Baltimore, or visit before 11 am or after 3 pm.

Outside the aquarium entrance, harbor and gray seals cavort in an outdoor rock pool, where you can watch them without paying admission.

Try as we might, we can never spot the giant 16-foot anaconda that cleverly disguises itself as a jungle vine, but we've spotted a number of other creatures, including funny-shaped fish and several species of turtle.

The 335,000-gallon Atlantic Ocean tank features the most authentic Atlantic coral reef ever fabricated, and is alive with bright tropical fish. "Open Ocean" is a wrap-around tank that visitors view from the center, as several species of shark, sand tigers and others swim around them.

Above, at the top domed level, grows a South American Rain Forest, where sloths hang languidly from branches overhead and tropical birds, frogs, monkeys, and fishes live in the pools and greenery. Listen for the screaming piha, the loudest bird for its size in the animal kingdom. If you are trying to locate a particular creature, or if you need help identifying one you see, ask one of the enthusiastic naturalists who are stationed throughout the rain forest.

Although these tropical and exotic habitats are the more dramatic displays and the real crowd-pleasers, Maryland and Chesapeake Bay habitats get major attention in exhibits, too. Several explore local ponds, rivers, tidal estuaries, salt marshes, the bay and the ocean.

Connected to the main aquarium by an elevated walkway, the 1,300-seat Marine Mammal Pavilion is where dolphins perform at daily 25-minute shows. This is an interactive show, always a highlight for children. Call ahead for schedule of shows. Hours vary seasonally, usually 9-6 in summer (later on weekends); 10-5, September through June. Call ahead for exact times.

Wheelchairs are provided at the Aquarium, and both buildings are fully accessible. Strollers are prohibited, but backpack carriers are available.

PORT DISCOVERY
35 Market Place
☎ 410-727-8120
Admission: $10, adults; $7.50, ages three to 12

An outstanding – one of the nation's largest – children's activity and learning center, Port Discovery is designed for ages five-13. Everything is interactive, stimulating kids' imagination with unique and surprising activities. Little visitors can crawl into a giant kitchen sink and down the drain or star in a show in the TV studio. Port Discovery is open Tuesday through Sunday, 10-5:30.

MARYLAND SCIENCE CENTER
601 Light Street
☎ 410-685-2370
Admission: $9.50, adults; $7, seniors, military personnel and children ages four-17

Hands-on activities and live demonstrations are the focus of the three floors of exhibits, and a demonstration theater features electricity and other subjects hourly from 10:30 to 1:30 weekdays, 10:30-5:30 weekends. Chesapeake Bay's diverse ecology is covered, along with other environmental issues, in exhibits designed to appeal to all age levels; these are not just for children. Learn about space exploration at the visitors center for the Hubble Space Telescope. The IMAX Theater's five-story-high screen features films that make the most of its larger-than-life capabilities, and shows in the Davis Planetarium explore the sky and outer space. Summer hours are Monday through Thursday, 9:30-6; Friday through Sunday, 9:30-8. Winter hours are 10-5, and until 6 on weekends.

BALTIMORE PUBLIC WORKS MUSEUM & STREETSCAPE
751 Eastern Avenue, past Pier 5, at the eastern side of Inner Harbor
☎ 410-396-5565
Admission: $2.50, adults; $2, seniors; $1.50, ages seven-12

You may or may not find trash disposal and water mains fascinating, but you have to admire this creative use of the elegant old 1912 brick pumping station. The urban environment – from the city's early days to the present – is explored in exhibits that feature photographs, diagrams and actual artifacts, such as wooden water pipes used here in the early 1800s. Streetscape examines what lies under the streets in a full-sized model. This is a museum for people who like to know how things work. The museum is open Tuesday through Sunday, 10-4.

Little Italy

Just across President Street from the Inner Harbor, the Italian quarter is filled with so many restaurants that local lore holds that the red sauce is piped in from a central reservoir. But there's more than *mangia, mangia, mangia* here. The neighborhood's two parish churches are the center of spiritual, social and cultural life for the many Italian families who live here, as well as those who have moved out of the inner city. Many descendants of the early Port of Baltimore immigrants have never moved any farther than the blocks close to High and Stiles streets. To reach Little Italy, walk east from the Inner Harbor on Pratt Street, crossing the wide President

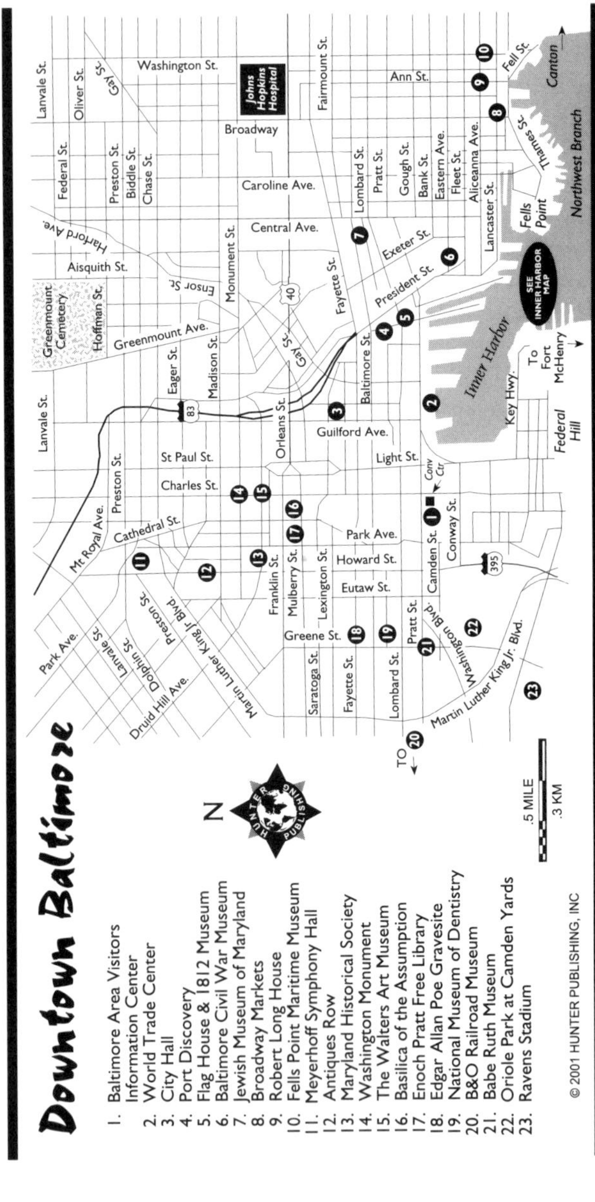
Downtown Baltimore
1. Baltimore Area Visitors Information Center
2. World Trade Center
3. City Hall
4. Port Discovery
5. Flag House & 1812 Museum
6. Baltimore Civil War Museum
7. Jewish Museum of Maryland
8. Broadway Markets
9. Robert Long House
10. Fells Point Maritime Museum
11. Meyerhoff Symphony Hall
12. Antiques Row
13. Maryland Historical Society
14. Washington Monument
15. The Walters Art Museum
16. Basilica of the Assumption
17. Enoch Pratt Free Library
18. Edgar Allan Poe Gravesite
19. National Museum of Dentistry
20. B&O Railroad Museum
21. Babe Ruth Museum
22. Oriole Park at Camden Yards
23. Ravens Stadium
N
HUNTER PUBLISHING
.5 MILE
.3 KM
© 2001 HUNTER PUBLISHING, INC
Inner Harbor
SEE INNER HARBOR MAP
To Fort McHenry
Federal Hill
Fells Point
Canton
Northwest Branch
Johns Hopkins Hospital
Greenmount Cemetery
TO 20

Street. A painted brick wall straight ahead tells you you've arrived in Little Italy.

Apart from the festivals that fill the streets with color, the best place to sense the soul of this neighborhood is at the **Bocce Court**, on Stiles Street. This sport is alive and well here, played by people of all ages. We like to watch the kids learning, with their grandfathers giving them tips on style. It's not just for neighborhood amateurs; tournaments during St. Anthony's Festival in mid-June and on Columbus Day in October bring pros to compete.

You'll need to wander these streets on foot, possibly as part of a tour called "A Taste of Italy," which will give you a lively and engaging introduction to both its history and its food; ☎ 410-547-0479.

FLAG HOUSE & 1812 MUSEUM
844 East Pratt Street, at Albemarle Street
☎ 410-837-1793
www.flaghouse.org
Admission: $4, adults; $3, seniors; $2, ages six-18

The brick home was built in 1793, and occupied by Mary Pickersgill, the ambitious seamstress who stitched the 30-by-42-foot flag that flew over Fort McHenry during the British bombardment in the War of 1812. The banner was so large that Francis Scott Key was able to see it still waving in the "dawn's early light" and knew Baltimore had not fallen. The Flag House is across the street from the big sign welcoming you to Little Italy. It is open Tuesday through Saturday, 10-4; guided tours are given between 10:30 and 3:30.

JEWISH MUSEUM OF MARYLAND
15 Lloyd Street
between Lombard and East Baltimore streets
☎ 410-732-6400
www.jhsm.org
Admission: $4, adults; $2, children

Two historic synagogues have been restored. The Lloyd Street Synagogue, built in 1845, and the B'nai Israel Synagogue, built in 1876, are both on the National Register of Historic Places. The museum also presents exhibits with artifacts from its collections relating to Jewish history, life and culture. The Golden Land is an interactive children's exploration of the turn-of-the-century immigrant experience, aimed at ages five-10. A research library, with extensive archives, is open by appointment. Museum hours are Tuesday through Thursday and Sunday, noon to 4, except National and Jewish holidays; guided tours are given at 1:00 and 2:30.

BALTIMORE CITY FIRE MUSEUM
Gay, Ensor, and Orleans Streets
☎ 410-727-2414
Free

The city fire museum is operated by the Box 414 Association, a non-profit group that borrowed its name from the first alarm that went off in the Fire of 1904. Here you can learn all about that historic disaster, as well as the telegraph fire communications system used across the city until just 20 years ago. If you have younger family members, then you must stop to see the old fire engines and pumps, many of which are still in operating condition. Extensive displays of antique firefighter's gear and equipment include brass poles that every kid will be fascinated with. The Old No. 6 Engine House, which was built in

1853, when all firehouses were volunteer, is topped with a 117-foot lookout tower. The museum is open Sunday, 1 pm to 4 pm.

BALTIMORE CIVIL WAR MUSEUM
601 President Street
☎ 410-385-5188
www.civilwarinbaltimore.org
Admission: $2, adults; $1, children

South of Little Italy, between Inner Harbor and Fells Point, this museum is in an historic train station that was also a stop in the Underground Railroad. That in itself is noteworthy, for two reasons. First, it's one of the few stops that was actually a railway station (the name "Underground Railroad" is a metaphoric one). Second, since the activities of the Underground Railroad were illegal and dangerous, there is very little written record to prove which buildings were involved. The old President Street Station is one of the few with such documentation. Historical exhibits explain the routes and methods used by escaping slaves and Baltimore's part in the Civil War, along with the role of African-Americans in the war. They are open daily from 10-5.

SHOT TOWER
801 East Fayette Street

Although you will still see it listed in some publications as being open for tours, this historic structure was part of the City Museums, and the entire complex has closed. You can still admire the tower from the outside, of course. Built in 1828, it is 234 feet high, using more than a million wood-fired bricks. It is one of the few remaining shot towers in the United States and was once a major supplier of lead shot. Molten lead was poured from the top of the tower, separating into small droplets as it fell. These cooled and became solid spheres when they hit the water in the bottom of the tower.

ST. VINCENT DE PAUL CHURCH
Fayette Street at Jones Falls Expressway
☎ 410-962-5078

Built in 1840, the distinctive church with its white tower is directly across from the Shot Tower. It is an outstanding example of Georgian architecture and Baltimore's oldest Catholic parish church. Tours are given on request after any services, which are held on Saturdays at 7:15 pm and Sundays at 9:00 and 11:45 am.

Fells Point

This old maritime neighborhood is still made up of homes built close to the docks by the merchants, shipwrights, carpenters – plus, we suspect, the successful madams whose business depended on sailors fresh off the boat after long months at sea. Its row houses, constructed in the 1700s and 1800s, have sheltered several waves of immigrants.

Very few maritime neighborhoods have survived in American cities In this case, although a preservation group saved it, Fells Point is not a museum-like enclave, tidied and gentrified into theme-park cuteness. It is very much a living neighborhood, self-sufficient with two of Baltimore's city markets on Broadway and a lively mix of shops, antiques stores, pubs and restaurants. Most businesses are on waterfront Thames and streets paralleling it, close to Broadway, the neighborhood's wide divided main street. Take the water taxi from Inner Harbor or walk, heading south from Little Italy along Caroline Street. You can also reach Fells Point from Inner Harbor by following the boardwalk along the water, a very pleasant stroll. On weekend evenings, especially in the summer, Fells Point is the playground of young people and students.

Fells Point has two adjacent market buildings on Broadway, a block from the waterfront. More than a place to shop for food or have lunch, the **Broadway Market** is a neighborhood institution. Its crowded rows of stalls sell everything from deli sandwiches and crab cakes to just-picked tomatoes and fresh-caught fish. In the north building look for Mrs. Parr's homemade fudge.

Broadway Market is open Monday through Saturday, from 7 am to 6 pm.

HELP, POLICE!

If you need help or want to pay a parking ticket, don't head for the clearly marked **police station** in the brick building on Thames Street between the wharves. Although it looks operative and appears freshly painted, you won't find a police officer there; in fact, you'll find the door locked. Don't blame Baltimore's finest for not being on duty. The station's a phony, created as a stage set when Fells Point was the setting for the filming of the NBC television series *Homicide: Life on the Street*. If you were a fan of the show, you'll recognize this block of Thames Street and the buildings across the street, too.

A two-hour walking tour of Fells Point can be arranged through Concierge Plus (☎ 410-547-0479); tours are for groups of 10 or more by prior arrangement. The Fells Point tour highlights the many movies that have been filmed there, including *Sleepless in Seattle* and *Avalon,* as well as the NBC series previously mentioned, and includes lunch at the *Homicide* cast's favorite hangout. Tours of other neighborhoods are also available.

ROBERT LONG HOUSE
812 South Ann Street
☎ 410-675-6750

Baltimore's oldest surviving urban home, the house dates from 1765. It is the headquarters of the **Baltimore Preservation Society**, and is restored and furnished with antiques of the 18th century. It was the home of one of Fells Point's leading merchants. You can take a self-guided tour of the house and of the garden, where herbs that were grown in the 1700s for food, medicine and dyes once again flourish. The house is open for tours on Thursdays at 10 am, 1 pm and 3 pm.

FELLS POINT MARITIME MUSEUM
1724 Thames Street
☎ 410-685-3750

A row of former mercantile buildings facing the docks in what was the shipbuilding and provisioning neighborhood of the city is becoming the new home of a distinguished collection of artifacts centering around Baltimore's long relationship with the sea. The Radcliffe Maritime Collection has been part of the Baltimore Historical Society Museum, but with expansion of that building to accommodate the acquisition of the former City Life Museums' collections, trustees of the society began to look for a new home for a separate maritime museum. What place could be more fitting than the docks and streets where the history happened?

The move is a work in progress, so you may want to check with the museum to see where the collections are when you visit Baltimore. Unless they are in trucks in transit, you will want to see them. Included are a complete boat shop and tools of the various maritime trades, ship artifacts, half-hulls, ship models and a fine group of artworks depicting ships and maritime subjects.

Federal Hill & Key Highway

The old neighborhood of Flemish-bond brick houses from the Colonial era, now a National Historic District, overlooks the Inner Harbor from a hill. Its workaday commercial streets are scattered with antiques shops and restaurants, and you'll see bright decorative banners fluttering from the lamp posts.

Cross Street Market, in its center at Cross and Charles Streets, is a noisy crowded tangle of meat and produce stalls interspersed with vendors hawking fast foods of every ethnicity. This, like others of the city's public markets, is so much a part of Baltimore culture that you'll find it crowded with shoppers nearly every morning and its snack bars and carry-out stalls filled during the lunch hour. It has a lively bar at one end where locals congregate after work and on Saturdays, too. The market is a good stopping place for a casual lunch or source of makings for a picnic in **Federal Hill Park**. Set at the hill's northern edge, where the land drops abruptly to the harbor, the park has a beautiful view of Inner Harbor and the downtown skyline. On hot summer days, you're more likely to find a breeze here than anywhere else on land. Key Highway separates the east side of Federal Hill from the harbor. You can reach this side of the harbor to visit its attractions via the Water Taxi.

AMERICAN VISIONARY ARTS MUSEUM
800 Key Highway, between Inner Harbor and Federal Hill
☎ 410-244-1900
www.avam.org
Admission: $6, adults; $4, seniors and students

If this were any city but Baltimore, the Visionary Arts museum would certainly be the city's most unusual. But this *is* Baltimore, so we'll skip the awarding of that title. Enough to say that we don't know of another museum like this in the United States. Touching at times to the point of heartbreaking, the displays are at the same time whimsical and joyous. Devoted to the work of artists untrained in the formal traditions of design, often working with found materials, exhibits include pieces by prison inmates, tortured minds, and those completely unfettered by artistic conventions. Shows have dealt with topics such as the unseen companions that inspire artists to creativity, art as a way of dealing with adversity, art as escape, art as a joyous outburst. You can see these works on the purely visual level or read the biographies of their creators to understand more about the forces at work within them. However you look at it, whether through your own or the visionary's eyes, you won't forget what you see. The Museum is open Tuesday-Sunday, 10-6.

BALTIMORE MUSEUM OF INDUSTRY
1415 Key Highway
☎ 410-727-4808
Admission: adults, $5; seniors and children, $3

Many visitors buzz right past without stopping at this wonderful museum in their haste to get to Fort McHenry, which we think is a shame (in fact, even though we're inveterate history travelers, we think this place is much more interesting to visit than the fort). We can't think of another place in the city where you'll find the embodiment of what Baltimore is all about more clearly represented.

Begin with its venue, a circa-1870 oyster cannery with much of its original equipment, including a belt-driven machine shop. Here you may find a blacksmith working on replacement parts, or perhaps someone who was once employed here, ready to explain its workings. Possibly the most boggling artifact of all is the giant pressure cooker that holds more than 100 cans at once and is lowered into a pit in the floor to heat. The walls are decorated with the colorful labels of products canned in Baltimore, along with large photographs of the workers (many of them children), showing the grimmer side of industrialization.

Other sections of the museum are devoted to more of the industries that made Baltimore great and shaped its gutsy blue collar culture. Entire shops are shown – the garment industry display has the original cutting tables, a tailor shop and pattern-making tools. Interpreters are on hand to describe the work or to answer questions as you wander through at your own speed.

> **DID YOU KNOW?**
>
> Standardized sizes and patterns for clothing began during the Civil War, when the Union Army needed a lot of uniforms all at once and there was no time for custom tailoring to fit each person.

Baltimore became a printing center because of the demand for labels on the local foods canned here.

In the print shop you can see the evolution of typesetting from the old hand-set type to linotype machines. A press is usually working, so you can see how it operates, and displays include many of the products of Baltimore's printworks.

Baltimore's place in industrial technology is graphically shown with a mural based on Baltimore products and Baltimore firsts. Modern engineering and manufacturing gets its due, too, with a series of displays on local products from Head skis to spacecraft.

In the harbor alongside the museum is a 1906 steam tugboat, which is open for tours.

The Museum of Industry is open Tuesday-Friday, noon-5; Saturday, 10-5; winter hours are shorter.

FORT McHENRY NATIONAL MONUMENT AND HISTORIC SHRINE
End of East Fort Avenue
☎ 410-962-4290
Admission: adults, $5; under 16, free

You won't be in Baltimore long without hearing the story of the city's favorite native son, but it's a good story and it's true (which sets it apart from many "historic" tales you hear while traveling). The fort's location gives it almost total command of the sea approach to Baltimore, which is how it saved the city from the British fleet in the War of 1812. The British, you will remember if you read the history section of the introduction to this book, had their sights set directly on destroying the city that had sent so many privateers after its ships during the Revolution. But this circa-1790 star-shaped brick fort withstood the attack.

Francis Scott Key, a Maryland attorney, was on board a ship trying to secure the release of an American doctor who was being held by the British. While he was serving as a mediator, the British attacked the city and Key was detained on board, within sight of Fort McHenry. All night he heard the rockets exploding as the British shelled the city from the harbor. But they couldn't take the fort, which kept them from getting close enough to capture the city, and at daybreak Key saw the "broad stripes and bright stars" of Mary Pickersgill's 30-by-42-foot flag, still flying over Fort McHenry, and knew that Baltimore had not been taken. So moved by the sight, he wrote the poem that would later be set to the tune of a British pub song and designated as our national anthem.

Stop at the visitors center between 9 am and 4 pm to see the displays and a film that describes the battle and the fort's significance, then tour the fort itself to see officers' quarters, guardrooms, a restored powder magazine, cannons and earthworks. On summer weekends, interpreters in period uniform re-enact life in the garrison. Fort McHenry is open daily from 8 am-4:45 pm; summer hours may be longer.

Camden Yards

Once the center of Baltimore's railroads, Camden is now its sports neighborhood. Even its museums reflect these past and present roles, featuring Babe Ruth and the B&O Railroad. Reach this area by walking west from Inner Harbor, past the Convention Center.

A few blocks north of Camden Yards are several other attractions that are quite close to each other, and which we have included here.

ORIOLE PARK AT CAMDEN YARDS
333 West Camden Street, at Eutaw Street
☎ 410-685-9800
Admission: $5, adults; $4, seniors and children under age 12

The home field for the Baltimore Orioles is a must-see for any sports aficionado, especially if you can get in for a game. Chances are, your bleacher seats will have a great view – the stadium is known for its unobstructed playing field. Maybe you'll even get a chance to be in one of the orange seats, which mark moments in Oriole record-breaking on the seat, such as Cal Ripken's 278th homer, which broke the record for a shortstop, or Eddie Murray's entrance into the 500 Homer Club.

A statue of Babe Ruth, who was born close by, greets sports fans as they enter the stadium. If you know baseball, you may wonder why the great lefty is wearing his glove on the wrong hand. It's no mistake; fans who really know their stuff will recognize that this statue represents the teenage boy who had to borrow his equipment and take what he could get, unable to afford the proper mitt. He'd have liked the new 48,000-seat stadium, the home of the Baltimore Orioles. Daily tours include the dugout, scoreboard control room, press box and other facilities; call ☎ 410-547-6234.

BABE RUTH BIRTHPLACE & BALTIMORE ORIOLES MUSEUM

216 Emory Street
☎ 410-396-6310
Admission: $5, adults; $3, seniors; $2, children

This house is indeed the place where the baseball legend was born in 1895, and his childhood room has been re-created for visitors. You'll learn historical details about his life and see plenty of memorabilia spanning his entire career from the small-time teams to his heyday playing with the Red Sox and the Yankees.

Three other row houses adjoin the one in which Babe Ruth was born, creating a museum not only of his life, but of Baltimore baseball. You'll find photographs, programs, memorabilia and artifacts associated with other great Baltimore players, as well as film footage to watch. The home is furnished in the style of the late 1800s. The museum is open daily; April through October, 10-5; November through March, 10-4. On days when the Orioles play home games, the museum stays open until 7 pm

B&O RAILROAD MUSEUM

901 West Pratt Street at Poppleton Street
☎ 410-752-2490
www.borail.org
Admission: $6.50, adults; $5.50, seniors; $4, children ages three-12

It's hard to say what's the most striking part of the museum – the beautifully restored giant roundhouse or the shining circle of rolling stock that fills it. You can climb aboard many of the 120 cars and locomotives for a closer look. This was the site of the Mount Clare Station, dating from 1829 and America's first passenger railway station. It served the B&O (Baltimore and Ohio), America's oldest railroad. Among the collections are some of America's oldest steam and diesel locomotives, passenger cars and freight wagons. Displays highlight various aspects of the railroad, such as pullman service and dining cars. and the museum has a collection of model trains. The Railroad Museum is open daily, from 10 am-5 pm.

MOUNT CLARE MUSEUM HOUSE

Carroll Park
1500 Washington Boulevard at Monroe Street
☎ 410-837-3262
Admission: $6, adults; $5, seniors; $3, students with ID; $1, under age 12

The only mansion in Baltimore that predates the Revolution, Mount Clare was completed in 1760 and was the summer residence of Charles Carroll, Barrister.

Mount Clare, along with Homewood (see page 87), is one of the nation's finest examples of Georgian architecture; it is furnished with an outstanding collection of 18th- and 19th-century furniture original to Carroll and his wife, whose portraits by Charles Willson Peale hang in the parlor. In addition to the home's original furniture – some fine examples of Chippendale and Hepplewhite pieces – are distinguished furnishings used by later generations of the family. It is rare to see a house museum of this era that contains so much of the original family's belongings, and this one is made even more interesting because it contains not only the show pieces, but things used by the Carrolls in their daily lives. Mount Clare was once surrounded by an 800-acre plantation, part of which is now Carroll Park. The orchards and vineyards are under restoration.

Tours of the house are given Tuesday through Friday, every hour on the hour from 11-3; and on weekends at 1, 2 and 3. Mount Clare is closed in January.

WHICH CHARLES CARROLL?

This Charles Carroll, the builder of Mount Clare, used "Barrister" as part of his name to avoid being confused with a more famous relative known as Charles Carroll of Carrollton (see the Charles Carroll House in *Annapolis*, page 187). The latter was a financier and the only Catholic signer of the Declaration of Independence; he was also the father of Charles Carroll, Jr., for whom he built Homewood.

BROMO SELTZER TOWER
Eutaw and Lombard Streets

Although this tower is not open to the public, and has actually been renamed the Baltimore Arts Tower by the city, it is still a Baltimore landmark, as well as a reminder of American ingenuity and marketing. The tower was commissioned by Isaac E. Emerson to advertise and house his product, Bromo Seltzer, which was an innovative cure for upset stomach and headaches. The building, designed by architect Joseph Evans Sperry, was topped with a tower inspired by the Italian Palazzo Vecchio. The clock face was designed with characters spelling out the product's name, instead of numbers. The company was eventually bought out and then moved, and today the building is the venue for many functions of the Mayor's Advisory Committee on Art and Culture; an appropriate use, we think.

A BEACON IN THE NIGHT

Unfortunately (some will disagree here) you're not seeing the full effect of the original beacon. The tower was once topped with a 51-foot cobalt blue Bromo Seltzer bottle, which rotated and was bathed at night in lights. When lit, the big blue bottle could be seen from well out into the Chesapeake Bay. What a comfort it must have been to sailors headed into port and for the dives of East Baltimore Street, to know that relief would be at hand for their hangovers the next morning.

NATIONAL MUSEUM OF DENTISTRY
31 South Greene Street
☎ 410-706-0600
www.dentalmuseum.umaryland.edu
Admission: $4.50, adults; $2.50, seniors, children ages seven-18, and students; free, under age seven

You'll never believe what a setting and nicely designed displays can do for a subject until you see this museum. It makes teeth and dentistry interesting, fun, even nostalgic.

Along with the set of dental tools kept solely for use in the royal mouth of Queen Victoria, you can see tooth cleaning and repair equipment from historical times and listen to old radio toothpaste jingles played by a jukebox shaped like a giant art deco mouth. This museum certainly gets the prize for clever and classy presentations and displays.

Be warned that if you bring children, they will certainly want to put on white coats and become dentists in the scaled-down offices, examining your teeth as you recline in a dental chair. A library provides a place for you to read to them from an astonishing number of children's books that involve teeth and dentistry. The museum is open Wednesday-Saturday, 10-4; and Sunday, 1-4.

Possibly the best-known display at the Museum of Dentistry is George Washington's false teeth, which were not made of wood.

WESTMINSTER HALL BURYING GROUND AND CATACOMBS
Fayette and Greene Streets
☎ 410-706-2072
Free

The 1852 Presbyterian Church, now inactive, is best known as the burial place of Edgar Allan Poe, but its interest goes far beyond that. It has one of the city's oldest burial grounds, with graves of many other prominent Marylanders. When the grounds are not open, you can see Edgar Allan Poe's monument right in the corner. Tours lead through the catacombs and feature interesting historical sidelights. Poe was not a Baltimore native, but he lived, worked and died here. He achieved his first literary recognition in

Baltimore, for the short story *MS. Found in a Bottle*. Westminster Hall is open daily, except holidays, 8 am to dusk. Tours are held the first and third Friday and Saturday of each month, April-November; reservations are required.

FIRE MUSEUM OF THE BALTIMORE EQUITABLE SOCIETY

21 North Eutaw Street
☎ 410-727-1794
Free

In the days before public fire departments, insurance companies kept their own brigades, which responded to fires at the homes and businesses of their insured. Not many museums let you play with the exhibits, but here you can try on some of the old fire helmets and – best yet – sound some of the alarm devices. Some people (like us) never grow up. The Fire Museum is open weekdays, 10-4.

LEXINGTON MARKET

400 West Lexington Street
☎ 410-685-6169

If you're visiting in March, you may meet Barnum and Bailey's elephants, who come to parade and dine in Lexington Market. Hey, this is Baltimore!

About 140 food merchants sell fresh produce, fish, meat,and baked goods along with ready-made foods of every ethnicity in the largest of Baltimore's city markets. Stop here for lunch or just to sample a slice of Baltimore life. The busy market gets even crazier on its festival days, when you trade personal space for the excitement and bustle reminiscent of the 200-year-old market's earlier days. The market is open Monday-Saturday, 8:30-6.

Mount Vernon & Vicinity

High society chose the high ground, where they could overlook the affairs of the harbor without actually having to live there. Early Baltimore's most prestigious in-town neighborhood, Mount Vernon still has the rarified air of old money, despite the mix of businesses and residences. A thriving center for the arts and culture, it features fine shops, "Restaurant Row" and art and history museums. At its center is the Washington Monument, set in a gracious park-filled intersection at Charles Street and Mount Vernon Place. The neighborhood's name derives from the name of George Washington's home.

The Mount Vernon Cultural District makes it easy to visit its attractions with a brochure that not only describes them but locates them on a handy map. You can pick up a copy at the Baltimore Area Visitors Center at Inner Harbor or at many shops in the neighborhood. Most of the places you'll want to visit are along Charles Street or close to the park-like squares flanking the Washington Monument. Mount Vernon Place, just to the west of the monument, is lined with fine row houses, the most outstanding of which is now occupied by the Engineering Club at numbers 7-11, a single mansion built from 1884 to 1904.

Nearly every building here has a story to tell, and you can hear the most romantic of them in a walking tour, offered by the Mount Vernon Cultural District, that explores Mount Vernon's past. The neighborhood's two best known love stories are those of Jérôme Bonaparte (Napoleon's brother) and Betsy

Patterson, and the Duke and Duchess of Windsor; ☎ 410-605-0462.

A LOVE STORY

While the story of the Duke and Duchess of Windsor is familiar to nearly everyone, that of the unfortunate Betsy Patterson is not. In 1803, the Emperor Napoleon's brother Jérôme was traveling in Maryland, where he met and fell in love with the lovely Betsy Patterson. Although both Napoleon and Betsy's father objected strongly, the two married within the year. Napoleon eventually cut off Jérôme's money and summoned him home. Betsy was refused permission to enter France. She bore Jérôme's child, but she never saw her husband again. You'll hear of Betsy again in the Maryland Historical Society Museum.

The museums in Mount Vernon join neighborhood shops, cultural centers and restaurants in **First Thursdays**, 5:30-7:30 on the first Thursday evening of each month. Free concerts and museum admissions, receptions and exhibits in the art galleries and special prices in cafés, theaters and restaurants bring both locals and out-of-towners to sample the neighborhood on these evenings.

WASHINGTON MONUMENT

North Charles Street at Mount Vernon Place
☎ 410-837-4636
Admission: $1

In case you wonder about such things, the statue of Washington atop the monument weighs 30 tons.

This was the first architectural monument in America honoring George Washington, and was completed in 1829. Another Maryland monument, a stone tower in the Appalachian Mountains, west of Frederick, was completed two years earlier in 1827, but is not an architectural design, hence the distinction. Sorry, but there's no elevator inside, so you'll have to climb the monument's 228 spiraling steps to reach the bird's-eye view of the city that you can see from the four windows at its top. The monument is open Wednesday through Sunday, 10-4.

THE WALTERS ART MUSEUM

600 North Charles Street
☎ 410-547-9000
www.thewalters.org
Admission: $5, adults; $3, seniors, students and young adults; $1, ages six-17; children under six, free

General admission to The Walters is free on Saturdays from 11-1 for all age groups.

The figures are staggering – 30,000 art objects representing more than five millennia – but they don't begin to prepare you for the degree of artistic achievement represented here. Baltimore-born Henry Walters amassed his collections with a critical and well-trained eye, then presented them to the city, creating what many experts consider one of the nation's top art museums. We'd have to agree. The collections span ancient Egypt to art nouveau, and highlights are the Fabergé eggs, medieval armor and Asian arts, which are shown separately in the adjoining Hackerman House. The museum is under renovation as we write, to create better exhibition space, but portions of it will remain open during this process. See their Web site for information about current exhibitions.

It's nearly impossible to list all the specialty collections, but among the most outstanding are the ancient Egyptian artifacts, European porcelains, gold work from the Renaissance to the early 20th century, classical antiquities, medieval illuminated manuscripts and Fabergé eggs.

An extraordinary set of Asian collections fill the adjoining Hackerman House, whose fine interior architecture is worthy of museum status itself. In its center, a spiral staircase rises, topped by a Tiffany skylight. The museum shop on the first floor of Hackerman House is quite nice, too, with a good selection of jewelry based on the collections, books for both adults and children and tasteful decorative arts. The Walters is open Tuesday through Friday, 10-4; Saturday and Sunday, 11-5; and the first Thursday of each month, 10-8.

The Walters Art Museum is undergoing extensive renovations, which will take several years, but the highlights of its collections are displayed in the sections that are not under reconstruction, and what you will see still outweighs the collections of most art museums.

MARYLAND HISTORICAL SOCIETY MUSEUM & LIBRARY
201 West Monument Street
☎ 410-685-3750
Admission: $4, adults; $3, seniors and children

This excellent repository of much of the state's historical artifacts is in the process of assimilating and interpreting the materials that were formerly in the

Baltimore City Life Museums, now sadly closed. The Historical Society's expanding facility is impressive in its size alone, and when you consider that they cannot display most of the collections for lack of space, you get some idea of the riches it contains. The original manuscript of Francis Scott Key's *The Star Spangled Banner* is shown here, in a room dedicated to the War of 1812 in Baltimore. Despite the surfeit of artifacts it could show, the museum concentrates in most of its galleries on interpreting the materials and tying them together in ways that represent some facet of history, whether it is early furniture, social life, the founders or craftsmen. The American decorative arts are exceedingly well represented, and the museum has the world's largest collection of paintings by Charles Willson Peale and the nation's largest collection of 19th-century American silver.

A suite of furniture from the home of Betsy Patterson (wife of Napoleon's brother Jérôme), a gallery devoted to children's toys and furnishings, exhibits on Eubie Blake and other Baltimore jazz musicians, the Enoch Pratt House and a gallery on the Civil War are among the collections.

As the renovations and expansions are completed, displays will change, but it is likely that the exhibit on the city drawn from the collections from the former City Life Museums will continue. This nicely presented exhibit blends a fine collection of historic photographs with artifacts to illustrate the city's rich past and present, from its founding and its immigrant influx to the funkiest of its quirky traditions. The museum and library are open Tuesday through Friday, 10-5; Saturday, 9-5; and Sunday, 11-5.

GEORGE PEABODY LIBRARY

1 East Mount Vernon Place

☎ 410-659-8179

The statue of Peabody in the park in front of the library is a copy of one in London, where George Peabody lived late in life.

What looks on the outside like a relatively predictable Renaissance revival building fairly soars once you step inside. The surprises continue, for after you've signed in at the desk in the elegant reading room, you can proceed to what we think is Baltimore's most stunning interior, the library room itself. Pictures simply do not prepare you for the six layers of library stacks, on galleries supported by cast iron columns and edged by iron railings. These rise to support, in turn, the iron roof trusses that hold double skylights.

The room itself is well worth the stop, but those of a literary bent will appreciate the changing exhibits in display cases around this and the reading room. These may highlight the library's collections or some literary great, such as John Dos Passos, who used the library. Even many readers who frequent the library don't know about the other treasure hidden inside the building: the bronze replica of Lorenzo Ghiberti's doors from the Baptistery in Florence, Italy. These are on the second floor of the Conservatory of Music, next to the library. The entire complex was the gift of a generous New Englander, George Peabody, who spent 20 years in Baltimore and shared his largess between that city and the colleges of Harvard and Yale, whose extensive museums he also founded. The Peabody Library is open Monday through Friday, 9 am-3 pm.

MOUNT VERNON PLACE UNITED METHODIST CHURCH
10 East Mount Vernon Place
☎ 410-685-5290
Donations welcome for guided tours

You really need to see this church's exterior in all kinds of weather, since its striking green serpentine marble with brown sandstone trim deepens in color when it is wet. Built in 1872, the church is on the site of the house where Francis Scott Key died in 1843. The interior of the Victorian Gothic building is filled with delicate wrought iron scrollwork; the balconies are supported by almost fragile-looking cast iron pillars. The effect is quite handsome. The church is open Monday through Friday, 9-3.

THE MOUNT VERNON MUSEUM OF INCANDESCENT LIGHTING
717 Washington Place
☎ 410-752-8586 or 410-323-2454

Like dentistry, the incandescent light bulb is not something you'd expect to find a museum devoted to. But in Baltimore the mundane often mixes with the sublime. We love this little museum, partly because it's the lifetime passion of one man, who has collected an astonishing variety of artifacts that bring incandescent lighting from its earliest invention to the present. Dr. Hugh Hicks, who will show you through the collection himself (which is why you need to call first for a reservation), is so recognized an authority on the subject that the Smithsonian comes to him for help. You will see only the cream of Dr. Hicks' 60,000-piece collection, which includes the largest and smallest lightbulbs ever made, as well as the earliest. Along with the lightbulbs – in every size and shape you can imagine – come the fascinating story of their invention and evolution, told with both enthusiasm and humor. He casts a new light on Thomas Edison and his methods and tells the role that Japanese inventors played in the race for light. Christmas decorations include an impressive collection of early German figural Christmas tree lights as well as later ones, such as comic strip character Betty Boop. The museum is open Monday through Saturday, 9-5, and you must call for a reservation; it may take you a few calls to reach Dr. Hicks, but it's worth persevering.

BASILICA OF THE NATIONAL SHRINE OF THE ASSUMPTION OF THE BLESSED VIRGIN MARY
Cathedral and Mulberry Streets
☎ 410-727-3564

The first Metropolitan Roman Catholic Cathedral in the United States, the Basilica was built between 1805 and 1821. Its designer was Benjamin Latrobe, architect of the US Capitol in Washington; the basilica is considered not only Latrobe's masterpiece, but one of the world's best examples of neoclassical architecture. Despite the long controversy over whether the towers were designed by Latrobe, it is now generally believed that these and their Islamic-inspired domes were his. The interior demonstrates Latrobe's artistry best, we think, with the brilliant use of a variety of design elements to create a unified space. Unlike many churches, where it is the decoration you remember instead of the architecture, here it is the design concept that triumphs. The Basilica is open Monday through Friday, 7-5; Saturday and Sunday, 7-6:30; tours are given following the 10:45 Sunday Mass (about noon) or by appointment.

ENOCH PRATT FREE LIBRARY
400 Cathedral Street
☎ 410-396-5430

The present art deco building was constructed in the 1930s, and was quite a departure from traditional library designs with their imposing giant staircases lifting them far above the street. This library was designed not to intimidate, but to encourage people to enter and use the books. The design of the Pratt Library, one of the largest in America, has served as the inspiration for libraries across the country. Although its best known collections – on Edgar Allan Poe and H. L. Mencken – are not open to the casual visitor, permanent exhibits highlight these and other collections, including Maryland history. The library is open Monday-Wednesday, 10-8; Thursday-Saturday, 10-5; and, from October through April only, Sunday, 1-5.

Bolton Hill & Mount Royal

Continuing north and west from the Inner Harbor and Mount Vernon are the quiet streets of Bolton Hill, whose restored brownstone and brick homes breathe gentility with a healthy mix of the arts. The former home of F. Scott and Zelda Fitzgerald, and the Victorian wooden home of Wallis Simpson's aunt are here.

> **☛ DID YOU KNOW?**
>
> F. Scott Fitzgerald used his first initial and middle name to disguise his full name – Francis Scott Fitzgerald – and his kinship with the illustrious ancestor for whom he was named.

Mount Royal is the area directly north of Mount Vernon, near the University of Baltimore and Penn Station. If any one neighborhood in this theater-scattered city could be called the concert and theater district, it would be this one, where it blends in with the northern edge of Mount Vernon. Within a few blocks you will find the Meyerhoff Symphony Hall, the Lyric Opera House and the Charles Theatre.

MARYLAND NATIONAL GUARD MUSEUM
Intersection of Preston and Howard streets
☎ 410-576-1441

The Fifth Regiment Armory is the home grounds of the Maryland Fifth Regiment, the same one that held the line against the British to allow George Washington and his army to reach safety after the Battle of Long Island. The regiment's history predates the Revolution, and collections in the museum relate to all wars involving American troops. The strongest coverage is of the World War II era. The museum is open by appointment.

BALTIMORE STREETCAR MUSEUM
1901 Falls Road, northwest of Penn Station
☎ 410-547-0264
Admission: $5, adults; $2.50, seniors and ages four-11; $20 maximum for families

The museum admission allows you to climb aboard and ride historic streetcars all afternoon in the company of uniformed conductors, with all bells clanging just as they did when these cars carried Baltimoreans along their city's streets. Exhibits and a video tell about the history of Baltimore's streetcar system, and more restored cars are there to inspect, but the rides are the big draw. To reach the museum, take an MTA bus to the corner of Maryland and Lafayette avenues; follow Lafayette west to Falls Road, then turn right on Falls Road towards the museum. From June-October, they are open Saturday and Sunday, noon-5; from November-May, it is open Sunday only, noon-5.

DIME MUSEUM
1808 Maryland Avenue, near North Avenue
☎ 410-230-0263
www.dimemuseum.com
Admission: $4, adults; $3, children

Step right up, folks, and see the amazing devil-man and the Samoan Sea Wurm! No matter that the wurm is created from the top part of a monkey joined to the body of a fish, nor that the nine-foot mummified Amazon is shown in a display case custom made to fit her and provided by her manufacturer. Such bogus creatures are relics of the dime museums, forerunners of the circus sideshow tents. These dubious museums are long gone, but two avid collectors have traveled the country in search of the exhibits that once drew admiring crowds at the outrageous admission price of a whole dime.

The owners, one of whom is often dressed as a sideshow barker, will tell you about their bizarre artifacts, some of which are actually what they claim to be. They may even tell you how some of them were made, and they will certainly draw your attention to the faded script that authenticates the source of their prized memento of Abraham Lincoln. We haven't had this much fun in a museum in a long time – and we like museums. The Dime Museum is open Wednesday through Friday, noon-3; and weekends, 11-4.

Hampden & Uptown

North of Bolton Hill, Hampden is far removed from the sparkling newness of the revitalized Inner Harbor and has retained more of the character of old "Bawlmer" than any other enclave. The neighborhood clearly marches to its own drummer, who seems to be playing music from the '70s. It takes its role seriously (well, as seriously as Hampden can take anything) as home to the classic Baltimore "Hon" – big-haired and gum-snapping, with long fingernails painted bright red.

Several museums are spread out in the area that surrounds the Homewood campus of Johns Hopkins University and the Druid Hill Park neighborhood. These are some distance apart, so this might be a good place to get the car out of your hotel's parking garage and try your skills at navigating Baltimore traffic. Or you can take a bus to the two of these that are close together – the Baltimore Museum of Art and Homewood – and take taxis to the rest.

BALTIMORE MUSEUM OF ART

Art Museum Drive, Charles Street at 31st Street
☎ 410-396-7100
Admission: $6, adults; $4, seniors and students; free, under 18

With the riches of the Walters Art Museum fresh in mind, it may be hard to believe that an even larger treasury of the world's great artworks is only a bus or cab ride away. Maryland's largest art collections are at the Baltimore Museum of Art, with permanent collections of more than 85,000 works. The Cone collection of Post-Impressionist and modern art is the core of its holdings, and features 500 works by Matisse alone. Picasso, Cezanne, Renoir, Gauguin and Van Gogh are all represented by major works; this collection alone includes about 3,000 pieces.

MTA buses number 3 and 11 stop near the Baltimore Museum of Art.

But the list goes on. The Saidie May Collection of Ancient Mosaics and both fine and decorative arts of the Renaissance and Gothic periods was added in 1951, along with May's outstanding examples of modern art. She made a serious effort to obtain works that would complement the Cone collection, so that when her bequest was received by the museum, the two collections would form a comprehensive overview of Impressionism through modern art. In doing so, she added major pieces by Kandinsky, Miró, Braque, Klee, Ernst, Mondrian, Chagall and others. The museum continues to acquire works to enhance its collection representing the last half of the 20th century, including those by Warhol, Pollock and O'Keeffe.

Several other collections include prints from the Old Masters to the present, including examples by Rembrandt, Dürer, Whistler, Cassatt, Manet and Daumier.

Other galleries display major collections of more than 1,600 examples of African arts, such as masks, tools, textiles and jewelry, along with Pre-Columbian, Oceanic and Native American works. Asian art is highlighted by large collections of Chinese ceramics, Japanese textiles and prints. The displays of American decorative arts are especially interesting, since they are arranged chronologically in a way that shows the changes in tastes, styles and craftsmanship.

American furniture pieces include the works of all the major cabinetmakers.

While you may think this is enough, we have not yet described all the major holdings. You'll find paintings by the Old Masters – Hals, Raphael, Van Dyck, Titian, Rembrandt and Canaletto – and 2,000 years of textiles and needlework. Highlights of the latter are the Baltimore album quilts, a rare and important representation of this uniquely American art. Roman mosaics from the city of Antioch that date from the first through fifth centuries include more than 30 design fragments depicting everyday life and mythology. The museum is open Wednesday through Friday, 11-5, Saturday and Sunday, 11-6; and – with free admission – from 5-9 pm on the first Thursday of each month.

HOMEWOOD HOUSE

3400 North Charles Street
☎ 410-516-5589
Admission: $6, adults; $5, seniors; $3, ages six-17 and students with ID

Homewood was the original "money pit" house, or so it must have seemed to Charles Carroll of Carrollton, who built the country home as a wedding present to his somewhat profligate son, Charles Junior. Although he was the wealthiest man in America at that time, and obviously fond of his son and his new daughter-in-law, Charles Senior repeatedly asked his son to consider the cost of both the building itself and its decoration and furnishings. To the benefit of students of Early American interiors, Junior largely ignored his father's request, ordering the finest materials from England to build and furnish his home.

Today it is one of the most remarkable examples remaining of Federal architecture in all America, a perfect gem of a hyphen-and-wing house, restored to the period of its construction in 1801.

Although Homewood has been used for everything from offices to a school, its architecture – both interior and exterior – has remained intact, even to original moldings and mantels.

The outstanding decorative detail is one thing that sets the house apart from others of that time; each mantel has a different treatment, a virtual catalog of early 19th-century styles and craftsmanship. In the bedroom, notice the variety of decorative motifs on the mantel carving, almost as if the builders were trying out designs to be used elsewhere in the house. You will see some of them repeated on other mantels, so this may well have been a sort of sampler.

Not so lucky with the furnishings, the restoration turned up only one armchair original to the house. But Carroll's records survive, and were meticulous, so some of the furnishings are known to be just like those which the Carrolls used. Other items, such as bedcurtains, are of Carroll family provenance. The French traveling bidet was once owned by Betsy Patterson, but is identical to one in Carroll's house inventory.

The central reception room shows off the elegance of Georgian simplicity, with floorcloths repeating the black and white squares of the marble portico. Even the faux-mahogany painting on the doors is original. The guiding principle of Georgian architecture is its symmetry, but it creates a remarkably livable arrangement of rooms, each one entered through a central hallway. Today, visitors enter through the museum shop, in what was once the kitchen, located at the far end of the house to keep its cooking fires from heating the rest of the house in the summer and to lessen the chance of involving the whole house in a kitchen-started fire.

Below the house, the wine cellar has been restored, and you can see some of the archaeological evidence that was turned up by workers during the restoration. On the grounds, the tiny brick house was originally the privy. Homewood is open Tuesday through Saturday, 11-4, and Sunday, noon-4 (last tour at 3:30).

EVERGREEN HOUSE
4545 North Charles Street
☎ 410-516-0341
Admission: $6, adults; $5, seniors; $3, ages six-18

Three things appeal to us – and to everyone who visits, we suspect – about this 48-room Italianate mansion. First, the house is a remarkable architectural and decorative treasure-trove. Each room has its own special attractions: the vivid red walls and Moorish-style carved transom screen of the entrance hall, lattice-patterned stucco walls and magnificent carved mantel and ceiling in the reception room, mosaic marble floors and gilt of the gold bathroom, the surprising warmth of the large drawing room. Our favorites (Okay, so we're bookish) are the intimate Reading Room with its charming painted scenes of cities where Ambassador John Garrett served during his diplomatic career, and the larger Great Library, whose American walnut shelves and panels are lightened by the huge windows. So inviting is this room that it's hard to restrain yourself from pulling a book from the shelf and sinking into one of the chairs for the afternoon. In the library is a portrait of the man whose sanctuary this was. He is casually dressed, with a book in his hand. By this point in the tour (guides here are excellent, by the way) visitors have begun to know Ambassador Garrett and his lively, extroverted wife, Alice.

Their personalities and interests are the second fascination of the house, which reflects them, their times and their personalities in ways most grand mansions do not reveal their owners. Never do you feel the intrusion of a decorator here, unless it's with Alice's firm guiding hand or John's gentle bookish insights. Alice is most evident in the theater and its lobby, an astonishing place designed by Leon Bakst, a set designer for the Russian ballet companies. Here, Alice, who loved to dance, performed for guests at their parties on a small stage built for one.

A former bowling alley underneath the wing was adapted to create a display room for the Garretts' collection of Japanese netsuke, inro and laquerware. This and other collections are the third fascination of Evergreen. The art collection pieces are used throughout, and so neatly worked into the décor of the home that you almost fail to focus on them as collections. We stood for some time in the entrance hallway before we realized that we were looking at Dufy paintings. More are in upstairs rooms. The drawing room is hung with Vuillards and works by Picasso, Bonnard and Degas. Collections of Tiffany glass and paperweights were not the Garretts', but are displayed here by the college. We leave Evergreen House regretting that we didn't live in Baltimore society in the 1930s, when Alice Garrett might have invited us to dinner and one of her performances.

The gardens at Evergreen are among the country's finest examples of Italianate landscaping.

The house sits in 26 acres of gardens, which include formal Italianate portions and are often the venue of sculpture shows. A good brochure offers a self-guided tour of the gardens. The brochure helps you see them as they were in the Garretts' time, and to picture the teahouse, studio, fountain and other features that once graced them. Some of these are being restored.

To reach Evergreen from the Baltimore Beltway (I-695), take Exit 25 onto Charles Street and head south about seven miles, where you'll see the entrance sign on your left. From the city, Evergreen is on the right, just north of the Loyola College campus. It is open Monday through Friday, 10-4; weekends 1-4; tours begin on the hour, with the last at 3 pm.

LACROSSE HALL OF FAME MUSEUM
113 West University Parkway
☎ 410-235-6882
Admission: $3, adults; $2, under 16

Admittedly, this museum is for sports fanatics only, as it follows 350 years of lacrosse history through uniforms, programs, equipment and old photographs. You can also see a videotape of the highlights of play in past championship games. It is open March through May only, Monday through Friday, 9-5; and Saturday, 10-5.

THE BALTIMORE ZOO
Druid Hill Park
☎ 410-366-5466
Admission: $8.50, adults; $5, seniors and ages two-15

More than 2,000 mammal, bird and reptile species make their homes in the 200-acre park, where strong importance is placed on creating wildlife habitats that are as close to the animal's native one as possible. The African Watering Hole is a free-range area covering six acres, with rhinoceros, zebra and gazelle in residence. Starring among the big cats are Siberian tigers. The Children's Zoo is not just for kids, although they love its hands-on activities. So do we, especially the Baltimore oriole's nest that is large enough to fit Big Bird. June through Labor Day, the zoo is open Monday through Friday, 10-4; Saturday, 10-8; Sunday, 10-5:30; in winter, they are open daily, 10-4.

BALTIMORE CITY CONSERVATORY
Druid Lake Drive
☎ 410-396-0180
Free

The Victorian "glass house" was built in 1888, and Baltimoreans have been going here to sample a bit of the tropics ever since.

We especially like it in the winter, when a dusting of snow outside reminds us that we are not living in the tropics, but inside all is steamy and green with luxuriant big leaves of trees and plants from warmer climes. Seasonal displays include flowering bulbs in the spring, chrysanthemums in the fall and poinsettias in the winter. Other greenhouses display orchids, begonias and desert plants. An adjoining outdoor garden shows seasonal plantings. The conservatory is on Druid Lake Drive, between Gwynns Falls Parkway and McCulloh Street. It is open Thursday-Sunday, 10-4.

CYLBURN ARBORETUM
4915 Greenspring Avenue
☎ 410-367-2217
Free

The Cylburn Mansion, begun in 1863 and finished in 1889, is one of several grand estates that once stood on the outskirts of Baltimore, surrounded by acres of gardens and estate lands that have since become city parks. Many of the mansions are gone, but the stone Cylburn survives and has been completely restored on the outside. The interior awaits restoration, and is now used as park offices and as a small nature museum featuring birds and interpreting the park's environment. It is worth seeing, even unrestored, for its parquet floors in patterns of oak, black walnut and maple, as well as the mirrors and the ornate dining room, with carved paneling and a marble fireplace.

The extensive grounds are now a nature preserve, planted with majestic oaks and accessed by wandering paths, all designed by the Olmsted brothers. Several gardens feature roses, herbs, All-America selections and the Garden of the Senses, designed for physically impaired visitors. The arboretum is reached via I-83, between Exits 9 and 10, north of

Druid Hill Park. It is open daily, 6 am to 9 pm in summer; dawn to dusk winter; the house is open Tuesday and Thursday, 10-3.

PIMLICO RACE COURSE
5210 Park Heights Avenue
☎ 410-542-9400

Any racing enthusiast will be fascinated by the exhibit set up on the club house's second floor, which details not only this track but the whole state's history of racing. Pimlico is the oldest race track in the country still in continuous use. You'll see a 19th-century betting machine, photographs, and even a note from George Washington, detailing his losses. Let that be a lesson to you. The exhibit is open for viewing from 11:30 am-5:30 pm on racing days, from March to mid-June.

SHERWOOD GARDENS
Stratford Road, just west of Route 45 in the neighborhood of Guilford
☎ 401-323-7982
Free

This small (seven acres) park is filled in the spring with an astonishing display of flowering bulbs. In late April the park bursts into bloom with 80,000 tulips, interspersed with other colorful bulbs. Flowering trees and shrubs, such as dogwood, cherry, azalea and magnolia, complete the colorful display. The gardens are open dawn to dusk.

Sherwood Gardens is fully wheelchair accessible.

Elsewhere in the City

Not all of the places you may want to see in Baltimore lie within or close to these defined neighborhoods. The two that follow are a long distance apart and not close to any other attraction but they are worth the extra travel time needed.

GREAT BLACKS IN WAX MUSEUM
1601 East North Avenue
☎ 410-563-3404
Admission: $5.75, adults; $5.25, seniors and college students; $3.75, ages 12-17; $3.25, ages two-11.

We admit to a general dislike of wax effigies of the famous, but this well-done display really does give a good picture of Baltimore's – and the nation's – African-American history and culture. Life-sized figures depict prominent people of African descent in historical settings, from ancient Africa to modern political figures. A 30-foot replica of a slave ship commemorates the many who arrived as victims of the slave trade. The role of Baltimore in the Civil Rights movement is well represented in the displays. The museum hours are Tuesday-Saturday, 9-6; Sunday, noon-6.

SS *JOHN W. BROWN*
Pier One, 2000 South Clinton Street, Canton, across the Harbor from Fort McHenry
☎ 410-661-1550

The John W. Brown *is one of only two surviving Liberty Ships of the original 2,500 to have been restored, and the only one on the East Coast.*

Project Liberty Ship maintains this historic vessel as a maritime museum and memorial to those people who built, sailed and defended Liberty ships during World War II.

Liberty ships were built as transport ships from 1941 until the war ended, each carrying 8,500 long tons of cargo that supplied allied fighting forces all over the world. The *John W. Brown*, built in Baltimore, took part in the invasion of southern France, as well as shuttling back and forth across the Atlantic filled with troops and war supplies. It is planned that the ship will have a regular schedule of day cruises in the Chesapeake, but for now it contains exhibits and is open for tours on Wednesday and Saturday, 10-2; call first to confirm.

Outside of Baltimore

FORT MEADE NSA CRYPTOLOGIC MUSEUM
Colony 7 Road, Fort Meade
☎ 410-688-5849
Free

The art and science of cryptography – the making and breaking of codes – is explored in depth in a fascinating museum. Books, computers, and other related equipment tell stories of critical intelligence work done by the military, and of people involved in the work. The highlight to most visitors is the now-famous Enigma machine, used by the Germans in World War II to decipher the code they were convinced could never be broken. The theoretical number of variations possible with the machine is so large that it has 115 digits – that's a trillion with another 34 sets of three digits tacked on. Of course, the allies did break the code, and from information they continued to receive – plans the German Army thought were close-held secrets – were able to shorten World War II by many months. But this is only one of the stories you'll hear in the guided tour, or read about if you choose to explore the museum on your own. The Cryptological Museum is open Monday-Friday, 9-3; Saturday, 10-2.

Fort Meade is southwest of Baltimore, via the Baltimore-Washington Parkway (also called 295, or the Spellman Parkway).

BROOKSIDE GARDENS
1500 Glenallen Avenue, Wheaton
☎ 301 949-8230
Free

These gardens are a bit of a trip from Baltimore, but they are so outstanding that anyone who loves gardens will not want to miss them.

Brookside looks so much like the carefully restored gardens of a fine old estate that it's hard to believe the gardens are only about 20 years old.

Full-grown tree specimens form their arboretum, which features not only Maryland species, but exotics as well. Asian trees grow on the island in the Japanese Garden. This nine-acre section adjoins a pond filled with bright carp, and has traditional pools, walks and a Japanese bridge and teahouse. Formal parterre beds, a stunning rose garden, lively special garden exhibits for children, an herb garden, an aquatic garden and several other specialty gardens are interspersed throughout beautifully landscaped grounds. The glass conservatory is often filled with special exhibits, which may be anything, from seasonal plants to butterflies. A full schedule of garden-related activities features seasonal subjects and includes classes, clinics and workshops on gardening and plant crafts. In December, the gardens become a wonderland of outdoor lighting displays.

The gardens are open daily all year. From Baltimore, take I-95 to the Washington Beltway (I-495) and go west to Exit 31, following Route 97 (Georgia Avenue) north. Pass Wheaton and Arcola Avenue and the park will be on the right before Randolph Road.

SIX FLAGS AMERICA
Route 214 (Central Avenue), Largo
☎ 301 249-1500
Admission: $30, adults; $15, kids under 48 inches tall; discounts for seniors and kids under three.

The granddaddy of all theme parks, with all the latest thrill rides and cartoon-based activities designed for youngsters. Rides, shows and shops are gathered into themed areas, so you'll find Main Street 1776 (it may take a little imagination) and Coyote Creek and Southwest Territory, with an oil drilling and gold mining theme. Looney Tunes Movie Town features all the Looney Tunes critters. You can try at least a half dozen roller-coaster-style rides, a miniature train ride, a swinging carousel and other rides appropriate for all age groups. Seasonal activities dress the park in everything from Christmas glitter to spooky tombstones and giant cobwebs. If theme parks are your stuff, you'll have a good day here.

The park is open weekends only in April, May and September through December; from late May through August it is open daily. From Baltimore, take I-95 to the Washington Beltway (I-495) and go east to Exit 15, following Route 214 (Central Avenue) east at Largo. The park is five miles east of the exit just past the Arena.

Spectator Sports

You won't be in Baltimore long before you learn that its residents are avid fans of their hometown teams, the Ravens (NFL football) and the Orioles (baseball). This is, of course, the city where Babe Ruth was born and whose Ravens (named for Edgar Allan

Poe's poem, *The Raven*) won the Superbowl in 2001. Both teams have new state-of-the-art stadiums for their home games. To catch a glimpse of the baseball players up close, stop at Orioles' Sports Bar, in the Sheraton Inner Harbor Hotel, the "official" bar of the Orioles.

Baseball

The Light Rail stop for Oriole Park is called Camden Yards, and the MARC Camden Line ends at Camden Station; bus lines 210 and 27 also stop near the stadium.

ORIOLE PARK AT CAMDEN YARDS
333 West Camden Street, at Eutaw Street
☎ 410-685-9800

The diamond that is the Orioles fan's best friend is Oriole Park at Camden Yards, a few blocks west of the Inner Harbor, past the convention center. If you go to a game here, even your bleacher seats will have a great view – the stadium is known for its unobstructed playing field. See *Attractions*, page 66, for more information on the stadium and to learn about tours.

Outside the stadium, you can get just about anything to express your support of the team, as well as a good selection of ballpark food. Look for Boog Powell's own BBQ, maybe even served by Boog himself, almost as much a legend here as The Babe.

The nearest Light Rail station for PSINet Stadium is Hamburg St., but the train stops only during stadium events. Buses 27 and 210 also stop nearby.

Football

PSINET STADIUM AT CAMDEN YARDS
Hamburg and Russell Streets
☎ 410-261-RAVE or 410-261-FANS

PSINet Stadium is the still-quite-new home to the Baltimore Ravens, the city's NFL team, and also hosts many other types of entertainment in the off-season. Designed by the same team of architects as Oriole Stadium a few blocks to the north, this sports center has a distinctive look, with brick arches and cutaway corners for sweeping city views from the inside. Even more distinctive are the 69,000 seats, all painted purple. As with any stadium, there are plenty of vendors, but the food here is considered above average.

Horse Racing

PIMLICO RACE COURSE
5210 Park Heights Avenue, near the northern boundary of the city.
☎ 410-542-9400

Pimlico, the oldest race track still in continuous use in America, is home of the Preakness Stakes, the second race of the Triple Crown, run on the third Saturday in May. It also has races throughout the summer. Upstairs in the clubhouse is a small museum (see page 93).

Buses 27, 91 and M3 stop near Pimlico.

Lacrosse

HOMEWOOD FIELD
Charles Street at University Parkway
Johns Hopkins University
☎ 410-235-6882

Lacrosse is a major sport at Johns Hopkins University, where some of the nation's top players are members of the Blue Jays (why do Baltimore's home teams all have bird names?).

Recreation

Golf

Baltimore has several public golf courses nearby, although none within the city limits. **Beechtree Golf Club**, north of the city in Aberdeen, is one of the best in the Middle Atlantic states, with a country club atmosphere and an outstanding layout and clubhouse. It's at 811 Stepney Road; ☎ 410-297-9700.

Another up-market club is nearby in Havre de Grace, **Bulle Rock Golf Course**. Also public, this par-72 course was designed by Pete Dye and has won several awards. 320 Bleinham Lane; ☎ 410-939-8887.

Tours

We like to meet a city on foot, but a good tour can give you a basic overview and show you the neighborhoods you'll want to return to on your own. This is particularly true in Baltimore, and happily there is a very good tour which emphasizes this neighborhood factor.

On Land

HARBOR CITY TOURS
Harborplace Pier
☎ 410-254-TOUR (8687)

The company is owned and run by Fran Zeller, whose witty and often irreverent commentary includes a lot of stories about growing up here. You'll learn about the city's unique culture and character – such things as formstone and painted window screens and marble steps – along with the more serious history. Her keen interest in the past has led her to research her information thoroughly, not just pass along the urban myths and tour-guide tales. Tours ($10) leave from Harborplace four times daily and can include pick-ups at downtown hotels. They last about 90 minutes and include on-and-off reboarding, in case you want to stop for a while to explore on your own.

★ TIP

For $5 more, buy a combination ticket that adds a one-hour narrated harbor cruise to your Harbor City Tours bus itinerary. You can do them on separate days.

On Water

BALTIMORE HARBOR TOURS
301 Light Street (Opposite Visitors Center)
Inner Harbor
☎ 410-783-4660 or 800-831-TOUR

Very reasonably priced 60-minute narrated cruises operate in conjunction with Harbor City Tours. For a package price of $15 you can get both land and sea tours. Boat tours alone are $9 and can also be combined in a package ticket with admission to the museum ships.

CLIPPER CITY
Harborplace Pier, next to the Science Center
☎ 410-539-6277
www.sailingship.com

The topsail schooner offers two-hour and longer sailing tours, Monday through Saturday at noon and 3, Sunday at 3 and 6; the cost is $12 for adults and $2 for children. Sunday brunch and weekend evening sails are $30 and $20 respectively, and feature live Caribbean music.

NIGHTHAWK
Thames Street, Fells Point
☎ 410-276-7447

The Nighthawk *is available for private charters during the day, for up to 48 people.*

The schooner *Nighthawk*, a classic tall ship, takes passengers on Saturday evening Moonlight Buffet cruises, from the first Saturday in May through the last Saturday in September, for $39.50 per person. They also have a Murder Mystery Dinner cruise the first Sunday of each month from May through October, for $49.50 per person.

HARBOR BELLE

Henderson's Wharf, at the end of Fell Street
Fells Point
☎ 410-764-3928

A replica of the paddlewheeler steamboats that once plied Baltimore's harbor, the *Belle* ends the work week right with low-priced after-work cruises on Friday, from 5:30 to 7:30; Saturday sunset cruises, at 7:15 pm, include a buffet dinner for about $30. Sunday Champagne brunch cruises board at 10:45.

BAY LADY AND *LADY BALTIMORE*

301 Light Street, Inner Harbor
Schedule, ☎ 410-347-5552
Reservations, ☎ 410-727-3113 or 800-695-LADY
www.harborcruises.com

Two-hour harbor cruises include lunch, Monday through Saturday, boarding at 11:30 am. Three-hour evening trips include dinner, Monday through Saturday boarding at 6:30, Sunday at 4:30. The costs are upwards of $25 and $35 respectively, with Monday's seafood dinner, Friday's crab feast and the Saturday buffet higher. Moonlight cruises without meals, on Friday and Saturday, 11:00 pm to 2 am, are about $25. On Wednesdays, June through August, you can cruise to Annapolis for the day, boarding at 8:00 am and returning about 5:00 pm.

Shop Till You Drop

Like everything else in Baltimore, shopping is largely defined by the neighborhoods, where local people still look first for their needs. Fells Point, Federal Hill and Mount Vernon are the primary neighborhoods for small boutiques, artisan studios and antiques shops, although Hampden has a number of unusual – some downright funky – shops that make it worth hopping onto a #27 bus and heading for 36th Street. There are two major shopping galleries near the Inner Harbor, and serious mall shoppers head for White Marsh, northeast of the city off I-95, just beyond the Beltway.

Inner Harbor

For mall shops, head for Harborplace Pavilion and The Gallery, connected by a skywalk.

HARBORPLACE
Pratt and Light Street Pavilions
☎ 410-332-4191
www.harborplace.com

Celebrate Baltimore, on the second level of the Light Street Pavilion, sells gifts that have a Baltimore theme.

These two glass pavilions house over 130 shops that overlook the harbor. The open atmosphere is delightful, and you will find many carts and vendors selling their goods in the old marketplace style. The food court is one of the few areas to remain unchanged and, although there are some shops that are permanent, the management likes to have variety for those who visit frequently. You can find almost anything here, including valet parking. Open Monday-Saturday, 10-9; Sunday 11-7.

THE GALLERY AT HARBORPLACE
Calvert and Pratt Streets
☎ 410-332-4191

Connected to Harborplace by a skywalk, the Gallery is a dramatic five-story atrium with about 70 shops. Most are specialty shops and upscale boutiques, and there are several choices of places to eat. You can buy everything here, from hats to gourmet dog biscuits.

Little Italy

Not a major shopping area, but convenient to Inner Harbor, Little Italy is also the place to look for imported Italian goodies.

WATER FROM THE MOON GALLERY
217 Albemarle Street
☎ 410-727-6380

This lovely gallery's name says it all, as it suggests the finest and most elusive – here you can find all sorts of rare and exquisite pieces of craftsmanship, with heavy emphasis on American artists. The art glass is nothing short of spectacular.

Fells Point

Fells Point is a good place to find studios and shops featuring handwork. Also browse in Fells Point's cobbled streets for antiques and original art. The area is known for more affordable antiques than the pricier Antiques Row. You'll find small shops along Broadway and Thames Street, as well as in the smaller streets that radiate from Broadway and Thames, such as Aliceanna and South Anne. On the second Sunday of each month from April through October, Broadway Market Square – the open space between the market and the Recreation Pier of Thames Street – is filled with antiques and collect-

Some Fells Point shops are closed on weekdays in the winter.

ibles vendors for the **Second Sunday Antiques Market**. Hours are 8 am to 6 pm; ☎ 410-675-4776.

BAY AND COUNTRY CRAFTS
1635 Lancaster Street
☎ 410-342-3317

Fine arts and carefully selected crafts relating to the Chesapeake Bay fill this tasteful shop. Waterfowl art (too fine to be called decoys any more), prints and paintings of bay scenes, mostly the work of local artists and craftsmen, range from jewelry and small items to museum-quality works. Bay and Country Crafts is open Thursday-Sunday, 11-5.

ANOTHER PERIOD IN TIME
1708-10 Fleet Street
☎ 410-675-4776
www.anotherperiod.com

Another Period in Time offers a staggering quantity of items.

This multi-dealer, two-level antiques store offers pretty much anything you could want, from jewelry to furniture. Another Period in Time is open Monday-Thursday, 9-5; Friday and Saturday, 10-6; Sunday, 12-5.

FLASHBACK
728 South Broadway
☎ 410-276-5086

This store is perfect for the nostalgic. If you're a John Waters film fan this is a must-stop, as it is now owned by Edith Massey's former business partner (if you're not a Waters fan, Edith was his favorite star). Lots more Baltimoriana is on the loose in Flashback. Travel back into the era of real rock 'n roll, back when girls were girls, boys were boys, and vinyl was your only choice. The atmosphere alone makes stopping here worthwhile. They are open every day, but hours vary quite a bit; we recommend that you call ahead.

SARATOGA TRUNK
1740 Aliceanna Street
☎ 410-327-6635

This quirky little shop is an interesting mix of assorted old stuff, big and small, and a small pottery studio in the back. Here you can find a veritable Noah's ark of clay animals, plus some Noah never dreamed of. Saratoga Trunk is open Friday through Sunday, noon-6.

ELZEARD POTTERY
602 South Ann Street
☎ 410-732-2928

Pottery can be both functional and decorative, or it can be unabashedly one or the other. Whatever your preference, you'll find it here, along with jewelry and furniture. Elzeard Pottery is open Thursday through Sunday; call for hours.

TEN THOUSAND VILLAGES
1621 Thames Street
☎ 410-342-5568

Handmade gifts, clothing and furnishings from around the world help support indigenous crafts and skills, while providing income to families in developing countries. Hours may vary seasonally but in general they are open Tuesday-Thursday, 11-7; Friday and Saturday, 11-9; Sunday, 1-5; closed Mondays.

.925 THE SILVER STORE

1640 Thames Street
☎ 410-327-0036

Handmade sterling silver jewelry in a wide variety of designs, including those that represent local motifs. A few other carefully selected items complement the jewelry. The shop is open until 7 pm daily.

GRRREAT BEARS

1643 Thames Street
☎ 410-276-4429

Bears from all over the world hibernate here, joining books and other toys and bear collectibles. You'll also find a complete line of Peter Rabbit items, and a whole section for everybody's favorite bear and his friends. Grrreat Bears is open every day, 9 am-9:30 pm.

Federal Hill & Key Highway

Practical neighborhood shops mix with the antiques and boutiques in this newly gentrified neighborhood. Cross Street Market has an excellent cheese shop.

THE ANTIQUE WAREHOUSE

1300 Jackson Street
☎ 410-659-0662

More than 30 dealers sell all sorts of antiques and collectibles in this multi-dealer gallery. The range includes everything from rare china pieces to yesterday's castoffs. The Warehouse is easy to reach by Water Taxi, at stop #9. The Antique Warehouse is open Tuesday through Saturday, 11-6 and Sunday, 12-5.

A COOK'S TABLE
717 Light Street
☎ 410-539-8600
www.acookstable.com

More than just a kitchen supply store, this shop is a gourmet feast in several ways. Here, among a wide variety of utensils and gadgets, you can find the perfect dishes for that romantic meal or a grand platter for your dinner party. And Cook's Table isn't just about the paraphernalia, it's about learning how to cook. Not only can you find an incredible selection of cookbooks for all levels of skill, but you can also enroll in one of their on-site cooking classes covering everything from international delights to the basics. A Cook's Table is open Monday and Wednesday-Saturday, 11-7; and Sunday, 12-5; closed Tuesdays.

GAINES McHALE ANTIQUES AND HOME
836 Leadenhall Street
☎ 410-625-1900

This is a large single-dealer antiques hall, filled with a wide selection of 18th- and 19th-century antique furniture and articles. Many of these are from the British Isles and France. McHale is also known for his ability to restore and adapt furniture into useful modern pieces, as well as for making authentically designed replicas from antique wood. The store is open Monday-Saturday, 9-6; Sunday noon-5.

Camden Yards

As you might imagine, sports rule even the shopping near the Orioles' home plate.

ORIOLES' BASEBALL STORE
B&O Warehouse, Camden and Howard Streets
☎ 410-332-4633, ext.158

This is where you find just about anything you want related to the city's favorite baseball team, from banners and beer glasses to clothing and photos, and it's all "official." You can't ask for better Baltimore souvenirs for baseball fans back home. The store is open Monday-Friday, 10-6; Saturday, 10-5; Sunday, noon-5.

GALLERY E
B&O Warehouse E, Camden and Howard Streets
☎ 410-547-6220

Baseball is not the only sport featured at Gallery E, despite the neighborhood.

Art meets sports in this unusual gallery of original sculptures, prints and paintings. Horse racing, fishing, golf, sailing, even racing cars and other active and spectator sports provide inspiration for the arts shown here, which range from Norman Rockwell prints to works with the paint barely dry. Gallery E is open Monday through Friday, 10-6; Saturday, 10-5; Sunday, 11-5.

Mount Vernon & Vicinity

Most Mount Vernon art galleries are open Tuesday through Saturday, 10-5.

North Charles Street is Mount Vernon's primary street for shopping, with galleries that feature fine arts, quality imports and crafts. The highest concentration of shops is between Pratt Street and Read Street.

Antiques Row runs along the east side of the 800 block of North Howard Street, between Read and Madison streets. It is the place to look for silver, Victoriana and furniture in the higher price ranges. Although the stores here specialize in antiques, they are certainly not limited to things previously owned. This district was once the craftsman's row, where furniture makers and other craftsmen lived and worked. Large portions of this old section were torn down for new structures, but the 800 block survives, restored as a reminder of the history of the neighborhood.

WOMEN'S INDUSTRIAL EXCHANGE

333 North Charles Street
☎ 410-685-4388

A period piece, this friendly shop carries handmade things you thought you'd never see again – delicately smocked dresses for little girls, hand-stitched heirloom christening outfits, handkerchiefs with crocheted lace edgings. It's irresistible. Dozens of rag dolls, stuffed toys, household linens, and knitted sweaters for all ages are only the beginning of this trove of needlework. It's by far the best source of baby gifts, and your purchase is going to a good cause as well, since the Exchange was founded more than 150 years ago to provide a respectable income for women who had fallen on hard times. The shop, which has a tearoom attached, also has a showcase filled with freshly baked pies, cakes, cookies, biscuits, breads and other baked goods. The Exchange shop is open Monday-Friday, 7-3. No credit cards.

One of the few such shops left in America, the Womens Industrial Exchange still provides widows, single mothers and other women a source of income.

BEADAZZLED
501 North Charles Street
☎ 410-837-2323

This specialty store sells only beads and jewelry-making materials, but it does it all the way. Here you will find over 4,000 varieties of beads, from common to rare and imported from all over the world. If you love beads but don't have the patience or the eyes to sit and fiddle with them, there are plenty of high-quality ready-made pieces available as well. Beadazzled is open daily, 10:30-6.

DUBEY'S ART AND ANTIQUES
807 North Howard Street
☎ 410-383-2881

Oriental furnishings and Chinese Export porcelain, as well as American and English furniture of museum quality, are the province of Dubey's. The shop is open 11-5, Monday through Saturday; noon-5, Sunday. Closed Sundays in August and September.

ANTIQUE TREASURY
809 North Howard Street
☎ 410-728-6363

This is a multi-dealer store, where collectors will be most likely to find Russian icons and Staffordshire-transferware china, as well as plenty of other antiques and collectibles ranging from jewelry to furniture. Antique Treasury is open 10:30-4:30 Tuesday through Saturday.

DRUSILLA'S BOOKS
817 North Howard Street
☎ 410-225-0277

This store is far beyond the typical endlesss stacks of disintegrating old books – Drusilla's specializes in collections, vintage books, and leather bound sets. If you are really into book collecting, you can buy books on your subject here as well, or even get her help looking for that elusive title or organizing and appraising your existing collection. Browse at Drusilla's Tuesday through Saturday, noon-5.

IMPERIAL HALF BUSHEL
831 North Howard Street
☎ 410-462-1192

This shop specializes in American silver and hollowware, as well as local Baltimore silver that is two centuries old. You may also find European silver here. Imperial is open 10:30-5, Monday through Saturday. In August it's open by appointment only.

Get a reduced parking rate at the Maryland General Hospital garage at Linden Avenue and Madison Street. Have your ticket validated at any shop in the Mount Vernon area.

E.A. MACK ANTIQUES
839 North Howard Street
☎ 410-728-1333

Mack's specialty is Early American and period furniture, including many pieces crafted in this very district during its heyday. Selections include some museum-quality pieces, and this is a favorite stop for dealers from all over the country.

BOGAT'S ANTIQUES AND RESTORATION
861 North Howard Street
☎ 410-728-4517

Bogat's biggest specialty is in fixing and restoring those treasured items that you thought were beyond hope, or giving that extra bit of attention to turn a nice antique into a gorgeous one. There are also antiques for sale here, but restoration is really their forté. Bogat's is open Monday through Friday, 10-4; Saturday, 10-5.

ZAKIYYAH'S ETHNIC VIBE
223 West Read Street
☎ 410-383-9141

Just around the corner from Antiques Row, you will find a great variety of African and African-American art and crafts. Many of the pieces from Africa are traditional work dating back to the early 1900s. The modern crafts for sale, including intricate beaded jewelry and silverwork, are made by local African-American artists. Call for hours.

Hampden & Uptown

You may have noticed that we like the funky neighborhood of Hampden. Apart from the Christmas decoration extravaganza on 34th Street, Café Hon and a pair of other memorable eateries, shopping is what Hampden is all about. That and having your nails done. Whichever direction you go on 36th Street, where almost all the shops are, don't miss Hometown Girl. And in case you wonder at the organization of this section, we're going up one side of "The Avenue" and down the other.

OH, SAID ROSE
840 West 36th Street
☎ 410-235-5170

Look here for great clothes, artsy, eclectic and quirky. The fine women's accessories and clothing are often handmade locally. You'll find dramatic jewelry and luscious drapey things in deep-toned velvets and other satisfying textures. Lots of hand-woven and hand-painted wearables. Hours may vary seasonally but in general they are open Tuesday-Saturday, 11-7; Sunday and Monday, 11-5.

HOMETOWN GIRL
1000 West 36th Street
☎ 410-662-4438
www.hometowngirlbalto.com

Look in this attractive shop for everything Baltimore, from high quality chocolates in the shape of crabs to books on Baltimore architecture. Locally made crafts, local foods to take home (cans of crab bisque, for example), Chesapeake Bay cookbooks, even Maryland fortune cookies. There's very little kitsch (fortune cookies are food, right?) in this tasteful collection of attractive gifts. Hometown Girl is happy to ship your order, too. The shop is open Monday-Wednesday, 11-8; Thursday 11-9; Friday and Saturday, 10-9; Sunday 10-6.

The book section at Hometown Girl is particularly interesting, with biographies that bring to life all those local names you meet in the museums.

Hometown Girl has an affiliated shop, Celebrate Baltimore, in the Light Street Pavilion in the Inner Harbor (see page 41), although we prefer the ambiance of the main store here in Hampden – and the chance to eat at Café Hon, next door.

GUSTAFSON'S
1006 West 36th Street
☎ 410-235-4244

There's no way to miss the changing window displays that fairly drag you into this shop. Here you'll find a little bit of everything, from nice antiques to the kind of junk that's sure to be another person's treasure. You may find yours. Call for hours.

PAPER-ROCK-SCISSORS
1111 West 36th Street
☎ 410-235-4420
www.paperrockscissors.com

The work of dozens of local artists and craftsmen, in many media, are shown in this attractive salon-style gallery. Textile arts, handmade paper, clothing and jewelry, stained glass, iron work and graphic arts join the paintings and drawings. Paper-Rock-Scissors is open Tuesday through Saturday, 10-6 and Sunday, noon-5.

FAT ELVIS
833 West 36th Street
☎ 410-467-6030

A description of this shop and its contents would not do it justice – but you can be assured that if it's bizarre, retro, and beyond your imagination, you can find it here. Vintage and nostalgia take over the selection of antiques and collectibles. The store is open Friday and Saturday, 10-6; Sunday noon-4.

THE PEARL GALLERY
815 West 36th Street
☎ 410-467-2260

The Pearl Gallery is filled with a lovely selection of various artwork and crafts. You may find the perfect pillows to go with that antique couch you just bought up the street, a striking sculpture to adorn the newly acquired art deco end table, or fine silver earrings to wear on your big night out in Bawlmer. The gallery is open Monday-Friday, noon-5; Saturday, 10-5; or mornings by appointment.

MUD & METAL
813 West 36th Street
☎ 410-467-8698

This shop is filled with all sorts of nifty pottery, ceramic, bronze, and copper work by local craftspeople. It's a good place for gifts or for decorating your house, with plenty of accessories to accent all types of decorating styles. Mud & Metal is open Monday-Saturday, 10-6; Sunday, noon-5; Friday evenings until 7. They may have extended hours during the holiday season.

THE TURNOVER SHOP
3855 Roland Avenue
☎ 410-235-9585

Not a bakery, but a consignment shop, the oldest in Maryland, Turnover is a good place to find all sorts of treasures, big and small. It appears that everybody brings their redundancies here. The shop is open Tuesday-Saturday, 10-5.

THE POTTERS GUILD OF BALTIMORE
Suite 101, Meadow Mill
3600 Clipper Mill Road
☎ 410-235-4884

Here you can not only buy the wares of Baltimore's potters, but also enroll in one of their classes to learn how to do it yourself. The shop is open Tuesday-Saturday, 11-4; Sunday, 12-5; call ahead for a schedule of classes.

All ages are welcome for classes at The Potters Guild.

ATOMIC BOOKS

1018 North Charles Street
www.atomicbooks.com
☎ 410-625-7955

This is a far cry from the average bookstore, and definitely one for the adventurous. Here you will find all of the books that weren't quite mainstream enough to make it into the big book stores, and some that are perhaps a little too daring to make it into the little neighborhood bookshop. Alongside the Betty Page pinup collections and extensive body art literature, you can find a great display of bizarre "things" that will make just about anybody squirm. Call for hours.

BALTIMORE MUSEUM OF ART MUSEUM SHOP

Art Museum Drive, Charles Street at 31st Street
☎ 410-396-7100

Purchases at the Baltimore Museum Shop help to support the museum.

If it's related to fine arts, especially the Impressionists and Post-Impressionists, you're likely to find it here. Works in the museums collections, as well as masterpieces from other museums, are represented. Posters and greeting cards, Museum reproduction jewelry, books about art and artists, and an array of other tasteful gifts fill the shop, which you can visit even if you are not touring the museum itself. The museum shop is open Wednesday through Friday, 11-5; Saturday and Sunday, 11-6.

EVERGREEN HOUSE MUSEUM SHOP

4545 North Charles Street, on the campus of Johns Hopkins University
☎ 410-516-0341

We don't even pretend to be unbiased; this is one of our favorite museum shops anywhere – and we love museum shops. Perhaps it's because they have such a plethora of material to work with – the subjects represented in the house itself are so broad and all-encompassing. But we've rarely seen such a tasteful and varied group of gifts, which range from fine china reproductions to art deco-inspired items. The book selection is also excellent, following both historical and artistic themes in the house. The Evergreen House museum shop is open Monday through Friday, 10 am-4 pm; weekends, 1-4 pm.

HOMEWOOD HOUSE MUSEUM SHOP
3400 North Charles Street
☎ 410-516-5589

Charming and tasteful Early American reproductions, paper goods and books highlight the attractive shop, which is located in the home's former kitchen wing, through which you enter the house. A number of selections here are suitable for children, too. This shop is within an easy walk of the Baltimore Museum of Art, so you can shop at both on one trip (and have lunch at Gertrude's, too (see page 170). Homewood House is open Tuesday through Saturday, 11-4 and Sunday, noon-4.

Cross Keys

The Village of Cross Keys is at 5100 Falls Road (Route 25), about 10 minutes north from the Inner Harbor. This clutch of specialty shops features clothing shops for all ages, several showing European designers, as well as accessories and gifts. A Radisson Hotel adjoins the shopping gallery (see *Best Places to Stay*, page 143).

HEIRLOOM JEWELS LTD.
14 Village Square
☎ 410-323-0100

As you might suspect from the name, Heirloom Jewels specializes in estate jewelry and wares, but there are also plenty of very affordable antiques as well. The shop is open from 10-5:30; Thursdays until 7:30; Sundays noon-4.

MANO SWARTZ
10 Village Square
☎ 410-825-9000
www.manoswartz.com

Here you can find anything your heart desires – as long as it's made of fur. They can also help bring your existing pieces back to life (the coats, not the critters, we mean) with alterations, restyling and skilled repairs. Mano Swartz is closed for vacation during the month of July. Call for regular hours.

THE PIED PIPER
32 Village Square
☎ 410-435-2676

Your kids or grandkids will love anything you buy in this upscale shop which offers sophisticated clothing and toys for children from birth to their pre-teen years. The Pied Piper is open Monday-Saturday, 10-6; Sunday, noon-4; and until 8 pm on Thursdays.

After Dark

Performing Arts

Baltimore is a very musically sophisticated city, with just about all bases well covered. This heritage of performing arts stems from many sources – the legacy of outstanding Black jazz musicians who made their names here, the largess of George Peabody in founding a well-respected conservatory, the musical traditions of the many European immigrant groups that poured into the city in the 19th century, and a long-standing tradition that encouraged the development of fine arts in all forms. On nearly any night you can find music and theater to suit almost any taste. For example, **The Handel Choir of Baltimore** (☎ 410-366-6544), a choir of about 75 singers, performs choral works at various venues – which may include concert halls or historic churches – with full orchestra and guest soloists.

Also listed in this section are three outstanding cinemas with specialized repertoires of art and foreign films, as well as those by local film makers.

Inner Harbor

MORRIS A. MECHANIC THEATRE
25 Hopkins Plaza, Baltimore and Charles Streets
☎ 410-625-4230
www.themechanic.org

The Mechanic Theatre's performance season runs from September through June.

This theater offers much more on the inside than its exterior suggests. The structure, which was opened in 1967 with the show *Hello Dolly*, was designed by architect John M. Johansen. His vision was not (and continues not to be) appreciated by many, but the theater itself is a very popular venue. Seating just over 1,600 people, the playhouse has seen a number of well known touring companies – including *Cabaret* – as well as several pre-Broadway productions.

BALTIMORE ARENA
201 West Baltimore Street
☎ 410-347-2000 for events listing
☎ 410-347-2010 for tickets

The Baltimore Arena seats over 11,000, and is accessible by Light Rail and bus – fortunately, since its parking garage holds only 840 cars. Here you will find anything from the Baltimore Blast (soccer) to Disney shows to wrestling.

TIP

Discounted tickets for concerts and other events are sometimes offered at the City Life Tickets kiosk, Inner Harbor Promenade, West Shore (between Harborplace and Maryland Science Center); ☎ 410-396-8342.

PIER 6 CONCERT PAVILION
Pier 6 (behind Pier 5 Hotel)
☎ 410-837-4636.

Summer concerts in the pavilion may be blues, country, rock or jazz, often featuring name performers and groups. Stars such as B.B. King and Willie Nelson have performed there.

HARBORPLACE AMPHITHEATER

Pratt and Light Streets
☎ 800-427-2671
Free

Concerts starring local performers and groups, and featuring all kinds of music, are presented in an open-air setting overlooking Constellation Pier, on Friday through Sunday, all summer.

Fells Point

THE VAGABOND PLAYERS

806 South Broadway, on the square
☎ 410-563-9135

Performances are usually Friday through Sunday evenings and Sunday matinées.

Year-round performances have been presented in this community setting for more than 80 years. Recent offerings have included everything from Moliere, to *The Haunting of Hill House*, to Broadway shows, all at affordable prices.

FELLS POINT CORNER THEATRE

251 South Ann Street
☎ 410-276-7837

This two-stage theater is in an 1859 firehouse, which has been renovated to suit its new use. Not only does the theater produce shows that are supported by area volunteers, but the company provides acting and various theater classes for both children and adults who want to get in touch with their creative side. The second stage is reserved for smaller performances and informal activities.

ORPHEUM CINEMA
1724 Thames Street
☎ 410-732-4614
Evenings and weekend matinees
$4.50 double feature, $3 matinee

Hollywood and cartoon classics as well as foreign films and independent releases are standard fare at this art theater.

Mount Vernon & Mount Royal

THE PEABODY CONSERVATORY OF MUSIC
1 East Mount Vernon Place
☎ 410-659-8124
www.peabody.jhu.edu

There are several performances during each semester at Peabody Conservatory.

Students of the nation's oldest music school, founded in 1857, present a full schedule of recitals and performances at the conservatory during the academic year. These include programs by the school's own symphony orchestra, its big band, its Renaissance ensemble, the opera department, and several student chamber groups. Guest artists also perform, in programs which have in the past included opera, symphony and recitals.

MARYLAND ART PLACE
218 West Saratoga Street
☎ 410-962-8565
www.MDartplace.org

The Art Place also presents a number of seasonal and annual art shows and exhibits.

The Art Place is just that, providing the area with not only some high quality entertainment, but also with workshops, a newsletter, and many other resources for both the artist and those who enjoy music, fine and performing arts. Live music, stand-up comedy, and films are just some of the programs found at the Art Place's 14Karat Cabaret. Art Place is open Tuesday through Saturday, from 11am to 5pm.

EVERYMAN THEATRE
1727 North Charles Street
☎ 410-752-2208

The Everyman Theatre was created as a vision of Vincent Lancisi to provide affordable theatrical entertainment. In this location since 1994, the theater is home to its own company, and performs many well known dramas, as well as newer works. Call for their performance schedule.

CHARLES THEATRE
1711 North Charles Street
☎ 410-727-3456,
www.thecharles.com
Two evening shows and weekend matinees
Evening shows $6, Matinees $4

This 486-seat theater was once the place to go to watch the newsreels, but now it's the place to go to watch the latest news in art films. The theater has recently opened a café, and four new small screening rooms to show smaller art films and low budget projects. The Charles also offers second showings of some of the better known art films, as well as newly released foreign and independent films.

LYRIC OPERA HOUSE

140 West Mount Royal Avenue, at Cathedral Street
☎ 410-685-5086 (Lyric Opera House main number)
☎ 410-494-2712 (for tickets to Broadway shows and other outside companies)
☎ 410-727-6000 (for Baltimore Opera Company information and tickets)

This lovely opera house, although wearing a modest exterior, was modeled after a 17th-century baroque theater in Leipzig, Germany. It's stage has seen many famous performers since its 1894 opening, during which time it has hosted not only the opera but also great orators and a variety of other entertainments. Today the Lyric is home to the Baltimore Opera Company, the city's resident company, and its orchestra. Recent performances have included Wagner's *Tannhäuser*, *Aida* and *La Boheme*. Grand opera productions often star international guest artists; English translation is projected over the stage. The Lyric Opera House also hosts outside theater companies from Broadway, as well as other types of shows.

JOSEPH MEYERHOFF SYMPHONY HALL

1212 Cathedral Street
☎ 410-783-8000

Even more impressive than its smooth modern architecture is the hall's ability to enhance the music played here and project its sound to every seat. This is one of the nation's most acoustically sophisticated music halls, with specially designed sound diffusing baffles and sound reflecting disks mounted at strategic points. And it is always busy, presenting an astonishing variety of well-known guest performers, both popular and classical; several regular series of concerts, including Classically Kids and Musical Adventures (classical daytime performances for children); Casual Series, SuperPops and Celebrity Series. It is not uncommon to find musicians of the quality of Yo-Yo Ma, Pinchas Zukerman, Itzhak Perlman, James Morris, the Canadian Brass Ensemble or the Vienna Boys Choir featured here, but concerts go far beyond the usual symphony hall repertoire. In 2000 alone, concerts included Gregory Hines in a song and tap dance recital, the Peking Acrobats, a big band swing concert, Ballet d'Afrique, and The Chieftains. Yuri Temirkanov became conductor in January of 2000. A number of city music groups, including the Baltimore Choral Arts Society, use the Meyerhoff as a performance venue.

ARENA PLAYERS
801 McCulloh Avenue
☎ 410-728-6500

The Arena Players are the country's oldest African-American theater company, and have been taking to the stage since 1953, back when Baltimore was still a segregated city. Facing financial problems, the company moved into an old church, which they eventually bought and renovated to turn it into a 300-seat theater. The Arena Players perform a wide variety of shows from classical and contemporary drama to comedy to musicals.

EUBIE BLAKE NATIONAL JAZZ INSTITUTE AND CULTURAL CENTER
847 North Howard Street
☎ 410-625-3113

The center honors not just Baltimore native composer Eubie Blake, but also the other big local names in jazz, including Billie Holiday, Chick Webb and Cab Calloway. Displayed here are Blake's original recordings and scores, as well as pictures and other memorabilia. Eubie Blake, who died in 1983 at the age of 100, was a ragtime pianist and vaudeville entertainer. He co-composed Broadway's first black musical, *Shuffle Along*, and wrote such hits as *I'm Just Wild About Harry* and *Memories of You*. This is also a place for students and artists to practice and share their talents and ideas.

Hampden & Uptown

THE SENATOR THEATRE
5904 York Road
☎ 410-435-8338
www.senator.com

The Senator Theatre is handicapped-accessible.

If you cherish the art deco style, you need to see this gem, on the National Register of Historic Places and considered one of America's best movie houses. Baltimore's own Barry Levinson and John Waters premier their films here, to the delight of audiences who recognize all their local icons. Look here also for art films and for premiers of other movies filmed in Maryland. Under its curved marquee with the streamlined neon lights, be sure to notice the **Sidewalk of the Stars**, with film logos and star signatures in the concrete.

Live Music

The venues listed here offer live music in settings other than concert halls or theaters, such as bars, pubs, restaurants and cafés where musicians add to the ambiance. Also included are places with dancing to live music. Some of these may have live performances only certain nights of the week, which we have tried to mention. But schedules change frequently, so it's always best to call and ask if musicians will be performing.

Inner Harbor

EXPLORER'S LOUNGE
Harbor Court Hotel, 550 Light Street
☎ 410-234-0550

This is a popular lounge where you may enjoy live music every night of the week while admiring the exotic and elegant African theme.

Fells Point & Camden

BOHAGER'S
515 South Eden Street
☎ 410-563-7220

This relatively small concert venue books some pretty popular acts, so be sure to check their schedule before coming to town, because it'll probably be sold out by the time you get there. Weekends, you can stop by and work off your overdose of crab cakes on the dance floor, to the music of DJs.

FULL MOON SALOON
1710 Aliceanna Street
☎ 410-276-6388 or 410-558-2873

The Full Moon Saloon is a Baltimore institution, famed for its selection of blues performances as well as spontaneous celebrity drop-ins. The atmosphere is priceless, too, and the down-home food is quite good. There are shows every night, starting at 9:30, or you can stop by on a Monday to watch freeform jams – you might be surprised by who shows up.

BAR HARBOR
2239 Essex Street
☎ 410-327-0100

Fun for weekend blues shows, real dancers will enjoy the swing or good jazz sounds in Bar Harbor's very comfortable atmosphere.

LISTA'S
1637 Thames Street, at Brown's Wharf
☎ 410-327-0040

This Tex-Mex restaurant has live jazz Friday evenings, when it serves meals until 11 pm. See *Best Places to Eat*, page 152, for a full description.

BERTHA'S
734 South Broadway
☎ 410-327-5795

On Tuesday, Wednesday and Thursday evenings you can "Eat Bertha's Mussels" to the strains of live Dixieland, blues, swing and jazz in the bar. See *Best Places to Eat*, page 155.

Mount Vernon

BUDDIES PUB & JAZZ CLUB
313 North Charles Street
☎ 410-332-4200

Although not your typical swinging jazz club, this comfortable pub offers more than just fish 'n chips. On Thursdays through Saturdays, to the beat of the Bing Miller Quartet, you can enjoy moderately priced seafood and pasta selections, as well as the expected pub fare for both lunch and dinner.

13TH FLOOR AT THE BELVEDERE
1 East Chase Street
☎ 410-347-0888 or 410-783-1332

Here you can dance to just about any kind of music, from jazz and blues to reggae and Latin music. When you get winded and have to leave the floor, you can withdraw gracefully by pretending to be distracted by the beautiful night views of downtown Baltimore. The 13th Floor is open Wednesday through Saturday; music starts at 9:30 pm.

Bars & Clubs

Fells Point

BIRDS OF A FEATHER
1712 Aliceanna Street
☎ 410-675-8466

Enthusiasts of the products of Scotland's best distilleries flock to Birds, a Scotch bar, where you'll find not only your favorite single malt, but everyone else's favorite, too. Birds is open Tuesday through Saturday evenings.

Camden

SLIDERS BAR & GRILL
Washington Boulevard
☎ 410-547-8891

Good sports bar for younger set enthusiasts.

STRIKE THREE
633 Portland Street
☎ 410-539-9052

Nice, friendly, and a less sports-infused atmosphere for casual socializing.

ORIOLES' SPORTS BAR
Sheraton Inner Harbor Hotel
☎ 410-962-8300 ext. 7168

This is the official bar of the Orioles, and a good place to watch for your favorite players if you're a fan.

Mount Vernon

THE BREWER'S ART
1106 North Charles Street
☎ 410-547-6925
Moderate

Not known for its food, although it offers some interesting combinations in a European-country sort of style, Brewer's draws a crowd to its huge rathskeller in the evening to sample the Belgian-style ales brewed there.

MICK O'SHEA'S
328 North Charles Street
☎ 410-539-7504
Inexpensive to moderate

The Irish music gives O'Shea's its lively character.

This unabashedly Irish pub serves the old pub favorites, plus some Chesapeake fare, such as crab cakes. But beer is what people go for – and the Irish music. Its location on Restaurant Row makes it a good late-evening winding-down stop after headier dinners up the street.

Sunset & Dinner Cruises

HARBOR BELLE
Henderson's Wharf, at the end of Fell Street
Fells Point
☎ 410-764-3928

A replica paddlewheeler steamboat, *Harbor Belle* cruises on Friday from 5:30 to 7:30 with bar service for an on-the-water happy hour or two. Sunset dinner cruises are on Saturdays at 7:15 pm. Cruise and buffet dinner are about $30.

CLIPPER CITY
Harborplace Pier, next to the Science Center
☎ 410-539-6277
www.sailingship.com

The topsail schooner offers weekend evening sails featuring live Caribbean music. Tickets are about $20.

BAY LADY and ***LADY BALTIMORE***
301 Light Street, Inner Harbor
Schedule ☎ 410-347-5552, reservations ☎ 410-727-3113 or 800-695-LADY
www.harborcruises.com

Three-hour evening trips include dinner, boarding Monday through Saturday at 6:30, Sunday at 4:30. Monday's menu is a seafood buffet, Tuesday, Thursday and Sunday a mixed buffet and Wednesday features beef, all priced in the low $40s. Friday's crab feast (June through September only) and the Saturday Admiral's buffet reach the $50s. Moonlight cruises without meals, on Friday and Saturday, 11:00 pm to 2 am are about $25. All evening cruises include dance music.

NIGHTHAWK

Thames Street, Fells Point
☎ 410-276-7447

The schooner *Nighthawk*, a classic tall ship, takes passengers on Saturday evening Moonlight Buffet cruises, from the first Saturday in May through the last Saturday in September, for $39.50 per person. They also have a Murder Mystery Dinner cruise the first Sunday of each month from May through October, for $49.50 per person.

Best Places to Stay

The lodging crunch in Baltimore is easing at last, with the building of new in-town properties. Rates are easing, too, with more special package deals that bring room costs down sharply. It is important to ask what special packages might apply during the time of your stay. Unless a big convention is in town, it is possible to find a package at even Inner Harbor hotels that will bring rates down into the moderate or even inexpensive range. The rule: the more expensive the hotel's rack rates, the greater the discount you're likely to get. But you probably won't get it unless you ask. Rates quoted are for one standard double room.

ACCOMMODATIONS PRICE SCALE	
Inexpensive	under $100
Moderate	$100-$200
Expensive	$201-$300
Deluxe	more than $300

Inner Harbor

PIER 5 HOTEL
711 Eastern Avenue
☎ 410-539-2000
Moderate to expensive

Balconies of this modern building overlook the harbor and the aquarium or a lighthouse and more water. But it's the interior architecture and décor that marks it – for better or for worse. Step inside to admire the atrium murals by Sam Robinson, which depict the views in each direction around the harbor and city. Below, in conversation groups, are cushy velour-covered chairs and sofas in sweeping art deco curves – an elegant look indeed.

Packages at Pier 5 include breakfast in the bright café and museum passes.

But this same soaring atrium, which eliminates the claustrophobic corridors of most hotels, also allows every sound from the lobby to drift upward and into guest rooms.

That aside, the rooms are as stunningly and innovatively decorated as the lobby, with custom-designed furniture and delightful touches – your wastebasket, for example, is a metal "paper" shopping bag. The faucets on the sink are elegant in delicate droplet shapes, also following the art deco theme. Nice bath amenities, roomy desks, a reading chair with ottoman, soft bathrobes, in-room safes, coffee makers, irons and ironing boards and other details show some thoughtfulness and style.

HYATT REGENCY
300 Light Street
☎ 410-528-1234 or 800-233-1234
Moderate to expensive

The location is tops, overlooking the harbor from its western side through great expanses of glass. Most rooms have good skyline or harbor views. A spa, tennis courts, fitness center and rooftop pool – the latter with a fine view and attractive landscaping – in addition to a full business services center, make the hotel attractive to business travelers. Continental breakfast and evening hors d'oeuvres are included with Regency Club floor rooms. The hotel has two restaurants. The bistro serves three meals daily, while Pisces (see *Best Places to Eat*, page 146) is one of the city's most acclaimed seafood restaurants.

TREMONT PLAZA HOTEL
222 Street Paul Place
☎ 410-576-1200 or 800-TREMONT
Inexpensive to moderate

Suites with fully equipped kitchens overlook the harbor, but the hotel is just enough removed from its hubbub to be quiet. A pool, sauna and fitness room, as well as the good deli in the building, make it convenient for business travelers or for those on an extended stay. Weekend packages offer some attractive bargains.

HARBOR COURT HOTEL
550 Light Street
☎ 410-234-0550 or 800-824-0076
Expensive to deluxe

You'll pay more for the smashing harbor-view rooms, but luxury and service are what this hotel is all about. Parking is included in some of the package rates, as is use of the fitness center, and these packages offer some substantial savings (bringing rates into the moderate level), so be sure to ask.

The Harbor Court is no run-of-the-mill hotel. It has a croquet court on the roof!

Fells Point

Fells Point is a short Water Taxi ride from all the attractions of Inner Harbor, and has its own enclave of excellent dining, shopping and night life.

THE ADMIRAL FELL INN
888 South Broadway (corner of Thames Street)
☎ (410) 522-7377
Moderate to expensive

We'll be honest from the start: this is our favorite place to curl up in comfort after a day in Baltimore. Not only is the staff warm and welcoming, but the location is A+ for people like us, whose day revolves around where we'll have dinner. Several of the city's best choices are nearby, and the waterfront streets of Fells Point are lively and interesting for an after dinner stroll. We enjoy just sitting on the dock, opposite the front door, and watching the boats go by. Quiet elegance and gentility pervade the inn, where some guest room furnishings include the antique wooden sea chests of the sailors who stayed here long ago, when the old brick building housed a much less sedate boarding house.

Parking is free at the Admiral Fell Inn.

The breakfast buffet is outstanding (and the staff just as bright and cheerful as the white-linen-set dining room itself). The bountiful table features fresh-cut fruit, a good variety of breads and pastries, European cheeses and creamy hot oatmeal in the winter.

Coffee and tea are available 24 hours a day in the spacious lobby, where several seating areas beckon with wing chairs and where, in cool weather, a fireplace warms the air. Guest rooms are equally large and uncluttered, with individual heat control, hair dryers, well-placed reading lights, phones, and televisions discreetly hidden away in armoires. Dormers create cozy nooks in some.

THE INN AT HENDERSON'S WHARF
1000 Fell Street
☎ 410-522-7777 or 800-522-2088, fax 410-522-7087
www.hendersonswharf.com
Moderate

Lushly decorated rooms and the elegant lobby overlook a garden-filled patio with a brick terrace of café tables. Somewhat disconcerting are the first-floor "cobblestone view" rooms facing directly onto the street, separated only by huge windows (and, of course, heavy drapes for total privacy). It's a quiet street, so it's not as though crowds of people were passing by, but it is a unique experience. Only a long block from the center of Fells Point's sometimes frenetic activity, Henderson's Wharf feels like a different world. Many of the rooms overlook the harbor and the inn's own marina. Boat slips or parking, as well as breakfast – an expanded continental buffet – are included in the room rates. The inn also has an exercise room.

ANN STREET BED & BREAKFAST
804 South Ann Street
☎ 410-342-5883
Expensive

Fireplaces grace the rooms of this vintage home just steps away from the busy-ness of Broadway and Thames Street. Take your morning coffee or afternoon tea into the garden in the summer to admire the flowers and enjoy the quiet.

Federal Hill

An historic neighborhood overlooking the Inner Harbor and close to its sights, Federal Hill is filled with restaurants, shops, even its own market.

SCARBOROUGH FAIR BED & BREAKFAST
One East Montgomery Street
☎ 410-837-0010, fax 410-783-4635
ww.scarborough-fair.com.
Moderate

This beautifully restored brick building is one of the oldest on Federal Hill, dating from 1801. It has been tastefully transformed into a B&B without losing its character; retrofittings are discreet and non-obtrusive. Six guest rooms have varied amenities. Some offer fireplaces, some whirlpool baths; all baths are private (for the use of a specific room), but not all are en suite. All rooms are decorated in a tasteful but practical blend of antiques and period reproductions.

Mount Vernon

Quiet gentility pervades this top-of-the-hill neighborhood, close to dining, antiques, art galleries and some of the best museums, but away from the busy Inner Harbor.

BILTMORE SUITES
205 West Madison Street
☎ 410-728-6550 or 800-868-5064
Moderate

For more than a century this brick hotel has been welcoming guests to Mount Vernon. Rooms are in two buildings joined by a leafy courtyard where guests relax in the summer at café tables. Architectural details are lovely and the public areas are decorated in antiques. So are some of the guest rooms, which are spacious, many with kitchenettes. Continental breakfast and a wine and cheese reception each evening are complimentary and, along with the personal service offered by an accommodating staff, add to the feeling that you are staying at your private club.

Bolton Hill

A bit out of the way (but the walk to Mount Vernon is all downhill), Bolton Hill is a perfect neighborhood for peace and quiet as well as for those who relish row on row of beautiful town homes set around well-kept park squares. Music lovers choose this neighborhood to be within walking distance of the Meyerhoff Symphony Hall and the Lyric Opera House.

MR. MOLE BED & BREAKFAST
1601 Bolton Street
☎ 410-728-1179, fax 410-728-3379
www.MrMoleBB.com
Moderate

Soaring ceilings, dramatic windows and grand original architectural elements combine for a "wow" first impression, even before you meet the effervescent Colin, who is your host. He's also the artist who did the wall paintings used with such flair throughout the building. Fine antiques and the owner's eccentric collections (such as miniature Adirondack furniture) combine with a highly creative and bold décor to make this one-of-a-kind home simply spectacular. Color and fabric treatments make each room unique, and two suites can each accommodate three guests, good for families (children over 10 only, please). Your host will doubtless point out the little quirks in the architecture and tell wonderfully funny tales that put the whole place into perspective. Taking it seriously is impossible with him to guide you through. Be sure to ask to see any rooms not yet occupied – the place is a big jar filled with eye candy, and it would be a shame to miss any.

Be aware that there is no resident innkeeper – although he lives nearby – and that arrivals are expected to check in between 4 pm and 6 pm. Free parking is included in the room rate.

ABACROMBIE BADGER BED & BREAKFAST
58 West Biddle Street
☎410-244-7227, 888-9BADGER, fax 410-244-8415, www.badger-inn.com
Moderate

Under the same ownership as Mr. Mole Bed & Breakfast, this more restrained property is directly opposite Meyerhoff Symphony Hall.

Elegantly decorated rooms include a few cozy singles, rare in a B&B, as well as large rooms with sitting areas and four-poster beds. Four-poster beds furnish some, all feature antiques and stylishly arranged collections. Reading lights shine wherever you would curl up with a book – two swing at the correct angle on either side of the bed. Some rooms have writing desks with lamps, even pen caddies with details such as scissors. Breakfast is what they term Dutch style, and includes cheeses and cold cuts, as well as fresh fruit and fresh-baked breads. Served in a trellis-painted room with bentwood chairs, it finishes with a sweet, which may be shoo-fly pie from an Amish farmers' market. For astute and discriminating suggestions on where to dine, consult Paul, the innkeeper. Or stay close to home and dine in the same building, beneath the B&B, at La Tesso Tana Restaurant (see *Best Places to Eat*). Be sure to make a reservation there for symphony nights, however.

There is no resident innkeeper (they live about four blocks away), and check-in time is 4-6 pm. If you must arrive at a different time, you will be given access instructions. Solo travelers uncomfortable with arriving at an empty house at night might consider another choice, but the attractive, inviting rooms in this B&B and its sister property are among the nicest you'll find. Off-street parking is free, too.

Uptown

DOUBLETREE INN AT THE COLONNADE
4 West University Parkway
☎ 410-235-5400 or 800-222-TREE
Moderate

Large guest rooms and elegant public areas – the décor echoes Classical Rome – characterize this continental-style hotel beside the Johns Hopkins University's Homewood campus. Some rooms have their own terraces, some have whirlpool baths. The glass-domed pool is surrounded by Italian marble. This is a good location for those who plan to spend a lot of time savoring the treasures of the Baltimore Museum of Art; several excellent restaurants are nearby.

Cross Keys Village

RADISSON HOTEL AT CROSS KEYS
5100 Falls Road
☎ 410-532-6900 or 800-333-3333
www.radisson.com/baltimoremd
Moderate to expensive

If you'd like to enjoy the city but prefer to retire at night to wider open spaces than a downtown hotel can offer, take advantage of the regularly scheduled complimentary shuttle to the Inner Harbor and stay in this resort. Rooms are large, in a tasteful French country décor, some with terraces. Gardens surround the large pool area and jogging trails adjoin the property. So do shops, in an atrium mall connected to the hotel.

Best Places to Eat

Restaurants tend to cluster into the same neighborhoods you'll want to visit for their other attractions. The thickest concentrations are in or near Fells Point and Mount Vernon, as well as the enclave of Little Italy. Although lots of eateries hug the Inner Harbor, most are of the eat-and-run or noisy bar variety – with a few stunning exceptions.

Call ahead for dinner reservations on weekends, during festivals or in the busy summer season, when the most popular and high-end restaurants will be crowded.

BALTIMORE CUISINE

Baltimore has its own food specialties, some of which, like crab cakes, it shares with the whole Chesapeake region, but others that are strictly its own.

- **Crab Cakes** – clusters of crabmeat (backfin is best) held together with as little breading as possible and very subtly seasoned, they may be fried or broiled.
- **Sour Beef** – Baltimore's own sauerbraten, served with dumplings.
- **Pit Beef** – slow-grilled top round, sliced paper-thin and served with onion and horseradish on rye or a kaiser roll.
- **Coddies** – fried codfish cakes served in a sandwich.
- **Lady Baltimore Cake** – white cake layered with pecans, dried (sometimes candied) fruit and boiled white frosting.

What have we left out? Somebody's favorite, you can be sure. Restaurants change, new ones open, chefs move, and no matter how hard we try to sample each one often enough to be able to describe and judge it fairly, we just can't keep up. We don't stop trying, of course, but we may have missed some really fine places, so be sure to ask local people you meet what their favorites are, too (and let us know if we should try it, too). Prices are for one entrée, without beverage.

DINING PRICE SCALE	
Inexpensive	Entrées are $10 or less
Moderate	Entrées are $11-$20
Expensive	Entrées are $21-$30

Inner Harbor

As you might expect from a refurbished and very active waterfront, fast-food spots, noisy café-pubs and twenty-something watering holes predominate here. But don't ignore the city's best view of the moonrise from Pisces, over some of the best seafood in a city famous for it. Ed Kane's Water Taxi (page 38) will take you to within a few steps of Joy America Café, on the other side of the harbor – just tell the skipper where you're going and the boat will stop at the nearest dock. Of all the Inner Harbor restaurants we've tried, these two rise well above the rest – literally and figuratively, since each is on an upper floor with water views.

PISCES
Hyatt Regency
300 Light Street
☎ 410-605-2835
Expensive

If the oyster is your world, look no farther. The raw bar here – or the sparkling menu choices – offer them from the best neighborhoods: from Prince Edward Island to Wellfleet to Chincoteague. The chef treats them well and, if you can't decide, opt for the sampler trio, baked with such accompaniments as crab-and-spinach or leek-and-fennel. Salads get the same attention as entrées; we liked the baby spinach and Asian pear combination with toasted pecans, and the selection of heirloom tomatoes and fresh mozzarella. The rest of the menu is inspired in tone and the chef has a keen sense of what flavors and textures bring out the best in each other. He also knows exactly when to pluck each morsel from the heat, so the scallops are like spun silk in the center, and the fish moist and lush.

Pisces' raw bar opens at 5; there's dancing some weekend evenings after 10:30.

Wild rockfish may be served with lump crabmeat, pinenuts and roasted tomatoes in a lemony sauce, or shrimps and scallops combined with roasted peppers and garlic in a tomato coulis. While we never tire of well-prepared seafood, others may not share our enthusiasm; honey and pecan roasted lamb chops or grilled veal chops in caramelized red onions and Burgundy are designed with these diners in mind. We're not usually dessert people, but our favorite waiter, Seamus, nearly always talks us into trying one; the crème brûlée is brilliant, with surprising twists, such as raspberry basil, roasted banana and papaya, or mango and pink peppercorn.

The service – in our experience – is excellent, offering just the right amount of informed guidance and advice and especially competent in pairing the excellent selection of wines to each dish.

JOY AMERICA CAFE
800 Key Highway, in the American Museum of Visionary Art
☎ 410-244-6500
Moderate to expensive

Latin American styles paired with Chesapeake ingredients are as good as fusion cooking gets, and Chef Jason Horowitz is a master of it. His bright new ways with old favorite crustacea and Eastern Shore chicken are a wonderful change from the ordinary.

Grilled salmon burrito with black beans, green rice and chêvre, for example, or a soft-shell crab sandwich enlivened by Key lime aioli, bring new zing to lunches. The dinner menu might feature a Caribbean lobster stew with plantains and sweet potatoes in a spicy tomato-coconut broth. Just as pleasing to the eye as to the palate, dishes are artfully arranged. Tamales are hand-rolled and may contain a combination of wild boar and dried cherries or less exotic black beans or fresh white cheese. A ceviche sampler includes coconut shrimp, rockfish in Key lime and red onion, and fresh salmon with green papaya. Chalupa crusts are mesquite grilled. Joy encourages patrons to order several of these and share as a meal. The margaritas get an unqualified *Olé*! Joy America is open for lunch and dinner Tuesday through Saturday, and for Sunday brunch.

Joy America's custom-made-at-your-table guacamole is perfect for those who know what they like (we like a little more jalapeño, please).

WAYNE'S BAR-B-QUE
Harborplace Pavilion, 301 Light Street
☎ 410-539-3810
Inexpensive to moderate

On quite a different note, this trendy, noisy barbecue place serves good ribs and offers a wide selection of beers, to the tune of country music. As you might expect, a young crowd wolfs down ribs, burgers and sandwiches here; open for three meals daily.

Little Italy

Restaurants in this colorful little enclave tend toward traditional Southern Italian menus, with a nod now and then to Northern Italian cuisines. There's no question that red sauce rules, but not everywhere. And, let us hasten to add, there's nothing wrong with tomato sauce, and the mamas and papas that make it here know how.

On weeknights, or in the winter, several of Little Italy's restaurants will send a car to your Inner Harbor hotel and take you home again. If you should drive your car into Little Italy to dine, most restaurants have attendants who will whisk your car away and retrieve it for you when you're ready to leave.

ALDO'S
306 South High Street
☎ 410-727-0700
Moderate to expensive

Begin with a look around this beautifully renovated pair of row houses, where dining rooms on two floors open onto a columned courtyard. Downstairs has a Roman feel, upstairs more La Belle Epoque. And below it all is a cozy dining table for two inside the well-stocked wine cellar. But you came for the food. Most of the old favorites are there, but you may not recognize them in the hands of this innovative chef, whose updated treatments are a welcome break from the neighborhood's marinara-sauce overdose.

Instead, the chef has returned to the origins of the great Italian comfort foods, with the freshest of locally grown ingredients and preparations that leave room for the natural flavors. The rack of lamb is beautifully presented and the gnocchi tender, although we have trouble choosing between those and the risottos – especially the mushroom one. The osso buco – hard to find in restaurants – is outstanding. A good selection of wines-by-the-glass provides a sampling of the extensive wine list. The cellar includes about 3,500 bottles, many of them from small vineyards.

Dinner is served daily from 5 pm and reservations are almost essential for Saturday evenings at any time of year, when they may be booked several weeks ahead.

DALESIO'S
899 Eastern Avenue
☎ 410-539-1965
Moderate

One of the few places here that specializes in the cuisines of northern Italy, Dalesio's is also unique in the neighborhood for its selection of lighter "spa" dishes. Don't envision Spartan – expect chicken with sun-dried tomatoes and mushrooms over whole wheat pasta following an appetizer of red and yellow bell peppers with fresh basil and anchovy. New takes on Italian traditions and creative use of local

At Dalesio's you can dine outdoors in the summer, and limo service from downtown hotels is available on weeknights.

ingredients mark this restaurant as the domain of a chef with ideas. Shellfish is treated to a Marsala glaze, crabmeat joins the fettuccine Alfredo, duck fills the ravioli. Both cigar smokers and those who think cigars foul will be pleased to note the Cigar Room all by itself on the third floor.

CIAO BELLA
236 South High Street
☎ 410-685-7733
Moderate, signature dishes expensive

The traditional Italian menu stars veal marsala – one of the finest of Italian dishes, we think, and served at its prime here, pale-colored, moist and fork tender. You can always depend on veal, whether it's rolled with prosciutto and provolone, paired with crabmeat or shrimp, in sage-scented saltimbocca or served cacciatore style. The atmosphere is all dark walls and crisp white linens, as befits the traditional special occasion menu, and service is attentive and warm. Open for lunch on weekdays, and for dinner nightly until 10 pm (11 on Friday and Saturday). On weeknights, they'll pick you up and return you to your downtown hotel.

AMICCI'S
231 High Street
☎ 410-528-1096
Inexpensive to moderate

Amicci's serves lunch and dinner daily.

If a restaurant can feel like home, this one does; the minute you put your elbows on one of its red-checkered tablecloths, you feel part of the family that owns it. We could skip the entrée and just keep ordering the appetizer shrimp and garlic in creamy sauce, served inside a scooped out loaf of crusty bread. It's enough for dinner, or you can share it to leave room for the gnocchi or tortellini with peas and ham. The often loud music may not soothe your soul, but the food will.

Fells Point

You may feel like you've strayed onto a college campus on a weekend night in Fells Point, as the very young set takes to the streets and bars. But some of the city's most stylish restaurants are here, along with its most rollicking pubs, music venues and other more adult occupations. Inside the cream of the restaurants you'll find a mixed crowd of in-the-know out-of-towners, yuppies and well-heeled gen-X-ers.

Although it's not in the heart of Fells Point, we've included Charleston (see page 154) in this neighborhood. In a few years, Charleston will be the keystone of a new neighborhood (it's prediction time, so listen well to your Baltimore soothsayers), but for now it's about halfway between Inner Harbor and Fells Point, a half-dozen steps from the Waterfront Promenade that connects the two. On a pleasant spring or summer evening it's a very easy walk from either, and a short cab ride back.

HAMILTON'S
Admiral Fell Inn
888 South Broadway
☎ 410-552-2195
Moderate to expensive

Creative and clever avoids becoming cute or contrived in the deft hands of Chef Jeffrey Crise, and however whimsical his presentations – foie gras in a tiny "sandwich" with apple and caramelized shallots

– the accent is on how well the flavors work together. And they do, with unerring aim. Pheasant stuffed with wheatberries may be served over bitter greens, spice-cured pork chop with Asian pears and couscous. A good wine selection includes a number of better ones by the glass. For dessert, look for an equally seasonal selection, an architectural tiramisu in the summer or warm apple and dried cranberry tarte in the winter. The downstairs dining room is formal, intimate and welcoming, with crisp white linens and excellent service.

LISTA'S
1637 Thames Street, at Brown's Wharf
☎ 410-327-0040
Moderate

Expect Lista's to be crowded and noisy on weekend evenings, especially in the summer, when tables spill out onto the wharf.

Haute cuisine it may not be, but Lista's is fun and the food is always good. Mexican and southwestern dishes often include Chesapeake ingredients, and the chef plays with the flavors and ingredients to create a few Lista originals, such as Margarita shrimp, salmon al ajo or tortilla-encrusted catfish. Vegetarians appreciate the hearty Potato Landscape, a mountain of garlic-mashed potatoes with asparagus, surrounded by meatless red chili. All the usual Tex-Mex suspects are lined up, too, including guac and chips, quesadillas, tamales, enchiladas, fajitas and flautas.

Lista's is open weekdays, 11-10; weekends, 11-11; and offers live jazz Friday evenings.

THE BLACK OLIVE
814 South Bond Street
☎ 410-276-7141
Expensive

Seafood with a Greek accent fills the long and ever-changing menu at this attractive little family-owned restaurant. Order whole fish from the display of daily catch at about $25 per generous entrée and choose from a selection of classic Mediterranean preparations. Begin with a mezze of grilled wild mushrooms, skewered grilled squid, mussels in ouzo or greens with goat cheese. Kakavia, a Greek version of langoustine-filled bouillabaisse; token offerings of red meat; and several vegetarian entrées complete the menu. To the best of our knowledge, this is the only place outside Highland Avenue where you can top off your meal with Greek yoghurt drizzled with mountain honey (reason enough to eat here, we think).

KALI'S COURT
1606 Thames Street
☎ 410-276-4700
Expensive

New and hip, Kali's draws the Polo Grill crowd to its Euro-stylish digs, a few blocks from Broadway. Seafood predominates – you can see it fresh before you order – as do Greek and other Mediterranean treatments. While we're not usually fans of octopus (in less than highly skilled hands it is reminiscent of garden hose on a hot summer day) Kali's is a sparkling exception, fresh from the grill and redolent of good olive oil with a hint of lemon. If you're still in doubt, go for the tuna carpaccio appetizer instead; they commit what is considered to be the greatest culinary sin in Italy – combining fish and cheese –

but they do it nicely with a shaving of asiago over the yellowfin.

Lunchtime selections may include brick oven pita filled with vegetables or smoked salmon, or swordfish, shrimp and fresh vegetables grilled on a skewer. Kali's is open every day for lunch and dinner.

CHARLESTON
1000 Lancaster Street, at the far west end of Shakespeare Street
☎ 410-332-7373
Expensive

Whenever annoying people from northern cities look down their noses at Baltimore cuisine – or at the South's in general, for that matter – we send them here. Then we rest our case. Chef Cindy Wolf and her restaurateur-husband Tony Forman have created together what neither could have done alone – a rare restaurant where everything is just right and a dining experience is seamless from start to finish.

Charleston's wine list has more than 500 selections. Tony has a talent for locating rare bottles, as well as for choosing high quality but affordable wines.

But it's the food you want to know about. New American doesn't quite fit, and New Southern doesn't come close to describing how Cindy plays the traditional Low Country comfort foods against a panoply of local ingredients, all fresh from the sea and local farms. And she obviously has fun doing it; this is food with a smile.

We seldom order foie gras because it has a three-second tolerance between under-done and over-done, but here the first bite, lightly laced with port sauce, sets the tone for an evening to savor. Whenever it's on the menu, we can't resist a second course of Cindy's signature fried green tomato sandwich, tangy slices fried crisp, sandwiching sumptuous lumps of crabmeat and lobster. Hearts of palm with heirloom tomatoes and lime vinaigrette are a back-up choice.

Medallions of venison are grilled and served with olives, roasted portobellos, and applewood-smoked bacon and cannelini beans with a balsamic reduction; juicy roasted veal tenderloin arrives with a trio of sauteed exotic mushrooms and a crisp grits cake. Roasted breast of duck is stuffed with pecans and sweet onions, and sauced in fresh nectarines and Armagnac. The cheese course is the perfect touch after this largesse: boutique cheeses from small farms in France and Italy, some we've never seen outside their home towns. After all this, we hope the dessert menu will offer fresh berries in Madeira sabayon, or a trio of house sorbets.

The details are all there – the well-chosen crystal and quality china, the crisp linens and commodious oak chairs, highly informed and professional service – but with a refreshing lack of pomp and pretension. Tony lets his ingredients for fine dining speak for themselves just as Cindy lets impeccable ingredients shine through her infinitely complex treatments. Charleston is open for dinner from 5:30 daily. Reservations at Charleston are almost essential.

BERTHA'S
734 South Broadway
☎ 410-327-5795
Moderate

"Eat Bertha's Mussels" admonishes a sign painted on the side of the building (and repeated on bumper stickers all over town). It's good advice. Bertha's renowned mussels are served with a choice of eight different sauces, from a delicate tarragon to assertive anchovy, at $9 for a large bowl, and fresh Italian bread on the side. Seafood – oysters with Smithfield ham in a cream sauce – and a few meat dishes – chicken with kumquat sauce and spicy kumquat relish – fill the ample menu. The inspiration is eclectic; you'll find paella brimming with chicken, shellfish and sausage along with the most traditional Chesapeake treatments. Sunday brunch (11:30 am until 2 pm) is a hearty affair with Welsh rarebit, country sausage and creamed oysters, for $8. Baltimore-brewed and British beers are on tap. Bertha's is open daily 11:30 to 11, until midnight on Friday and Saturday.

At Bertha's on Tuesday, Wednesday and Thursday evenings you'll hear live Dixieland, blues, swing and jazz in the bar.

TEA FOR YOU

Bertha's also serves Mrs. McKinnon's Scottish Afternoon Tea on Monday through Saturday afternoons, 3-5 pm, by reservation. Along with fresh-brewed tea you'll be served a platter of fresh-baked scones, sweets and savories, for $9.

PIERPOINT
1822 Aliceanna Street
☎ 410-675-2080
Moderate to expensive

Chef Nancy Longo was among the first to bring a new look to Baltimore menus, and she has thus secured her place in the city's culinary history. If her dishes no longer seem so cutting edge and creative, it's because so many other places have caught up to the pace she helped set. Watch her work in the open kitchen as you sample dishes such as Eastern Shore rabbit sausage, smoked crab cakes (she was really treading on thin ice when she first tampered with this sacrosanct number) and the dish most patrons rave longest about – crisp-fried oysters served over fried tomatoes. Presentations are important here, and you can enjoy watching them go past in the intimately sized restaurant. Lunch and dinner are served daily, plus brunch on Sunday.

PETER'S INN
504 South Ann Street
☎ 410-675-7313
Inexpensive

Really good food is served in bar-like surroundings at this unprepossessing little eatery. We do mean little – there are only about half a dozen tables. The kitchen might offer chicken in a mustard cream with crabmeat, or steak languishing in a bourbon glaze. Or ravioli filled with wild mushrooms served in a cream sauce perfumed with sage. No atmosphere, but great and creative food, with an eastern Mediterranean accent.

Don't confuse Peter's Inn with Wee Peter's Pub on South Broadway.

ZE MEAN BEAN CAFE
1739 Fleet Street
☎ 410-675-5999
Inexpensive to moderate

Eastern European influences are evident here, with pierogi, blinchika (filled with ricotta and wild mushrooms) and kielbasa with sauerkraut. But these dishes are not without a creative touch either. A Reuben is made with roast pork loin and red cabbage, the plate of grilled sausages includes some made with wild boar, pheasant and venison. We're fond of pierogi, those delectable dumplings stuffed with farmer's cheese or potato, and rarely like anyone else's as much as our own. But we order them here. Other dishes are Mediterranean- and New

Bring your own wine or beer to Ze Mean Bean.

American-influenced: rosemary-grilled chicken or sea bass with fennel and polenta, or duck with fig and pear compote. Live music fills the evening air in this informal, inviting café.

EL SALVADOR
207 South Broadway
☎ 410-522-3270
Inexpensive

Spanish is the predominant language at El Salvador.

Sample Salvadorian and other Latin American specialties are the focus at this ethnic enclave not far up Broadway from the market building. Combination plates, a good way to try unfamiliar dishes, are $6-$7, appetizers are $1.25 to $3. Papusas, enchiladas, tacos and Latin versions of local seafood are served to a salsa beat in an informal setting. El Salvador is open from 11 am until 10:30 pm on weeknights, and until 1 am on weekends.

OBRYCKI'S
1727 East Pratt Street
☎ 410-732-6399
www.obryckis.com
Moderate to expensive

Obrycki's has a mail-order seafood department that is open year-round. Order by phone or through their Web site.

Baltimoreans have been feasting on boiled crabs at Obrycki's since the 1940s and one gets the distinct feeling that not much has changed here since then. The menu still features hard-shelled crabs in the rough, crab cakes, or Obrycki's specialty, crab imperial. You'll also find crab in marinara sauce, stuffed and broiled, as a topping for shrimp, in a hearty cioppino, over linguine or in crab cakes. The atmosphere is hard to define: a cross between a shore dining hall with brown paper on the table and a place families choose to bring grandmother on her birthday. If you're going there in the daytime, you can walk up Broadway from Fells Point; we wouldn't at night. Obrycki's closes in the winter, but in season they are open daily; call for hours.

Canton

Canton is a bit out of the way, but the Water Taxi brings you here from the Inner Harbor or Fells Point. The dining choices are varied and you'll be sharing your restaurant with natives once you leave the area right near the old canning factory. In fact, even there you'll find few out-of-town visitors.

CLADDAGH PUB
2918 O'Donnell Street
☎ 410-522-4220
Inexpensive to moderate

If you long for a good, rollicking Irish pub, with no-nonsense Black Angus steaks, steamed mussels, shrimps or burgers to accompany your Murphy's, follow the shamrocks painted on the sidewalk. Black Angus burgers are a bargain on Saturday night.

HELEN'S GARDEN CAFE
2908 O'Donnell Street
☎ 410-276-2233
Inexpensive to moderate

You may hear about this out-of-the-way spot from natives, but they also might just keep it to themselves. Walk through the bar to the upstairs dining room. The menu defies categorizing, and may have anything from homey comfort foods to American fusion dishes inspired by styles and ingredients from the far corners of the earth. The wine list is outstanding and not too pricey, with an astonishing selection available by the glass. It's the only place we know in Baltimore where you can do flights. Breads are heavenly.

THE WILD MUSHROOM
641 South Montford Avenue
☎ 410-675-4225
Moderate

What you read on the sign is what you get inside. Begin with a delectable grilled portobello or one filled with tantalizing crab dip, then move on to a mushroom loaf or pasta-mushroom combination. From cepes to chanterelles, you'll find them here, lovingly prepared. Friday and Saturday lunches are a bargain for those with big appetites, with unlimited seconds.

SIP & BITE
2200 Boston Street
☎ 410-675-7077
Inexpensive

A diner, pure and simple, a favorite of the late-night set, with Greek and American comfort foods. It's open 24 hours every day. To get there, follow the waterfront through Canton, past the Cannery. It's quite a distance from anyplace else you'd be late at night, but if you have wheels and a consuming hunger after midnight, this is the place to go.

Federal Hill & Key Highway

On the other side of Inner Harbor, the Hill combines the ungentrified brashness of the typical old Baltimore commercial streets and market, with the sedate rows of refurbished Flemish-point brick townhouses. Like the architecture and culture, dining here is a mixed baguette. When looking for places in this neighborhood, remember Joy America Café, in the American Visionary Arts Museum on Key Road, which is described under Inner Harbor (see page 62).

ONE WORLD CAFE
904 South Charles Street
☎ 410-752-8561
Inexpensive

Baltimore isn't a city known for vegetarianism, but this café makes up for the city's shortcomings in that area. International and casual, the menu draws inspiration from the street foods of the world, with burritos bursting with black beans, pitas filled with hummus and even PB&J sandwiches – made from tasty organic peanut butter, of course. It's not all ethnic comfort foods, however – you'll find an up-to-date portobello sandwich, too. Drinks range from healthy juices to wines and microbrews. At breakfast, the Belgian waffles are splendid.

One World Café is open for three meals daily.

NICK'S INNER HARBOR SEAFOOD
Cross Street Market, Cross Street, Federal Hill
☎ 410-685-2020

A lunch-hour and Saturday morning favorite for crab cakes, Nick's isn't fancy, but it's reliably good.

PAZZA LUNA
1401 East Clement Street
☎ 410-727-1212
Expensive

Betwixt and between, this restaurant in a residential neighborhood between Federal Hill and Fort

McHenry serves southern Italian food, but it's distinctly out of the red-sauce zone. Every detail is thought out, with style and flourish. The veal scallopine is sumptuously flavored with shiitake mushrooms, and the grilled eggplant with Vidalia onion is a knockout appetizer. The owner is a Frank Sinatra fan, so you'll surely hear his music in the background.

Mount Vernon & Vicinity

This is the neighborhood to be seen in, and its restaurants represent all price and style ranges. Breakfast here at the homey Women's Industrial Exchange, lunch at cafeteria-style Sasha's or stray over to Lexington Market for crab cakes, and settle into a fine, exotic Afghan dinner at The Helmand. You'll have Baltimore dining in a nutshell.

Charles Street is often called Restaurant Row for its plethora of eating places. Several of the city's best are in this neighborhood, whose artistic predilections extend to the table.

MAISON MARCONI
106 West Saratoga Street
☎ 410-727-9522
Moderate to expensive

The décor, the service, the menu and the atmosphere personify the old-fashioned places where people always went on special occasions, in the days when American cities had little more than a smattering of upscale restaurants. Those continental and domestic favorites – sweetbreads bordelaise, lobster Newburg, vichyssoise – that you may not have seen on a menu in a decade are alive and well here, with heavy sauces lightened just a bit for modern sensibilities. Jacket and tie are required of gentlemen in the front, crystal-chandeliered dining room; appear without either and you'll be welcomed just as politely and shown to the second, less formal dining room.

MARTICK'S RESTAURANT FRANÇAIS
214 West Mulberry Street
☎ 410-752-5155
Expensive

You'd never call this place dull, with its folk art-meets-stained-glass décor, speakeasy entry (you ring the bell, please) and irrepressible chef-owner. You never know what will be on the menu, but it will be interesting. It will probably feature the bouillabaisse, because it's Morris Martick's signature dish. Service is often spotty, but good humored, so who cares?

SASHA'S
527 Charles Street
☎ 410-539-8880
Inexpensive

Caterers turned restaurateurs, Sasha's serves lunch cafeteria style, then turns into a classy little full-service restaurant in the evening. A rack of florist-fresh bouquets ($5) sits Parisian-style against one wall. Sparkling and arresting modern décor in good colors – deep red and yellow – create a compatible setting in which to enjoy a sampling of what Sasha's calls Taste Plates. Like generous tapas, these plates are designed to be combined into a meal of any size, one for a light meal, two or three for a heartier one. It's a concept we applaud, especially as we dip into

Sasha's serves cafeteria-style lunches Monday through Friday, 11 am-4:30 pm.

charred tuna bites, or the garlic plate, with roasted garlic, goat cheese, olive torte and roasted peppers.

RUBY LOUNGE
802 North Charles Street
☎ 410-539-8051
Moderate

The chef creates dishes that seem Italian, then Spanish, then Southwest, all subtly flavored by her Louisiana background. It's currently the place to be seen in Mt. Vernon, but the food is good nonetheless. Look for meats grilled over chipotle peppers, fish paired with crabmeat and a good wine list.

THE HELMAND
806 North Charles Street
☎ 410-752-0311
Moderate

Whenever anyone tells you about The Helmand, they always suggest you begin with the pumpkin appetizer. You should follow their advice. Baby pumpkin is served with a garlicky yoghurt sauce, and it sets the tone for the happy surprises that will follow. Local ingredients like sea bass shine in Afghan dishes – stewed with ginger, mint, tomatoes and baby red potatoes, for example. We heartily approve of their invitation to order some of the main dishes in appetizer portions, a perfect way to sample several of them. Crisp white linens set the stylish tone of the dining room, but the food is the real star.

SOTTO SOPRA
405 North Charles Street
☎ 410-625-0534
Moderate to expensive

The influences are clearly Italian, but the chef isn't bound by the traditional ingredients. Oven roasted salmon is served with purple potatoes, patty-pan squash and a raspberry-juniper berry reduction, and tuna is encrusted with poppy and sesame seeds. Ricotta gnocchi are served as an entrée with roasted tomato coulis. In short, you'll find the happiest of marriages here between old country and new world. We always said good marriages were made in the kitchen. For a starter course, try the vitello tonnato, which we never find on American menus – tender braised veal in a sauce of tuna and anchovy. It's delectable. The lunch menu includes saltimbocca, pasta with wild mushroom sauce (also on the dinner menu) and filet of rainbow trout with pernod and dill.

FAIDLEY'S
Lexington Market
400 West Lexington Street
☎ 410-727-4898
Inexpensive

Faidley's is the only place in Baltimore where you can buy muskrat, a hunter's favorite that even city-type Marylanders long for occasionally. But you'll have to cook it yourself.

This is certainly Baltimore's most famous market stall. Faidley's appears on everybody's short list of "the best crab cakes in Maryland" – and rightly so. Obviously, you don't come here for gramma's birthday dinner, but if you want a good crab cake for lunch when you're downtown, you'll find it here. Those, like us, who prefer their crab cakes broiled, will be happy here, too. At Faidley's, you'll have to eat your crab cakes standing up, or carry your delectable bundle of lump crabmeat to a park or waterfront bench for a picnic.

WOMEN'S INDUSTRIAL EXCHANGE TEA ROOM
333 North Charles Street
☎ 410-685-4388
Inexpensive

The Women's Industrial Exchange Tea Room does not accept credit cards.

Comfort foods in a low-key lunchroom setting, served by a staff of cheerful women, some of whom began working here half a century ago. If they thought of changing the menu to replace the specialties, such as deviled eggs and tomato aspic, there'd be a revolution in Baltimore. The biscuits are scrumptious and tender, perfect for breakfast or a pick-me-up snack in the mid-morning. You can also buy cookies, cakes and other baked goods in their period-piece shop. Open for breakfast and lunch only, Monday-Friday, 7-2.

KAWASAKI
413 North Charles Street
☎ 410 659-7600
Moderate

The sushi and beef tataki are just as perfect now as when this was the only Japanese act in town. The atmosphere is right, too, with tatami mats and cushions, hushed service and an air of calm. Kawasaki serves lunch and dinner, Monday through Saturday.

Bolton Hill

This neighborhood has a more sparse offering of restaurants, and they are nearly always crowded when there's a concert at the Meyerhoff Symphony Hall. If you're not bound for a concert, plan on dining late, since there's a mass exodus just before the orchestra tunes up, at around 8:00. Reservations are always a good idea on Bolton Hill.

SPIKE & CHARLIE'S
1225 Cathedral Street
☎ 410-752-8144
Expensive

Basic ingredients, deftly combined and artfully served, have made this restaurant's name – and its owners – synonymous with fine dining for Baltimore's hip crowd. The menu changes with the market, but you might find a duxelle-stuffed loin of rabbit with its juices held inside a packaging of bacon, or roasted wild boar may be on the night's menu. Simple pleasures like fried oysters join the more esoteric fare. Look for new twists on old themes, such as shrimp pot pie; they aren't afraid to experiment. You'll also see a serious emphasis on presentation.

LA TESSO TANA
58 West Biddle Street
☎ 410-837-3630
Moderate

Located in the ground floor of Abacrombie Badger B&B (see page 142), across the street from the Meyerhoff Symphony Hall, this restaurant is predictably busy on concert nights, but relatively quiet the rest of the time. The old Italian classics are well treated – veal Marsala, chicken piccata, saltimbocca, even spaghetti with meatballs – but they don't take over the menu entirely. The veal scallops with artichoke hearts, sun-dried tomatoes, toasted walnuts, capers and vermouth have a distinctly modern Northern Italian accent.

Hampden

Not a center for haute cuisine, but a lot of fun to wander around and shop in, Hampden's best known restaurant epitomizes the "Charm City" atmosphere of this cheeky Old Bawlmer enclave. Yes, they actually do call their city "Bawlmer" here, and they'll probably call you "Hon," too.

CAFE HON
1002 West 36th Street
☎ 410-243-1230
Moderate

On Mondays at Café Hon, you'll have a rare chance to sample sour beef, a Baltimore specialty based on German sauerbraten.

With tongue firmly in cheek, this hometown favorite both exalts and pokes good natured fun at all the old Baltimore traditions. Big hair and cat-eye glasses reign in this campy outpost in one of the city's last true holdout neighborhoods. Retro furnishings remind you of a diner, as might a casual look at the menu. All the old favorites are there – meatloaf, lasagna, chicken parmesan, crab cakes – but they're all a bit updated, the pasta is heart-healthy and there may be arugula in your salad. Weeknight blue-plate specials include Tuesday's fried chicken and Friday's fish & chips.

Even if you doubt that their meatloaf is really "Better than Mom's" as promised, stop in for a piece of pie (always several choices; we favor the apple ourselves) and a mug of coffee, especially during their annual search for "Miss Hon." Wear your big hair, capri pants and hot pink sweater and you could find yourself the star of the show. Stop in at the adjoining shop, Hometown Girl (see *Shopping*, page 115). Café Hon is open Monday through Thursday, 7 am-9 pm; Friday, 7-10; Saturday, 9-10; Sunday, 9-8.

SUZY SOBA
West 36th Street
No phone

Opposite Café Hon, this little Korean restaurant has a nice garden for al fresco dining. Korean dishes here show off this cuisine, which is quite different from either Chinese or Japanese, although it features many of the same ingredients.

HOLY FRIJOLES
908 West 36th Street
☎ 410-235-2326
Inexpensive

Tiny and a little crowded – often with hungry people eyeing your table in hopes you'll eat your chicken chimichangas a bit more quickly – Holy Frijoles serves home-style Mexican foods. As the name suggests, you can expect good hearty portions of black beans or salsa fresca to bring tears to your eyes as you crunch on nachos. Servings are quite large.

Uptown

Most visitors to the city are unlikely to venture out of the attractions of the downtown area just to find an eating place, but if you're headed out of town – or into town – or happen to be in the neighborhood visiting the many parks and museums here, these are well worth a stop. Visitors staying at the Inn at the Colonnade will find these especially convenient.

GERTRUDE'S
Baltimore Museum of Art
10 Art Museum Drive, off Charles Street
☎ 410-889-3399
Moderate to expensive

Look to Gertrude's for skilled treatment of some dishes you usually don't find on upscale restaurant menus – a feast of steamed hard-shell clams and oyster stew.

Don't mistake this for a museum café; it's far more than a place to rest tired feet after a few hours of galleries. In fact, you'd better have a reservation to sample John Shields's latest dinner menu. His mission – as you already know if you've watched his popular cooking show – is to bring the Chesapeake's products, from shellfish to farmhouse cheeses, to the culinary fame they deserve. You can choose from two (sometimes three) kinds of crab cake, including crabettes, which are bite-sized crab cakes that bite back. Rockfish may be presented with goat cheese and asparagus spears, and Eastern Shore chicken could be served in a Vietnamese five-spice with soba noodles or pan-fried with fresh buttermilk biscuits; real Maryland comfort food in good hands. The new menu invites you to build your own entrée, choosing sauces and sides to suit your own taste.

If you don't have room for dessert, return for afternoon tea, when you can sample some of the best, including their version of the famous Lady Baltimore Cake. It's a great improvement, replacing the cloying boiled frosting with white buttercream, and the tiresome candied citron with choice dried cherries, pears, apricots and cranberries, marinated in Cointreau. Candied violets decorate the top. And the tea in your full-sized china pot is real, made with water just off the boil. The setting is lovely, too, overlooking the gardens through a solid wall of glass.

ANGELINA'S
7135 Harford Road
☎ 410-444-5545
Moderate

Angelina's also serves good desserts.

Like Faidley's, Angelina's always appears on the list of crab cake greats, and for a good reason. With a little more class than Faidley's – at least you can sit down here to consume your little piece of Chesapeake heaven – Angelina's is beloved by natives and usually missed entirely by everyone else. Our cousins in Westminster drive all the way into the city to eat here. The rest of the menu marries Italian with Irish pub. Angelina's is open for both lunch and dinner.

AMBASSADOR
3811 Canterbury Road
☎ 410-366-1484
Moderate

Fragrant Indian cuisine is authentic and deftly prepared and served in a nice atmosphere. Wing chairs are comfortable indoors or you can dine in the courtyard overlooking the gardens, enjoying classics like a memorably seasoned lamb vindaloo. It's nice to see this cuisine accorded a setting and service equal to its lineage for a change.

POLO GRILL
4 West University Parkway
☎ 410-235-8200
Expensive

Opinion is divided as to whether the food here is that much better than a number of other places with lower tabs, but the be-seen factor probably makes up the difference for most of its devotees. As you might expect from the name, the atmosphere is that of a private club. American cuisine shines in the hands of a very competent chef, whose rendition of chowder based on corn and crabmeat is outstanding. Wines are well-chosen and service is appropriately correct and highly informed about the menu. Three meals daily.

Annapolis

It would be hard to picture a more appealing small city than Annapolis. It is just the right size to offer plenty of things to see and do, but small enough to get around easily. It is filled with history, and among the greatest of its charms are its historic streets, lined with comely brick buildings. This gives Annapolis its character and its aura of prosperous antiquity.

But despite its passion for historic preservation, Annapolis is a city of the present. Two campuses – St. John's College and the Naval Academy – border the center of town, and their students keep Annapolis forever young at heart. So does the constant buzz of boat-related activity at the City Dock.

A Brief History

The water was crucial to Annapolis from the very beginning, when nearly everything and everyone arrived by boat. The second Lord Baltimore wanted to secure this good harbor and the lands around it, so he offered land grants in **Providence**, as this new addition to his colony of Maryland was called, to Puritans uneasy with Virginia's tight Church of England controls. Along with the land came the promise of religious freedom. In 1695, Providence was renamed Annapolis, honoring Princess Anne, and it became the provincial capital.

DID YOU KNOW?

The city's claim to immortality in US history books took place in November of 1783, when Annapolis became the capital of the United States, a position it held until August of 1784. During that time the Treaty of Paris was ratified there, ending the Revolution.

Getting Here

By Car

US-301/50 runs east-west from Washington DC to the Eastern Shore via the Bay Bridge, skirting along the northern edge of Annapolis. **Route 2** and **I-97** connect that road to the Baltimore Beltway. To reach Annapolis from southern Maryland, use **Route 2**.

Getting Around

On Foot

Annapolis is easy to walk around in, with sights and activities gathered into close areas. The center of most activity, sightseeing and dining is in the old part of the town, clustering around the dock, the Capitol and the Naval Academy. It's pretty hard to get lost in the historic area, with the **State House**

Annapolis Area

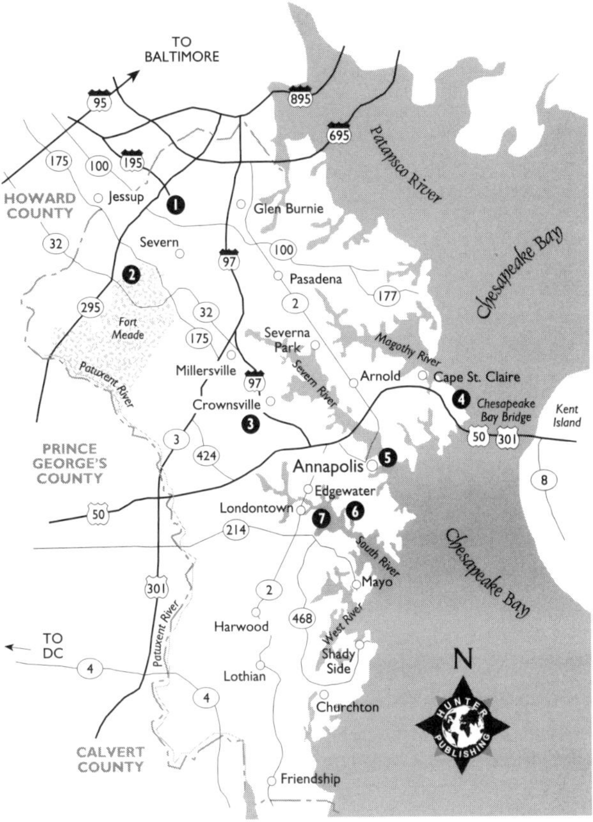

1. Baltimore-Washington International Airport
2. National Cryptologic Museum
3. Maryland Renaissance Festival
4. Sandy Point State Park
5. US Naval Academy
6. Truxtun Park; Quiet Waters Park
7. London Town (historic site)

and **Church Circle** uphill, the water downhill, and the **Academy** blocking off escape on one side and **Spa Creek** on the other. **Main Street** climbs the hill from the docks to Church Circle. **West Street**, with the Annapolis & Anne Arundel County Conference & Visitors Bureau (see page 177) and several restaurants, continues out of town beyond Church Circle. **Duke of Gloucester Street** runs at an angle from Church Circle to Spa Creek, meeting **Compromise Street** at the Spa Creek bridge. Compromise follows the water from the City Dock to Spa Creek.

By Car

Shuttles from the Stadium run from 6:30 am to 8 pm daily, May to mid-October; until 7 pm, weekdays only, the rest of the year.

The narrow old streets may give Annapolis its charm, but they are a pain in the neck to drive on, let alone park along. We suggest leaving your car at your hotel (those on the outskirts have courtesy buses to shuttle their guests to the center) or in the Navy-Marine Corps Stadium, near the Academy. You can park all day, taking a shuttle that stops at the visitors center, the Naval Academy and Main Street. Weekend parking is $4 all day, and the shuttle is free. Weekday parking is $3, with an added 75¢ for the shuttle. RVs, which are nearly impossible to get through the narrow downtown streets, are $8 a day.

Downtown parking garages, which are more expensive and may be filled on busy days, are located off Main Street and next to the visitors center, near Church Circle. The first hour is free and the daily maximum is $8 on weekdays, $4 on weekends. If you are shopping downtown, ask for validation to get discounted parking.

> **CAUTION**
>
> You must move your car from a metered spot after the two-hour limit. You can (and will) be ticketed for refilling an expired meter.

By Water Taxi

To reach the restaurants along Spa and Back creeks, take **Jiffy Water Taxi** (☎ 410-263-0033, which, from mid-May to early September, departs hourly from City Dock, Monday-Thursday, 9:30-midnight; Friday, 9:30-1 am; Saturday, 9-1 am; and Sunday, 9-midnight. It runs a more limited schedule from April through October, early and late in the season.

Information Sources

Annapolis & Anne Arundel County Conference & Visitors Bureau, 26 West Street, Annapolis, MD 21401, www.visit-annapolis.org, ☎ 410-280-0445, is just off Church Circle. Parking is in the lot behind the building. Open daily, 9 am-5 pm. An information booth is also on the City Dock.

The first hour of parking is free at the Visitors Bureau.

Sunup to Sundown

Recommended Sights & Activities

Since Annapolis sights require a lot of walking, we suggest beginning your day by touring on foot, then taking one of the water tours in the afternoon, when you'll appreciate the chance to do the rest of your sightseeing sitting down.

Allow half a day for the attractions at the **Naval Academy**, and half a day to visit the **Hammond-Harwood** and **William Paca** houses, longer if you plan to linger to admire the historic points along the walking tour of that neighborhood, or to add another historic home – the **Chase-Lloyd House**. Charles Carroll's home and the sights around the **hill** will occupy at least another half-day, as will a visit to **London Town** on the opposite side of the South River.

If you are in the area during the **Renaissance Festival**, you will want at least half a day there; most people enjoy a whole day, when they can take advantage of the many live performances, from Shakespeare to jousting matches, throughout the fairgrounds.

If you are not touring the Eastern Shore, you might earmark a day to travel by boat to **St. Michaels**, to see the town and its maritime museum.

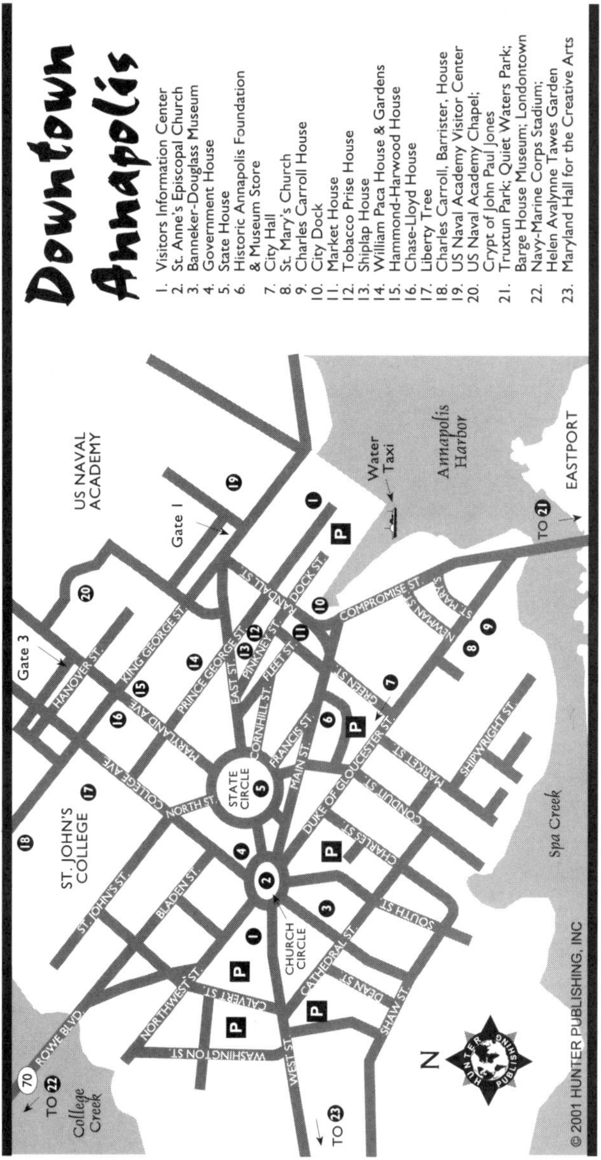
Downtown Annapolis
1. Visitors Information Center
2. St. Anne's Episcopal Church
3. Banneker-Douglass Museum
4. Government House
5. State House
6. Historic Annapolis Foundation & Museum Store
7. City Hall
8. St. Mary's Church
9. Charles Carroll House
10. City Dock
11. Market House
12. Tobacco Prise House
13. Shiplap House
14. William Paca House & Gardens
15. Hammond-Harwood House
16. Chase-Lloyd House
17. Liberty Tree
18. Charles Carroll, Barrister, House
19. US Naval Academy Visitor Center
20. US Naval Academy Chapel; Crypt of John Paul Jones
21. Truxtun Park; Quiet Waters Park; Barge House Museum; Londontown
22. Navy-Marine Corps Stadium; Helen Avalynne Tawes Garden
23. Maryland Hall for the Creative Arts
US NAVAL ACADEMY
ST. JOHN'S COLLEGE
STATE CIRCLE
CHURCH CIRCLE
Gate 1
Gate 3
Water Taxi
Annapolis Harbor
EASTPORT
Spa Creek
College Creek
TO 21
TO 22
TO 23
70
ROWE BLVD.
N
© 2001 HUNTER PUBLISHING, INC

A Walking Tour

While we encourage those with plenty of time to simply wander around the streets between the docks and the Naval Academy, stopping at historic houses as they happen upon them, those with limited time may want to follow a more structured tour route. The entire walk takes about half an hour if you don't stop and, although much of the route is on brick sidewalks, it is not steep. Note that hours of operation and contact information for these sights are in the *Attractions* section.

- Begin at the **City Dock**, where you may see the skipjack ***Stanley Norman*** or other sailing ship. Harbor and river excursions begin here. From the docks, visit the old **City Market**, then take the street behind it, next to Maria's Restaurant. This is Pinckney Street, and at the corner is the **Tobacco Prise House**, an early 19th-century warehouse. Next door, the **Shiplap House**, built about 1715 and one of the city's oldest homes, sits high above the street. When Pinckney Street meets East Street, take a right then a quick left to the **William Paca House and Gardens**, on Prince George Street.
- The other narrow old streets going up the hill – Cornhill and Fleet streets – are worth following, too, for the restored homes that line them. Continue on Prince George Street to Maryland Avenue at the end of the block, where a right turn brings you to the door of the 1774 **Ham-**

mond-Harwood House, an outstanding example of late Colonial architecture.

- Across the street, the 1769 **Chase-Lloyd House** stands behind a picket fence, through which you may see some of its famous roses. Maryland Avenue continues straight to Gate 3 of the **US Naval Academy**. Most of that institution's attractions are close to that gate, including the **Chapel** (on your right), with the Crypt of John Paul Jones, and the **Naval Academy Museum** (on your left). Return to Prince George Street and turn right at the corner with the Hammond-Harwood House, walking one block to College Avenue. Follow it to the left, past the campus of **St. John's College**, whose buildings date from as early as 1722. On the campus is the towering **Sons of Liberty Tree**, where patriots conspired during the Revolution.

- Turn left onto North Street to reach State Circle and the **Maryland State House**, which was the US Capitol in 1783 and 1784. Continue around State Circle to School Street, on the corner of which is **Government House**, the official residence of Maryland's Governor.

- School Street leads straight to Church Circle, with **St. Anne Episcopal Church** and its churchyard filling the center. On the other side of the circle is West Street, where you will find the visitors bureau and several restaurants in its first block.

- Heading downhill from Church Circle on Duke of Gloucester Street, which leaves the circle just to the right of Main Street you'll come to the **Charles Carroll House** at number 107, overlooking Spa Creek. Next to the house is **St. Mary's Church**, a Victorian Gothic building worth a stop to see its ribbed vaulting and carved altar screen. The church is usually open during daylight hours. From the end of Duke of Gloucester Street, go left on Compromise Street, which leads back along the waterfront to your starting point at City Dock.

Attractions

Even if you are not following the walking tour outlined above, the best place to begin touring the historic district of Annapolis is at the docks, the focal point and origin of much of the city's history.

The historic homes and locations that follow are arranged in a geographical sequence, heading from the City Dock, past the market building and up Pinckney Street, from the corner of Market Square behind the market.

Downtown Annapolis

TOBACCO PRISE HOUSE & SHIPLAP HOUSE
18 Pinckney Street, at the corner of Market Street
☎ 410-267-7619
Free

Right at the corner is the Prise House, a stone-ender that served as a warehouse for tobacco from the early 1800s. Exhibits describe the early tobacco trade, and include a large press that was used to pack tobacco leaves into hogsheads – large barrels for shipping. Next door is Shiplap House, built about 1715, and one of the oldest houses surviving in the city. An early tavern, it has had many uses before becoming the offices of the Historic Annapolis Foundation. Its terraced garden displays many of the plants common to late 18th-century herb gardens in Annapolis. Inside, changing exhibits highlight various historical subjects. The buildings are generally open Monday-Friday, 2-4 pm, from March to October. If the Prise House is not open, ask at the Shiplap House and someone will open it.

WILLIAM PACA HOUSE AND GARDENS
186 Prince George Street
☎ 410-263-5553
Admission: $7 for house tour and garden; $4 for garden only

This historic home and impressive two-acre garden complex was completed in 1765 for Maryland's Governor, William Paca. Beyond its historical significance and extensive gardens, this estate is a marvel of restoration. Over the years, the building and gardens fell into disarray, and a large hotel was built over the once-grand gardens, with the house used as a lobby. Through extensive research of historical evidence, the gardens and home have been returned to the most accurate state possible.

The 37-room Georgian house has been fully restored, and a third of its rooms are decorated and furnished as they were in Paca's time. There are tours available that last about 45 minutes and include a tour of the gardens. The visitors center, which is in the garden, not inside the house, holds exhibits on both the house and life of Paca, as well as the gardens and culture of the 18th century. These exhibits change regularly.

The gardens are the most impressive in Annapolis, covering nearly two acres. The terraced gardens can be explored on authentically located brick paths that were found in archaeological digs during restoration. There are plenty of places to sit and admire the terraces of roses, topiaries, orchards, and water gardens. A domed summer house by the pool caps off the far end of the gardens, and adds to the elegance of a garden-party atmosphere. This house was reconstructed from its representation in the background of a portrait of William Paca. House tours are given Monday-Saturday, 10-4; Sunday, noon-4; (in January and February, tours are Saturday and Sunday only). The garden is open the same hours as the house, and until 5 pm, April to October.

HAMMOND-HARWOOD HOUSE
19 Maryland Avenue
☎ 410-269-1714
Admission: $5, adults; $3, children

This fine 1774 home will delight anyone interested in period architecture. It is a highly regarded example of the late Colonial style, and is the last work of well-known architect William Buckland. Unlike some other historical homes of its time, this one has been preserved, instead of brought back from near ruin, and is still very close to its original state, due to upkeep instead of major restoration. Be sure to notice the lovely dining room with its hand-carved moldings and extensive woodwork. Look for the false window, which is actually the back door, called a jib door and fairly common to Georgian homes. The lower panel is filled in to create the illusion of a window and retain the symmetry that is the hallmark of Georgian architecture. The home is filled with antiques from its period, including portraits by several members of the Peale family. The furniture is original, and much of it is the work of the well-known Charles Shaw. Tours are given hourly, Monday-Saturday, 10-3:30; Sunday, noon-3:30.

The ornate Rococo style of the Hammond-Harwood House's first floor is particularly impressive for its handwork.

CHASE-LLOYD HOUSE
22 Maryland Avenue
☎ 410-263-2723
$2 donation is requested

This is another fine historic home, the work of architect William Buckland, although the house was begun before he was hired. As a result, it is mostly the interior that shows his work, such as the cantilevered stairway and the meticulous carvings. The impressive decorations are not for the minimalist. The house is open Monday-Saturday, 2-4 pm.

Garden lovers should be sure to visit the Chase-Lloyd's rose gardens in season.

MARYLAND STATE HOUSE
State Circle
☎ 410-974-3400
Free

The historic Maryland State House, still in use today, is the oldest continuously used in the country.

It is also the only state capital that once served as the capital for the nation.

The Treaty of Paris was signed at the Maryland State House, officially ending the American Revolution.

Both the historically minded and those who love antiques will want to see the State House for its collections of period furniture and military items, which include the USS *Maryland* silver service and several portraits by Charles Willson Peale. If you are not there when tours are offered, you may explore certain rooms on your own.

Outside on the grounds are a cannon, which was brought by the first settlers in 1634 aboard the *Dove*, and a small brick treasury building from 1737. The Maryland State House is open daily, 9-5, with 30-minute tours at 11 and 3.

GOVERNMENT HOUSE
State Circle and School Street
☎ 410-974-3531
Free

This residential home of Maryland's Governor is a fine Victorian mansion. You may visit the house during regular hours, or make an appointment ahead of time to see the collections of Maryland art and antiques. Government House is open 10-2, Tuesday, Wednesday and Thursday, from April to December; Tuesday and Thursday, from January to March.

St. Anne's was the home parish to three of the four Maryland signers of the Declaration of Independence.

ST. ANNE EPISCOPAL CHURCH
Church Circle
☎ 410-267-9333
Free

This lovely church sits at the top of the hill, overlooking the circle. Most impressive are the fine Tiffany stained glass and a silver communion service (which was a gift from King William). The St. Anne Memorial window, by Louis Comfort Tiffany, won first prize at the Chicago World's Fair in 1893. Historians will want to find the grave of the last Colonial governor of Maryland in the churchyard. St. Anne's is open daily, 8-6.

BANNEKER-DOUGLASS MUSEUM
84 Franklin Street
☎ 410-974-2893
Free

This museum, named for two well-known Maryland African-Americans, Frederick Douglass and Benjamin Banneker, is a center for both permanent and changing exhibits of African-American historical and art collections. With its focus on Maryland's own African-American heritage, this is the official state museum. It is housed in the former Mount Moriah African Methodist Episcopal Church, and is considered one of the most complete collections of its kind. The museum is open Tuesday-Friday, 10-3; Saturday, noon-4.

CHARLES CARROLL HOUSE
107 Duke of Gloucester Street
☎ 410-269-1737
Admission: $5, adults; $4, seniors; $2, ages 12-17

This is the birthplace of Declaration of Independence signer Charles Carroll of Carrollton. Carroll, one of the wealthiest and most productive men of his time, lived in this home until 1821. The house is still under restoration; gardeners will be especially interested in the terraces along the shore of Spa Creek. Charles Carroll House is open Fridays, Sundays and holidays, noon-4; Saturdays, 10-2.

Charles Carroll was the only Catholic to sign the Declaration of Independence.

ST. MARY'S CHURCH
109 Duke of Gloucester Street
☎ 410-263-2396
Free

This Gothic Victorian church sits next door to the Carroll house, but its cornerstone was not laid until 1858, by Saint John Newman. Step inside to see the impressive ribbed vaulting and the hand-carved altar screen. St. Mary's is open during daylight hours.

BARGE HOUSE MUSEUM
Bay Shore Drive, Eastport
☎ 410-268-1802
Free

This small museum is dedicated to exhibits and collections on the maritime history of the area, including the culture of the boat builders and sailors who spent their lives on the Maryland waterfront. The Barge house is open Saturday, 11-4, or by appointment.

HELEN AVALYNNE TAWES GARDEN
Tawes State Office Building, Taylor Avenue
off Rowe Blvd./Route 70, West Annapolis
☎ 410-267-8189
Free

The little-known garden is a must for both naturalists and garden-lovers. Covering six acres, the garden is set up to display examples of Maryland's native plants and natural habitats from the Chesapeake and river shores to the upland forests. The garden is open during daylight hours.

Outside of Annapolis

LONDON TOWN
Londontown Road
Londontown
☎ 410-222-1919
Free

London Town, on the bank of the South River opposite Annapolis, was the best crossing point from that side of the river to Annapolis. Here, the once-bustling town of 300 or so, then called London, was the unloading zone for ship merchants, including tobacco merchants from the south.

Only one original home (the William Brown house; see below) from the settlement stands in the historic site today, but extensive archaeological digs are underway to determine the exact location of buildings and to learn as much as possible about the lives of the people who lived here.

One ongoing dig at the site of the long-gone **Rumney's Tavern** has proven it to be a treasure trove, a time capsule of everything that was thrown away by the tavern. The cellar of the tavern would flood during big storms and, over time, the cellar silted up. Between the storms the tavern keeper threw the trash there, so each layer was preserved by the next flood. From this trash, historians can tell what dishes were used, what foods people ate, even who they traded with during several different periods. Archaeologists have found the entire Delft tavern service and quantities of wine bottles, bones and oyster shells that tell researchers what the tavern served. You can visit the dig sites when they are in operation.

The gardens that surround the visitors center and spill into the ravine that leads to the riverbank are best known for their rhododendrons, which spread huge clusters of flowers in the spring. There is also a wonderful shop at the visitors center, which sells books of historical and local interest, as well as nice replicas of period brass and china items. In the visitors center you can also see some of the artifacts found on the site. London Town is open year-round, Monday through Saturday, 10-4; Sunday, noon to 4.

WILLIAM BROWN HOUSE
Londontown Road
London Town
☎ 410-222-1919
Admission: $6, adults; $4, seniors; $3, children

The header bond pattern has the highest number of bricks laid with the small ends facing outward, so it uses more bricks.

This 1760 home is made entirely with header bond brick, which was the most expensive technique of its time, and is the only Annapolis building to be entirely made in this fine brickwork method.

William Brown was a man who suffered from more extravagant taste than his pocketbook could afford and, as a result, the interior of the home took many years to complete. Interestingly, however, Brown did not keep up the lavish detail when he came to the design of the house. Although outrageously expensive to construct with the finest brick available, the interior layout of the home was simple and unpretentious, designed in a practical manner with the grand stairways and wings typical of Georgian homes set aside for simple function to accommodate his large family.

In an attempt to pay back the large loans that he was obligated to for the building, Brown took advantage of his location at the ferry landing and opened the house as an inn. Unfortunately, by that time, the heyday of this port was over, and Brown finally went bankrupt in 1790, losing his dream home. It had several different owners from then until the 1960s, when it was recognized as historically important and its restoration began.

While touring the William Brown house, pay attention to the fine linen work done by volunteers; it's completely authentic and realistic to the era of the house.

Visitors are invited to touch and handle artifacts in some sections of the house. Don't miss the kitchen and spinning room, as well as a few rooms that have not been restored, which are reminders of the ravages of time on an old building. The house is open year-round, Monday through Saturday, 10-4 pm; Sunday, noon to 4 pm. In January and February, house tours are by appointment only.

MARYLAND RENAISSANCE FESTIVAL
Fairgrounds, Rte. 178, Crownsville
☎ 410-266-7304 or 800-296-7304
www.rennfest.com
Admission: $14, ages 16-61; $12, over 62; $5 ages seven-15

Permanent buildings in fanciful medieval and Renaissance themes stretch through a forest of tall pine trees and around an open field, simulating the colorful and lively atmosphere of a fair in 16th-century England. Spectator events – fencing matches, jousting tournaments, human chess games, magic shows, sword-swallowing acts, troubadours, madrigals – take place in open-air theaters, stages and in the arena, as well as randomly along the busy "streets." A replica of London's Globe Theatre has regular Shakespeare productions. Not all shows are repeated on all weekends; call for a complete program to time your visit for such special guest performers as the comedy-magic act of Tom Crowl and the Wench.

Shops and booths offer an amazing variety of hard-to-find goods, each of which must tie in some way to the medieval or Renaissance eras. Handmade replicas of period crafts include beautiful swords made by a blacksmith who has studied the art of early weaponry, pottery chalices and steins with dragons as handles, tapestry pillows, herbal and flower crowns, carnival masks and period costumes, as well as many items with a more tenuous connection to the eras. Moving through the crowds of modern travelers are magnificently attired kings and queens in velvets and brocades, monks in hooded robes, serving wenches, knights in armor, jesters with jingling caps, barefoot peasants in ragged sacks and minstrels carrying lutes.

Games of chance, free pony rides for kids, a maze and a chance to try your hand at archery are scattered throughout the five-acre fairgrounds. Food may be authentic or not, but the most popular items are the giant smoked turkey drumsticks, steak on a stake and meatpies. Spirited beverages abound, including ales, ciders and meads. It's not a theme park, but a lively hands-on re-creation in the spirit of four centuries ago. For creative anachronism, you can't beat it. The Festival is open on weekends from late August through October, 10:30 am to 7 pm.

The Naval Academy

US NAVAL ACADEMY VISITOR CENTER
Gate 1, 52 King George Street
☎ 410-263-6933
www.usna.edu/PAO/visitor.html
Free

Guided tours of the 338-acre training center and college, where more than 4,000 students prepare for careers as officers in the Navy or Marine Corps, begin at the center, where you can also see a free film about the academy. The Visitor Center is open daily, March through December, 9-5; January and February, 9-4. Guided tours are $5.50 for adults; $4.50 for seniors; $3.50 for students.

US NAVAL ACADEMY CHAPEL
Gate 3, at the end of Maryland Avenue
Free

You quickly sense the long history and traditions of the Academy inside the impressive Chapel, which is easy to identify by its large and imposing dome. At the rear of the center aisle, close to the entrance, you'll find a useful brochure about the chapel, explaining its art and a bit of its history. The brochure identifies the outstanding stained-glass windows, the artistic stars of the chapel. The Farragut window, on the right in the rotunda, depicts the Admiral in the rigging of his flagship, and the Archangel Michael guiding ships through the mine-studded Mobile Bay. To its right is a window by the Tiffany studio. Opposite these, across the rotunda, is an earlier Tiffany window of the Angel of Peace and depictions of Saints Peter and Andrew mending nets. Sir

Galahad, to the left, is the oldest Tiffany work here, intended originally for an earlier chapel.

Underneath the chapel, reached by inside stairs to the left of the entrance or from an outside door, also to the left of the main entrance, is the small, dark and intimate St. Andrews Chapel. Its baptismal font is made of wood from the USS *Constitution*. The chapel is open Monday through Saturday, 9-4; Sunday, 1-4.

CRYPT OF JOHN PAUL JONES
Under the Naval Academy Chapel
Gate 3, at the end of Maryland Avenue
Free

The whereabouts of John Paul Jones remains was unknown when the chapel was built. But Ernest Flagg, the architect, so admired this naval hero that he designed a vaulted crypt under the rotunda in the hope that his remains would someday be located. They eventually were discovered in France, and were returned on a navy ship to be laid to rest here, both to honor the hero and to serve as a role model for midshipmen. To reach John Paul Jones' crypt, you must go outside the chapel and around to the left (it's on the right as you face the chapel steps), entering a small door underneath the center of the chapel. The crypt is open Monday through Saturday, 9-4; Sunday, 1-4.

ACADEMY MUSEUM
Gate 3, at the end of Maryland Avenue
☎ 410-263-6933
Free

At right angles to the chapel is a building housing artifacts of the history of the academy and of the US

Navy. The two overlap, of course, since many of the most famous events in naval history were under the command of men who studied and were commissioned here. The exhibit on Fleet Admiral Chester Nimitz, class of 1905, includes the uniform he wore, the pen he used, and the table on which he signed the Japanese documents of surrender, as well as photographs of the ceremony on board the battleship *Missouri* in Tokyo Bay, on September 2, 1945.

Downstairs is a collection of some very unusual ship models, each one made at the same time that the original ship was built. Many of the ships have not survived, so these models, some several centuries old, are all that is known of the details of those vessels. The oldest model was made about 1650, and many of them are so detailed that they have working parts hidden below the decks.

TIP

Although the free printed guide to the model ships is designed for parents to use while touring the Academy's collection with children, you will find it useful yourself, as it points out details such as the evolution of decorative elements and rigging techniques.

Even more unusual is the collection of rare prisoner-of-war art, beautiful ship models carved from bone saved from their rations by French sailors interned in British prison ships between 1756 and 1815. Bone pieces were applied over wooden hulls and the rigging is of human or horse hair. These were made using handmade tools formed from nails and pieces of glass. Nearly a dozen of these ships are here, one nearly a yard long.

The museum reflects life at the academy, naval art, great naval explorers and survivors, war at sea and important naval figures.

In the same building is the **US Naval Institute Bookstore**, which will attract those interested in ships, the academy or naval history. Books, although the main focus, are not the only things sold here; prints, nautical gifts and Naval Academy insignia items are here, too; ☎ 410-295-1043, www.usni.org. The Naval Academy Museum and shop are open Monday-Saturday, 9-5; Sunday, 11-5.

Tours

On Land

THREE CENTURIES TOURS OF ANNAPOLIS
48 Maryland Avenue
☎ 410-263-5401
Admission: $8, adults; $3, children

Guides in Colonial costume escort informative two-hour tours of the Naval Academy and the historic district. Tours are for groups of 10 or fewer, on a first-come, first-served basis. Tours are given daily, April through October, starting at 10:30 from the visitors center on West Street and at 1:30 from the information kiosk at City Dock. From November through March, tours start at 2:30 on Saturday, from Gibson's Lodgings at 110 Prince George Street. Private tours may also be arranged by appointment.

ANNAPOLIS WALKABOUT
223 South Cherry Grove Avenue
☎ 410-263-8253

Explore the buildings of the Naval Academy or the streets of the historic district with an architectural historian. We promise that by the end of the tour, you won't have to ask again what Flemish bond brickwork is. Tours are given Saturdays and Sundays, April through October, starting from the visitors center on West Street. Times vary; call for reservations.

HISTORIC ANNAPOLIS FOUNDATION MUSEUM STORE AND WELCOME CENTER
77 Main Street
☎ 410-268-5576

The voice of Walter Cronkite narrates a recorded self-guided tour of Annapolis, available as an audiocassette. Another recorded tour leads to places significant in Annapolis' African-American history and heritage. Audio cassette rental is $5. The center is open Monday-Saturday, 10-5; Sunday, noon-5.

On Water

If you have a chance to see the city from its waterways, we highly recommend it. You will find a side of Annapolis that is hidden away from the roads, and see the fine homes that stretch along the waterfront. Cruising the harbors can also bring you back in time to the days when the water was essential to the economy and social life of the city, and most travel was done by boat. The harbor offers plenty of options for the boat lover, including sightseeing cruises that give you a chance to see the skyline of the city, or fishing excursions for the more adventurous.

CHESAPEAKE MARINE TOURS
Slip 20, City Dock
☎ 410-268-7600
$6-$12 for cruise; $21.95 and up with lunch

This boat tour company offers choices to fit any schedule. A full day of cruising will bring you across the Chesapeake Bay to St. Michaels, on the Eastern Shore; a 90-minute cruise explores the Severn River and visits the Thomas Point Lighthouse; a pleasant 40-minute outing offers a view of nearby sights around the harbor. Chesapeake Marine gives tours and cruises daily, April to early October.

SCHOONER *WOODWIND*
Annapolis Marriott Waterfront Hotel
☎ 410-263-7837
Cost: adults, $24-$27; seniors, $2 less; children, half-price

This beautiful 74-foot yacht will take you on a two-hour cruise of the harbor and Chesapeake Bay, and on the surrounding waterways. While day-trips feature sightseeing, evening cruises feature on-board entertainment and theme nights. Wednesday evenings are a special treat, when you can watch the sailboat races right from the water. The *Woodwind* is available for cruises and day-trips Tuesday-Sunday, from May-September; less frequently in spring and fall.

BEGINAGAIN
City Dock
☎ 410-626-1422
Adults $55

This small 36-foot sailboat is an especially pleasant way to enjoy the waters of Annapolis. Ride for three hours around the harbor and up little waterways, exploring places that the bigger boats can't go.

Recreation

Sailing

Sailing is as much a part of Annapolis as water is to a bay, and it's a good place to learn the sport if you've never tried it. Wednesday evenings in the summer you can watch sailing races, or you can sail as a passenger, join as crew to learn the skills crew or rent your own sailboat.

ANNAPOLIS SAILING SCHOOL
601 Sixth Street, across the Spa Creek bridge
☎ 800-638-9192

Whether you've sailed before and need a brushup or you just want to get the feel of it without committing yourself to a full sailing course, join America's oldest sail-training program any summer morning at 10 for "Try-Sail." If you know how to sail, you can rent craft here.

J WORLD ANNAPOLIS
213 Eastern Avenue, Eastport
☎ 410-280-2040 or 800-966-2038

Weekend and week-long sailing courses are tailored to your own skill level in limited-sized classes. All sailing craft are late model.

SOUTH RIVER BOAT RENTALS
Pier 7 Marina, Route 2
Edgewater
☎ 410-956-9729

A fleet of Hobie Cats and sailboats are available for rent by the hour, day or week.

Canoeing & Kayaking

AMPHIBIOUS HORIZONS
600 Quiet Waters Park Road (in the park)
☎ 410-267-8742 or 888-I-LUV-SUN
www.amphibioushorizons.com.

This company operates throughout the state and offers day-long Saturday trips through the Susquehanna Flats. Cost of all day excursions is $75, and includes lunch at a waterside restaurant.

Wednesday through Monday, June-August; Friday through Sunday in April, May, September and October. Canoe and kayak rentals are available at Quiet Waters Park (☎ 410-222-1777), on Hillsmere Drive off Bay Ridge Road, where you can explore the flatwater of Harness Creek.

On alternate Friday evenings from May through September, at 6 pm, Amphibious Horizons offers guided kayak tours of the creek. The $35 fee includes boat, instruction and refreshments. Beginning and intermediate small-group or private lessons are offered on weekends. See their website for a complete list of trips and prices.

Fishing

With the Chesapeake Bay calling, it is hard for the fisherman to resist. If you have your own boat, there is a paved ramp at Truxtun Park, which is just off Hilltop Lane, or you can go to Sandy Point State Park to rent a boat, as well as find bait and anything else you might need for a day of fishing. If you are less confident about your boating skills than your fishing, plenty of excursions are available for fishing without the hassle of your own boat. Sportfishing licenses are needed for those ages 16 to 65, and they are available at any tackle shop and many local stores.

CHESAPEAKE BAY FISHING
Captain Clyde's Charters
☎ 410-974-4314
www.captclyde.com

Groups as small as two or as large as 20 can take either fishing or sightseeing cruises. Call for directions.

SEA VENTURE CHARTERS
Holiday Point Marina
3774 Beach Drive, Edgewater (south of Annapolis)
☎ 410-798-6459
www.baycaptains.com/seaventure
Half-day $240, full day $340

These charter fishing trips are for groups up to six, and provide not only the bait and tackle, but fishing permits and a well-informed guide who will enhance the trip.

> **CAUTION**
>
> It is recommended that you check with the Coast Guard at ☎ 410-267-8107 if you question a boat's current certification, since the status may change. It is considered the responsibility of each passenger to be aware of the certifications.

Beaches & Parks

SANDY POINT STATE PARK
East College Parkway, signposted from US-301/50 immediately north of the Bay Bridge
☎ 410-974-2149

Just off the Bay Bridge on Cape St. Claire, this park has day-use facilities, including a beach with changing rooms and food vendors, boat ramps, boat rentals and picnic areas. Along with swimming, the park has excellent windsurfing off its long elbow-shaped beach.

QUIET WATERS PARK
Hillsmere Drive, off Bay Ridge Road
☎ 410-222-1777
Admission: $4 per vehicle

Stretching along the scenic shore of South River, this attractive park has formal gardens, picnic sites, rowboat rentals, fishing piers and boat access. Walking trails are wide enough to share comfortably with bicycles, as they wander through woods and marsh and alongside a pond. A café serves healthy dishes made from fresh local ingredients.

TRUXTUN PARK
Truxtun Road, off Hilltop Lane
☎ 410-263-7958

Located at the end of Spa Creek, the park has boat access and fishing, with swimming in a pool.

Shop Till You Drop

Downtown Annapolis

Main Street is lined with interesting and attractive, if often pricey, boutiques and shops, and is always a pleasant place to browse. Antiques buffs as well as historical sleuths will be fascinated by the great variety of antiques shops in the area. The best places to go in search of shops are on **Maryland Avenue** near State Circle and the **Riggs Avenue** area of Baltimore-Annapolis Boulevard (Route 648), which is also accessible from the Baltimore-Annapolis Bicycle trail (although you probably won't do much serious antiques shopping on a bicycle). You will encounter plenty of shops in these areas, as well as open-air multi-dealer markets and specialty antiques shops.

ANNAPOLIS POTTERY
40 State Circle
☎ 410-268-6153

The store features an open workshop for those curious about how the pottery is made, as well as an extensive shop. Open Monday-Saturday, 10-6; Sunday, 10-5.

THE LEAGUE OF MARYLAND CRAFTSMEN
54 Maryland Avenue
☎ 410-626-1277

The association's shop displays and sells a wide variety of crafts by local artisans, including glasswork, handwoven baskets, woodworking, and pottery. The League is open Monday and Wednesday-Saturday, 10-5; Sunday, noon-5.

ANNAPOLIS ANTIQUE GALLERY
2009 West Street
☎ 410-266-0635

Features over 40 dealers' collections from tiny knickknacks and fine estate jewelry to mint-condition antique furniture. Open daily, 10-5.

HISTORIC ANNAPOLIS FOUNDATION MUSEUM STORE
77 Main Street
☎ 410-268-5576

The Museum Store is particularly interesting for those who enjoy maritime history.

The Museum Store sells models of ships and plenty of other related books and gifts. The store also offers products reminiscent of other aspects of Annapolis history, including reproductions of housewares and other local antiques. The store is open Monday-Saturday, 10-5; Sunday, noon-5.

SAVE THE BAY SHOP
188 Main Street
☎ 410-268-8832

Proceeds from sales at the store are donated to the Chesapeake Bay Foundation, which is dedicated to preserving the environment of the bay. Save the Bay is open Monday-Saturday, 10-5; Sunday hours vary.

Ecologically conscious shoppers will enjoy Save The Bay.

Outside of Annapolis

AAA ANTIQUES MALL
Intersection of Routes 175 and 295
just outside of Fort Meade
☎ 410-551-4101

Traditionally one of the biggest and varied multi-dealer malls in the area, you can find nearly anything here, from the finest china to sentimental "junk." Offers 58,000 square feet of browsing space in a casual atmosphere for both the serious collector and the curious passerby. AAA Antiques Mall is open daily, 10-6.

ANNAPOLIS FARMERS' MARKET
Corner of Riva Road and Truman Parkway

Local farms sell fresh seasonal produce here. The market is west of Annapolis, and is open Saturdays, 7 am to noon.

PENNSYLVANIA DUTCH FARMERS' MARKET
Annapolis Harbor Center, Solomons Island Road
☎ 410-573-0770

This farmer's market offers more than just produce – there are home-baked goods, private farm cheeses, and meats among the goodies found here. They are open Thursday, 10-6; Friday, 9-6; Saturday, 9-3.

After Dark

Performing Arts

MARYLAND HALL FOR THE CREATIVE ARTS
801 Chase Street
☎ 410-263-5544
www.mdhallarts.org

The major performance venue for concerts, road shows and a variety of performing artists.

ANNAPOLIS OPERA, INC.
☎ 410-267-8135
www.mdhallarts.org

The outstanding group maintains a year-round schedule of grand opera, operetta and Broadway musicals, which they perform at Maryland Hall and other venues.

ANNAPOLIS SYMPHONY ORCHESTRA
Maryland Hall for the Creative Arts
☎ 410-269-1132

Professional musicians perform a classical repertoire, and chamber concerts are designed to attract family audiences. Performances are held October through May.

THE ANNAPOLIS CHORALE
Maryland Hall for the Creative Arts
☎ 410-263-1906

A 150-voice full chorus, a smaller chamber chorus and the Annapolis Chamber Orchestra join to perform popular and classical works from September through May.

ANNAPOLIS SUMMER GARDEN THEATRE
143 Compromise Street
☎ 410-268-9212

Thursday through Sunday, from late May through Labor Day, Broadway musicals are presented in a 200-seat theater under the stars.

BALLET THEATRE OF ANNAPOLIS
☎ 410-263-8289

This professional dance company performs classical and modern ballet at Maryland Hall for the Creative Arts, and occasionally at other locations.

COLONIAL PLAYERS
108 East Street
☎ 410-268-7373

Five annual productions are performed in a theater-in-the-round setting.

Live Music

In this section are included bars and clubs where live music is performed in other than a concert hall setting.

CHESAPEAKE MUSIC HALL
Exit 29, off US-50
between the Severn and Bay Bridges
☎ 410-626-7515
www.toad.net/~musichall

The hall is open Thursday-Saturday evenings and Sunday at 1 pm. Musical shows are accompanied by buffet dinners, in a cabaret setting.

MIDDLETON TAVERN OYSTER BAR
Dock Street
☎ 410-263-3323

Open Monday-Friday, 11:30 am to 2 am; Saturday-Sunday, 10 am to 2 am. In the summer the bar is outside on the porch, overlooking the market square; live entertainment year-round.

RAM'S HEAD TAVERN
33 West Street
☎ 410-268-4545
www.ramsheadtavern.com

A schedule of performances is available on the Ram's Head Web site.

A separate entertainment area, with bright décor and cabaret seating, is used for a regular schedule of performances that include well-known area jazz artists. The tavern is open Monday-Saturday, 11 am-2 am; Sunday, 10 am (for brunch) until 2 am.

49 WEST
49 West Street
☎ 410-626-9796

The café and wine bar features live classical music Tuesday evening, jazz Wednesday through Friday.

Bars

RIORDEN'S
26 Market Space
City Dock
☎ 410-263-5449

Although Riorden's is a restaurant and raw bar, too, we include it here for the old-time saloon atmosphere of its bar, where you can order from a selection of nearly two dozen draft beers, several of which are brewed in Maryland microbreweries.

Evening Cruises

SCHOONER *WOODWIND*
Annapolis Marriott Waterfront Hotel
☎ 410-263-7837
Cost: adults, $24-$27; seniors, $2 discount

Evening cruises on board the 74-foot yacht come alive with entertainment and theme nights on board. On Wednesday evenings you can watch the sailboat races right up close. Evening cruises are given May-September, Tuesday through Sunday; less frequently in spring and fall.

Best Places to Stay

ACCOMMODATIONS PRICE SCALE	
Inexpensive	under $100
Moderate	$100-$200
Expensive	$201-$300
Deluxe	more than $300

Lodging Services

During very busy seasons – Commissioning Weekend at the Academy, St. John's College graduation (both in late spring), the boat shows and major football games (in October) – lodging in Annapolis can be very hard to find. At these times and whenever you are looking for small B&Bs that may not advertise or may be open only seasonally, these three lodging services might be useful to know about.

AMANDA'S BED AND BREAKFAST REGIONAL RESERVATION SERVICE
3538 Lakeway Drive
Ellicott City 21042
☎ 443-535-0009, fax 443-535-0009
email amandasrs@aol.com
www.amandas-bbrs.com

ANNAPOLIS ACCOMMODATIONS
41 Maryland Avenue
Annapolis 21401
☎ 410-280-0900 or 800-715-1000

Downtown Annapolis

HISTORIC INNS OF ANNAPOLIS
58 State Circle
☎ 410-263-2641, 410-269-0990, or 800-847-8882 (reservations only)
www.annapolisinns.com
Inexpensive to expensive

Three 18th-century buildings on State Circle – the **Maryland Inn** (44 rooms), **Governor Calvert House** (54 rooms), and **Robert Johnson House** (25 rooms) – are all within a few blocks of each other and share a single check-in area and guest services. The Governor Calvert House is the center for bell service and valet parking ($12) for all three buildings. Room sizes and levels of décor and ambiance vary between the buildings, as do the room rates. The newly renovated Robert Johnson House, furnished in antiques and reproductions, is our preference.

FLAGG HOUSE INN
26 Randall Street
☎ 410-280-2721 or 800-437-4825
Moderate

In the center of the historic district, between City Dock and the Academy, this gracious mansard-roofed home has nicely appointed rooms. The off-street parking is a real plus in this neighborhood.

GIBSON'S LODGINGS
110 Prince George Street
☎ 410-268-5555
Moderate

Three historic-district houses combine to form a single inn, with 21 rooms, just a few steps from the City Dock. Rooms are lovely, with period antiques and tasteful décor. In good weather, you'll enjoy your continental breakfast (included in the room rate) in the garden.

WILLIAM PAGE INN
8 Martin Street
☎ 410-626-1506 or 800-364-4160
www.williampageinn.com
Moderate to expensive

Antiques and fine reproductions furnish this attractive inn, which also has off-street parking. A full breakfast is included with your room. If you're feeling energetic and extravagant, go for the third-floor suite, which features a sleigh bed, window seats and whirlpool tub.

HARBORVIEW BOAT AND BREAKFAST
City Dock
☎ 800-877-9330
www.harborviewbnb.com
Moderate

If you've never been lulled to sleep by the gentle bobbing of a boat, you should opt for this opportunity. A fleet of several classic yachts has cozy staterooms where you can spend the night and have breakfast in the morning. Evening and morning cruises are available as an option.

SCHOONER *WOODWIND*
☎ 410-263-8619
www.schooner-woodwind.com
Moderate to expensive

This 74-foot schooner has sleeping accommodations for eight guests in four air conditioned double-berth staterooms. Lodging is available weekends only, and includes a sunset cruise. This experience is especially nice for a family group or several couples traveling together.

Outside of Annapolis

COUNTRY INN AND SUITES
2600 Housley Road, near the intersection of Route 2, US-301/50 and I-97, just east of the city
☎ 410-571-6700 or 800-456-4000
www.countryinns.com
Moderate

Each suite has two commodious rooms with thoughtful extras, including in-room irons and ironing boards. The location is convenient to downtown and to the Renaissance Faire-grounds and vans shuttle guests to the historic district. The inn has an indoor pool, free parking and a continental breakfast.

Best Places to Eat

DINING PRICE SCALE	
Inexpensive	Entrées are $10 or less
Moderate	Entrées are $11-$20
Expensive	Entrées are $21-$30

City Dock & Market Square

Market Square faces the City Dock, and is almost filled by a small but unmistakable market building. A bakery, deli, raw bar, pizzeria, sandwich bar and ice cream stand are all contained inside. This is where locals go for a quick breakfast or lunch in a mellow market atmosphere, as well as for fresh seafood and vegetables for dinner.

AROMI D'ITALIA CAFE
8 Dock Street (behind the information kiosk)
☎ 263-1300
Inexpensive to moderate

The location of this European-style café couldn't be much better, facing the docks with sidewalk tables snuggled against its brick wall. Gelato in the showcase is available in so many delicious-sounding flavors – we like the nocciola, a toasted hazelnut flavor – that the line is always being slowed down by someone who simply (and understandably) can't make up his or her mind. Light dishes and panini sandwiches, salads and pizza are served in a gleaming setting, along with a few full meal specials each day from 11:30 to 3 at very low prices, which do not rise dramatically at dinner time. Aromi is open Monday-Thursday, 10-10; Friday, 10-midnight; Saturday, 8 am to midnight; Sunday, 8 am to 10 pm.

MIDDLETON TAVERN OYSTER BAR AND RESTAURANT
Dock Street
☎ 410-263-3323
Moderate to expensive

The circa-1750 building overlooks the City Dock, and in the summer its lounge and bar occupy the spreading front porch. Dinner specialties feature Chesapeake Bay seafood – soft crabs, rockfish stuffed with crabmeat or broiled in butter – cooked in both traditional and updated styles. Cajun dishes may spice up the menu with choices such as blackened shrimp and scallops served over pasta. The tavern is open Monday-Friday, 11:30-2 am; Saturday-Sunday, 10-2.

MARIA'S
12 Market Space (facing the City Market)
☎ 410-268-2112
Moderate

Southern Italian, but not all marinara sauce by any means, Maria's menu blends Italian cooking styles with local bay bounty. Veal is paired with jumbo shrimp and sautéed in lemon butter, rockfish is sautéed in white wine and capers, red snapper is napped with caper marinara sauce with clams. In warm weather, tables from the casual downstairs dining room spill onto the sidewalk. Upstairs, the more formal dining room overlooks the docks. Maria's is open for lunch and dinner.

GRIFFINS

22 Market Space
☎ 410-268-2576
Moderate

Griffins is known for a good selection of beers.

A menu of mixed influence with few surprises, but a good variety of items combines pasta dishes, local seafood favorites, steaks and chicken entrées. The latter may be cooked with a hot habañero sauce or with Jamaican jerk spices.

BUDDY'S CRABS AND RIBS

100 Main Street
☎ 410-626-1100
Moderate

High above City Dock, this second-floor dining room is big, noisy, and casual, with plenty of window tables for views of the waterfront. We like their delicately seasoned crab cakes and the just-crunchy softies, although the ribs are succulent. At lunch on weekdays, Buddy's serves an inexpensive buffet 11 am to 2 pm. Sunday breakfast buffet, 8:30 am to 1:30 pm, includes fresh fish, custom-built omelets, Belgian waffles and corned-beef hash, also inexpensive.

YIN YANKEE CAFE

105 Main Street (opposite Town Dock)
☎ 410-268-8703
Inexpensive to moderate

Traditional Maryland meets Japanese at this informal little café, where fish & chips, steamed shrimp, and ribs share the menu with sushi or udon noodles with chicken, vegetables or shrimp. A few sidewalk tables are out in good weather.

Main Street

CAFE NORMANDIE

185 Main Street
☎ 410-263-3382
Moderate to expensive

Candlelight dining and its provincial French ambiance makes this restaurant a romantic choice for dinner. But consider it, too, at breakfast or lunch, when you can order their crêpes. As you might guess, the menu is largely French, featuring veal, filet mignon, tournedos with bordelaise sauce, roast duck and bouillabaisse.

GOVERNOR'S GRILL

Main Street (at Conduit Street)
☎ 410-263-6555
Expensive

Dark mahogany-paneled walls give this upscale restaurant an aura of quiet gentility, but the atmosphere is not stiff or formal. Lamb chops with rosemary often highlights the meat side of the menu, while shrimp stuffed with more fresh seafood is a favorite on the seafood side. The Grill is open daily for lunch, 11:30-3; Sunday-Thursday, 5-9 and Friday-Saturday, 5-10, for dinner.

Governor's Grill offers complimentary valet parking on Friday and Saturday evenings – a blessing in Annapolis' parking-poor downtown area.

THE TREATY OF PARIS

16 Church Circle (at Main Street)
☎ 410-263-6340
Moderate to expensive

With its environment redolent of Colonial times, this is the sort of place locals who don't want to cook on Thanksgiving Day choose for an elegant dinner. The Maryland Inn, which houses the restaurant, is

The Treaty of Paris Restaurant serves three meals daily.

indeed from the 18th century. Look for the elegant showpiece dishes, such as beef Wellington, along with steaks, chops and, of course, Maryland crabs.

West Street

RAM'S HEAD TAVERN
33 West Street
☎ 410-268-4545
www.ramsheadtavern.com
Moderate

The Fordham Brewing Co., housed in the tavern, is the only microbrewery in Annapolis, and tables surround the two giant copper vats. Each of the dining areas has its own character, from the casual patio and tavern to the more elegant little tearoom. The music from the adjacent performance area (see *Live Music*) doesn't pervade the dining rooms. Sandwiches are served all day, and at dinner you can choose from old-time pub and tavern favorites – shepherd's pie, shellfish pie, crab cakes – or steaks, Jambalaya or baked chicken breast stuffed with crab imperial. Ram's Head is open Monday-Saturday, 11 am-2 am; Sunday, 10 am (for brunch) until 2 am.

CIAO!
51 West Street
☎ 410-267-7912
Moderate to expensive

With one of the city's more innovative menus, Ciao! draws inspiration from several European and eastern Mediterranean cuisines. Several Mediterranean-rim influences combine in an appetizer of hummus enlivened by roasted red peppers and garlic.

Roast duck breast is served over a potato galette with a brandied fruit demiglace. Paella joins French traditional dishes not often found in restaurants: cassoulet and bouillabaisse. The classy fusion menu fits well with the smart bistro surroundings. Ciao is open for dinner only, Tuesday through Sunday, from 5:30.

Eastport

CARROL'S CREEK RESTAURANT
410 Severn Avenue, just over Eastport/Spa Creek drawbridge
☎ 410-263-8102
Moderate to expensive

The setting overlooking the marina and harbor, as well as the glass-encased smart interior, promises a memorable experience, and the food lives up to the promise. We head for the nightly specials, which may include broiled shrimp and scallops on an orange coulis. Lamb loin is encrusted with pecans before roasting, a medallion of tuna sits on a risotto cake. Their cream of crab soup is justly famous as a beginning, and the dessert cart may include an elegant coeur à la crème with mascarpone or espresso crème brûlée. Carrol's Creek is open Monday-Saturday, 11:30-4 and 5-8; Sunday brunch, 10-2.

The Northern Chesapeake Bay

The coastal towns north of Baltimore were once larger and more important than Baltimore itself. From their ports sailed ships laden with products of the fields, mines and mills of northern Maryland and Pennsylvania. But mining and agriculture took their toll on the rivers that carried all these goods, and the fine harbors silted. Their ports declined as Baltimore continued to grow, fed by the new railroads. A canal system improved shipping along the Susquehanna River in the middle 1800s, but rail transport left the canals obsolete.

A Brief History

Meanwhile, across the bay, Chesapeake City was booming. The building of the Chesapeake & Delaware canal allowed ships to pass directly from the Delaware River into the Chesapeake Bay, without having to sail south to the mouth of the Potomac, to reach Baltimore and Washington DC.

Both sides of the northern Chesapeake Bay enjoyed a relatively quiet history, except during the War of 1812, which left Havre de Grace in flames and many of the river ports of the eastern shore of the Bay badly damaged. But the Civil War passed this part of Maryland by; most of the action it saw was as a route for escaping slaves heading north.

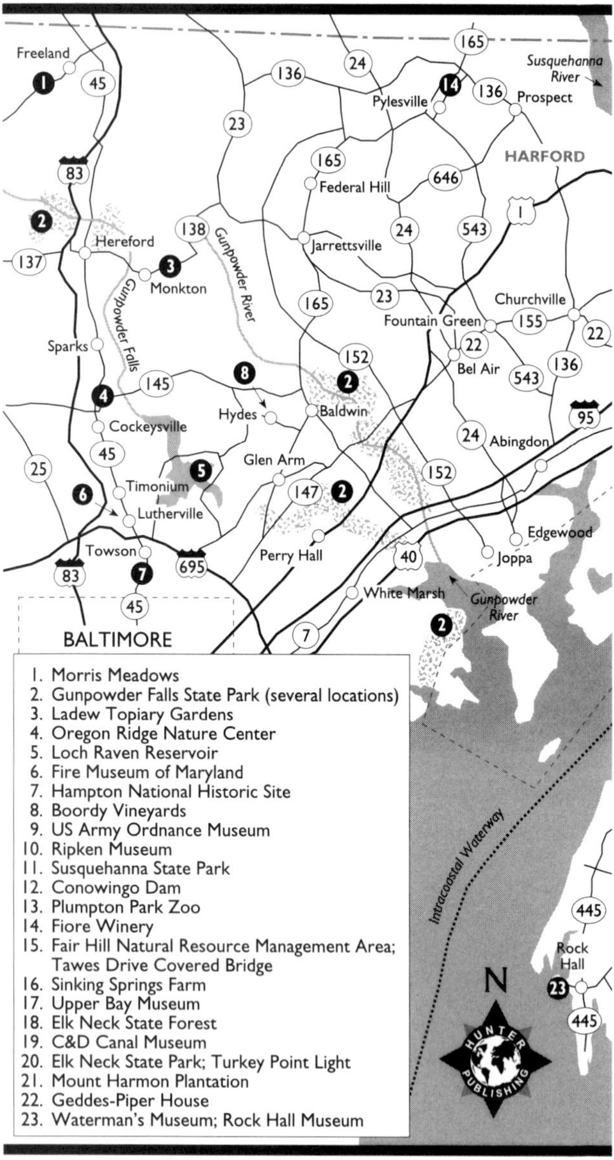
Freeland
Susquehanna River
Pylesville
Prospect
HARFORD
Federal Hill
Hereford
Jarrettsville
Monkton
Gunpowder River
Gunpowder Falls
Churchville
Fountain Green
Sparks
Bel Air
Hydes
Baldwin
Cockeysville
Abingdon
Glen Arm
Timonium
Lutherville
Edgewood
Towson
Perry Hall
Joppa
White Marsh
Gunpowder River
BALTIMORE
Intracoastal Waterway
Rock Hall
N
HUNTER PUBLISHING
1. Morris Meadows
2. Gunpowder Falls State Park (several locations)
3. Ladew Topiary Gardens
4. Oregon Ridge Nature Center
5. Loch Raven Reservoir
6. Fire Museum of Maryland
7. Hampton National Historic Site
8. Boordy Vineyards
9. US Army Ordnance Museum
10. Ripken Museum
11. Susquehanna State Park
12. Conowingo Dam
13. Plumpton Park Zoo
14. Fiore Winery
15. Fair Hill Natural Resource Management Area; Tawes Drive Covered Bridge
16. Sinking Springs Farm
17. Upper Bay Museum
18. Elk Neck State Forest
19. C&D Canal Museum
20. Elk Neck State Park; Turkey Point Light
21. Mount Harmon Plantation
22. Geddes-Piper House
23. Waterman's Museum; Rock Hall Museum

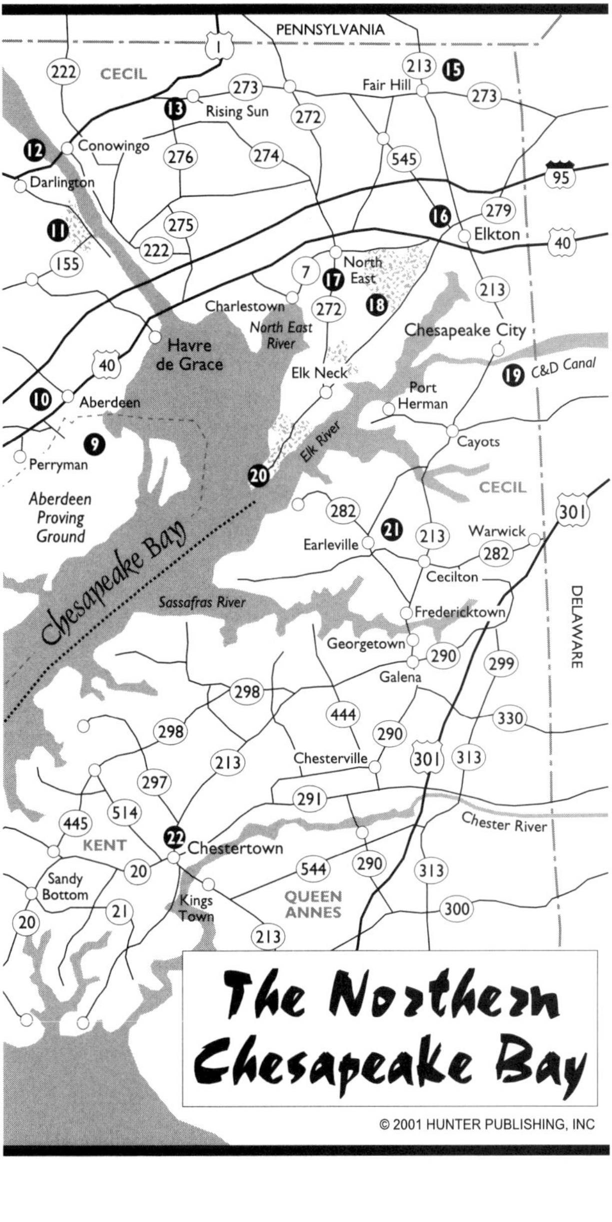

PENNSYLVANIA
CECIL
Rising Sun
Fair Hill
Conowingo
Darlington
Elkton
North East
Charlestown
North East River
Havre de Grace
Chesapeake City
C&D Canal
Elk Neck
Port Herman
Aberdeen
Cayots
Perryman
Elk River
Aberdeen Proving Ground
CECIL
Chesapeake Bay
Earleville
Warwick
Cecilton
Sassafras River
Fredericktown
DELAWARE
Georgetown
Galena
Chesterville
Chester River
KENT
Chestertown
Sandy Bottom
Kings Town
QUEEN ANNES
The Northern Chesapeake Bay

Since the Civil War, the military presence has been strong in the northern part of the Bay. The Edgewood Arsenal and Aberdeen Proving Ground take up a large part of the west shore of the bay and both have played major roles in the development of the weapons that have defended the United States for the past century.

Tourism, too, has largely bypassed the Northern Chesapeake Bay area. People traveling up or down the eastern seaboard whiz right past on I-95 and US-40 without any idea of what they are missing. This leaves the charming Eastern Shore town of Chestertown and the historic port of Havre de Grace – each with impressive historic districts – the province of local travelers on weekend trips from Wilmington, Philadelphia, Washington and Baltimore.

Orientation

This area encircles the northern end of the Chesapeake Bay, and most attractions lie within a few hours of Baltimore or Annapolis. The north edge of the region is the **Pennsylvania border**, also known as the Mason-Dixon Line to history buffs. **Baltimore** and **Harford counties** lie directly north of the city of Baltimore, with the big **Susquehanna River** serving as their eastern border. On the other side of the river, **Cecil County** sweeps around the head of the bay, squeezing between the Elk River and the Delaware border. The **Elk River basin** is the dominant feature of the southern part of the county, reaching inland deeply in several places. South of the **Sassafras River** (which cuts inland almost to the Delaware border) lie **Kent County** and the northern part of **Queen Anne County** with its access to the Bay Bridge, providing an easy route back to Baltimore.

Getting Here

Two Interstate highways head from Baltimore into these northern counties: **I-95**, following the Chesapeake Bay shore northeast toward Wilmington and Philadelphia; and **I-83**, heading straight north into Pennsylvania. Old **US-1** runs between them, also headed northeast, but inland of the newer Interstate. Smaller roads leave Baltimore like wheel spokes, leading into every corner of this rolling landscape of farms and forests. **US-50/301** crosses the bay at Annapolis, then splits on the other side, with 301 heading northward and 50 going south.

Getting Around

In general, the north-south roads are the most direct, with few routes cutting across. You may often find that your best way to travel east or west is to return to the larger north-south artery rather than head off as the crow flies. River valleys and uneven terrain, along with the historic needs that spawned road building, have contributed to this irregular road pattern.

If you are looking for a direct but non-Interstate route through the westernmost area covered in this chapter, consider taking **US-1**, which swings north and inland before turning east. Follow **Route 273** for trips to Rising Sun or Fair Hill. **Route 213** south from Fair Hill will take you through the heart of the region "across the Bay" and on to **Route 301**, if you are heading west, or **Route 50**, to continue south.

Information Sources

Baltimore County Conference & Visitors Bureau, 118 Shawan Road, Hunt Valley Mall, Baltimore 21030; www.visitbacomd.com, ☎ 410-329-1001, 877-STAY-N-DO, fax 410-329-1188.

Discover Harford County Tourism Council, Inc. 121 North Union Avenue, Suite B, Havre de Grace 21078; www.harfordmd.com, ☎ 410-939-3336 or 800-597-2649.

Havre de Grace Tourism Commission, 224 North Washington Street, Havre de Grace 21078; www.hdgtourism.com, ☎ 410-939-3303 or 800-851-7756.

Cecil County Tourism, 129 East Main Street, Elkton 21921; www.ccmagazine.org/visitcecil.htm, ☎ 410-996-5303 or 800-CECIL95.

Kent County Office of Tourism, 400 High Street, Chestertown 21620; www.kentcounty.com, ☎ 410-778-0416.

Sunup to Sundown

The region on either side of the northern waters of the Chesapeake is ideally designed for a circular touring route. Several inland attractions to the north and northeast of Baltimore are also worthy of day-trips – the Fire Museum in Lutherville, Ladew Topiary Gardens in Monkton, and the stunning Hampton National Historic Site in Towson are three of these, and between them could easily occupy a whole day, even if you don't get sidetracked shopping at White Marsh.

Recommended Stops

For those interested in history, **Havre de Grace** is an important stop, perhaps a good place to remain overnight, since it has several historic B&Bs. Military history gets the spotlight in nearby **Aberdeen** and the little Upper Bay Museum in **North East** concentrates on the watermen.

Chesapeake City is a good base for visiting the parks at the head of the bay, and for antiques shopping. The Chesapeake and Delaware Canal, known as the C&D, cuts across the narrow neck of the Delmarva peninsula between the Delaware River and the upper reaches of the Chesapeake Bay on the Elk River. The 14-mile canal saves ships a 300-mile voyage around the peninsula to Chesapeake Bay ports, including Baltimore.

★ TIP

The more than 15,000 vessels that pass through the C&D canal each year make Chesapeake City a good vantage point for watching the barges go by. Both of the two excellent local restaurants take advantage of that with views overlooking the water.

Historic sites and plantations are scattered between Chesapeake City and **Chestertown**, another good stopping point, which – like Chesapeake City – offers good food and lodging. From Chestertown it's a short way back to Annapolis and Baltimore, via the beautiful tidewater lands along the narrows.

☛ DID YOU KNOW?

The history of Havre de Grace is fascinating. During the Revolution, General Lafayette was here several times. On one such occasion he said that the port reminded him of Le Havre, a seaport in his native France. At another time the town vied to be the state capital of Maryland, losing to Annapolis. The War of 1812 brought a British attack and most of the town was destroyed. The Brits were probably angry because they couldn't get to Baltimore.

Museums

Just Outside Baltimore

FIRE MUSEUM OF MARYLAND
1301 York Road, Lutherville
☎ 410-321-7500
www.firemuseummd.org
Admission: $6, adults; $4, ages three-18

Even if you think you're not interested in fire fighting, this museum is exciting for both adults and kids. The staff is so well informed that you are sure to leave knowing a lot more than when you entered. For example, did you know that before the Civil War firemen, not horses, pulled the fire wagons? The meticulous and ornate painted decoration on hand-drawn fire fighting equipment from the 1800s is worth the visit. Kids can learn in the Discovery Room, where they can climb on a real fire truck and try on real gear. It's okay to give in to temptation and pull the alarm box lever here. Throughout the museum are old-fashioned red call boxes, and when an alarm is pulled you should hurry to the Fire Alarm Office to see how the city responded to it and kept track of which trucks were where. This is the original equipment used in Baltimore until the 1980s, when 911 replaced the old technology. From the Baltimore Beltway (I-695), take Exit 26-B North, marked York Road/Lutherville. The museum is behind the Heaver Plaza Office Building, a short distance from the highway. The museum is open Tuesday through Saturday, 11-4, June through August; Saturday only in May, September and October.

> **DID YOU KNOW?**
>
> Early fire hoses were made of leather, kept flexible by rubbing with pig fat? How firemen maintained a grip on them is beyond us.

Aberdeen

US ARMY ORDNANCE MUSEUM
Aberdeen Proving Ground
☎ 410-278-3602
www.ordmusfound.org
Free; donations accepted to support restoration.

Note the donation box at the Ordnance Museum. Although the museum is free, the restoration and maintenance of the artifacts are paid for by private donations.

Here on the banks of the Chesapeake Bay is the place where some of the US military's most powerful weapons were developed and tested. Captured enemy weapons were also brought here for evaluation so the Army could determine their strengths and weaknesses. World War II German weapons helped to strengthen our defense and examination of Russian arms helped in our defense of Korea.

The weapons on display provide an interesting insight into the history of firearms and show how even obsolete and outdated weapons prove useful in solving problems in the design of modern arms. The range of materiel here is immense, from rare examples of breech loaders, revolvers and other early arms to row upon row of tanks and heavy artillery, the **Mile of Tanks,** and a 25-acre tank/artillery park. The museum is a must for anyone with an interest in the military. Among the exhibits is one that shows how military technology has had direct impact on civilian life – the Jeep, for example, or the SUV. Visitors are welcome to photograph any of the collections. The museum is open daily, 10-4:45. From I-95, take Exit 85; follow Route 22 east, crossing US-40, to the Proving Ground Gate. The museum is to the right.

RIPKEN MUSEUM
Aberdeen Municipal Building
3 West Belair Avenue (Route 132)
Aberdeen
☎ 410-273-2525
Admission: $3, adults; $2, over 62; $1, ages six-18.

Perhaps the best-known Maryland professional baseball player ever is hometown hero Cal Ripken, Jr. In the Aberdeen municipal building, the small but very well-done exhibits show the highlights of his extraordinary career. This museum pays tribute to his entire family and the values and dedication that created this family heritage of baseball. At one point two Ripken brothers and their father were all active with the Baltimore Orioles. Personal items, photographs, videos, interactive trivia games, and mementos of the family, the Orioles and baseball come together here in a bright and attractive setting. There is a small gift shop for souvenirs. The museum is handicapped-accessible. They are open daily, June-August; Thursday-Monday during April & May; Friday-Monday the rest of the year.

The Ripken Museum is easy to spot; look for the bronze statue of Cal Ripken at the corner of US-40 and Route 132 in the center of town.

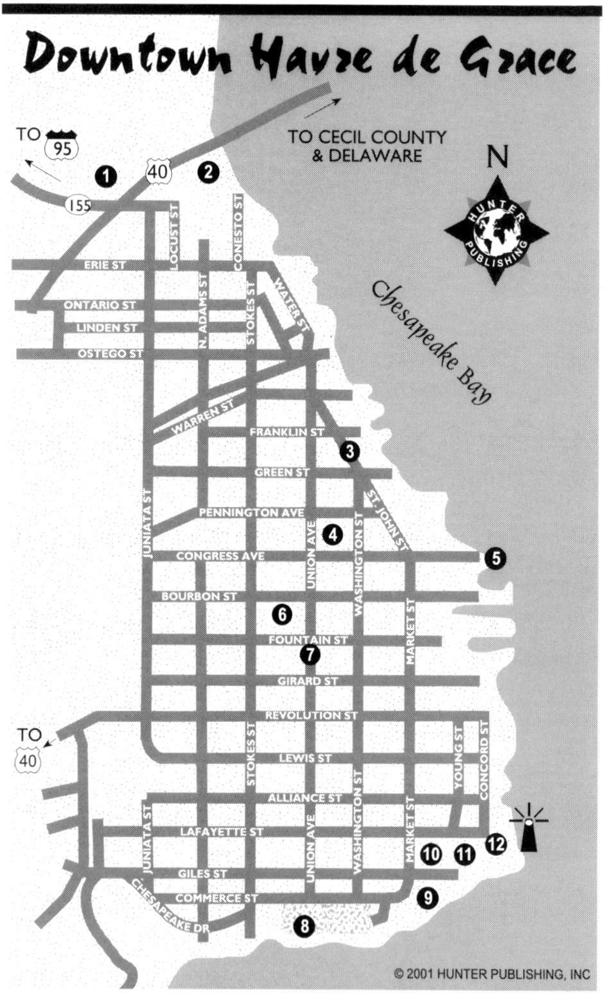

1. Steppingstone Museum
2. Susquehanna Lockhouse
3. Antiques Row
4. Old City Hall
5. Skipjack *Martha Lewis*
6. Vandiver Inn
7. Spencer-Silver Mansion
8. Tydings Park; *Applegarth*
9. Promenade
10. Decoy Museum
11. Maritime Museum
12. Concord Point Lighthouse

Havre de Grace

DECOY MUSEUM
215 Giles Street
Havre de Grace
☎ 410-939-3739
www.decoymuseum.com.
Admission: $4, seniors; $2, ages eight-11

Decoy carving is a Maryland art form, and Havre de Grace is still a center for the business. The museum features a number of the local artists and their work, as well as encompassing the well-known work of carvers from elsewhere in the state, such as the Ward brothers (see the Ward Museum, page 286). A well-done display describes the history of the art, and describes the materials used, species of birds and poses favored, and demonstrates the regional differences among decoy makers. A carver's shop has been reproduced.

The gallery dedicated to the history of waterfowl hunting on the bay is called "Gunning the Flats." Through the use of skiffs, blinds, calls and weapons the story of hunting on the bay is shown in a setting surrounded by a mural of the marshes. The museum has a gift shop featuring art, gifts and books with a waterfowl theme. The museum is open daily, 11-4, and is handicapped-accessible.

TIP

Three museums in this area, The Ripken, Army Ordnance and Decoy museums, are all fully handicapped-accessible, as is the fine boardwalk along the shore in front off the Decoy Museum.

SUSQUEHANNA LOCKHOUSE MUSEUM
Erie and Conesto Streets
Havre de Grace
☎ 410-939-5780
Admission: $2, adults; $1, seniors

The Susquehanna and Tidewater Canal, opened in 1840, connected Wrightsville, Pennsylvania with Havre de Grace, and the Chesapeake Bay. Its 29 locks lifted boats a total of 233 feet in 45 miles, connecting, via other canal systems, all of central Pennsylvania with the major ports of Baltimore and Philadelphia. The lockkeeper was an important personage who controlled access to the canal, collected the tolls and insured its maintenance. The lockhouse, built in 1840, was his home and office, with a door on one end of the porch leading to his office and another on the opposite end for access to his quarters. Both are furnished as they would have been during the mid-19th century. A video shows the history and process of the canal. Outside is the restored outlet lock and a reconstructed pivot bridge, designed to swing out of the way to allow canal barges to pass through. There is a small gift shop carrying books on local and canal history. The museum is open weekends, from May to October, 1-5 pm.

STEPPINGSTONE MUSEUM
461 Quaker Bottom Road
Susquehanna State Park
Havre de Grace
☎ 410-939-2299
Admission: $2, adults; children under 12 free

This working farm museum's mission is to preserve crafts and skills used between 1880 and 1920. But this is no mere static display; working craftsmen such as blacksmiths, coopers, woodworkers, wheelwrights, decoy makers, weavers and potters demonstrate their crafts to modern generations. The farm itself centers around a big brick farmhouse and the buildings, shops and sheds common to working farms – a dairy barn, corn cribs, wood shed, and ancillary buildings where the tasks of specific craftsmen were carried out. The carriage barn shows off a collection of carriages, wagons and sleighs, and in another barn is a re-creation of a general store and veterinarian's shop. Demonstrations of the many skills required of successful farmers are demonstrated in most of the buildings. The Steppingstone Museum is open weekends, 1-5 pm, from May through September.

☛ **DID YOU KNOW?**

It was so cold during the winter of 1852 that railroad tracks were laid across the frozen surface of the Susquehanna Flats, from Havre de Grace. Entire trains laden with cargo crossed on top of the ice. In January and February, 10,000 tons of goods were carried across by rail each month.

Chesapeake City Area

UPPER BAY MUSEUM
219 Walnut Street
North East
☎ 410-287-2675

For wooden boat lovers, this is a delightful collection of craft and memorabilia of the life and culture of the bay. One example, a double sinkboat that rode with its deck at water level in the days of commercial duck hunting, is among very few in existence. All the displays, craft and artifacts relate to the upper bay area and Susquehanna Flats. The exhibits cover boating and settlement history from Native American stone weapons to tools that are barely obsolete. There is a lot to interest boat lovers, including a skiff based on a Viking design, a decoy shop and collection and a display on drag seining. Historic photographs help visitors see how some of the artifacts were used. The Upper Bay Museum is open from Memorial Day to Labor Day, Saturdays, 10-3; Sundays, 10-4.

C&D CANAL MUSEUM
815 Bethel Road
South Chesapeake City
☎ 410-885-5622

Small, but very well designed, this museum shows how the canal works and how it was built, with engaging exhibits. The visuals are good, especially the model that shows how the original locks worked. The canal's two locks were removed in 1921. Visitors can track ships in the canal by viewing television monitors. It is located beside the canal, in the lift wheel pumping station that provided water for the locks. The huge wheel, which once moved 20,000 gallons of water a minute, and the original engine that ran it, are next to the museum and visitors can see them from catwalks and through windows. The museum is open Monday-Saturday, 8 am-4:15 pm. Even when the museum is closed, you can see the wheel through windows on the canal side.

Chestertown Area

WATERMAN'S MUSEUM

20880 Rock Hall Avenue
Rock Hall
☎ 410-778-6697
www.havenharbour.com/hhwatmus.htm

The exhibits are the tools and lore of the crabbing, fishing and the oyster fleets that once made this a thriving port. In summer, they are open daily, 8-5; in winter, Monday-Friday, 8-5; Saturday and Sunday, 10-4.

ROCK HALL MUSEUM

Town Hall
Main Street, Rock Hall
☎ 410-778-1399

This museum continues the story of the Waterman's Museum with model boats, shipping displays and equipment, as well as Native American artifacts. Call for hours.

Historic Sites

Just Outside Baltimore

HAMPTON NATIONAL HISTORIC SITE
535 Hampton Lane
Towson
☎ 410-823-1309
Admission: grounds, free; house tours, $5

The dining room at Hampton can seat 50 comfortably.

Dating from the end of the American Colonial period, the mansion is one of the great homes of America. The grand manor house, built between 1783 and 1790, is classically Georgian, with a central section flanked by two wings with hyphens, the whole capped with a perfectly proportioned cupola. But it is as noted for its gardens as for its buildings. Now a National Historic Site property, its 60 acres are only a remnant of the 24,000 acres once owned by its builders, the Ridgely family.

The Ridgelys' fortune began with iron mined and smelted on the property. This made them among the wealthiest families in the new United States. Later, they recognized that the future of agriculture and commerce lay in grain that could be shipped to markets all over the world from the excellent ports around them. Their fields were changed from tobacco to wheat, corn and other grains, which they shipped from Baltimore on their own merchant fleet.

The house itself is pink stucco; the color is original to the property and was caused by the oxidation of iron in the sands mixed into the original stucco. The rooms are furnished with exquisite antiques, all brought to the property by the long line of Ridgely descendants who have lived here. Many, for example the John Findlay drawing room set, were crafted on commission for this house; other rooms are furnished in pieces and styles of later descendants. Built for entertaining on a grand and impressive level, the house would hold 300 easily for parties. Hampton is open daily, 9-5, year-round, except major holidays. House tours are given on a regular schedule; the gardens are open at all times. From the Beltway (north) take Exit 27-B, which is Dulaney Valley Road, then an immediate right onto Hampton Lane.

TIP

Women should wear flat shoes when touring the interior of Hampton, to protect the original floors from heel marks.

Hampton is also notable for its complete ensemble of 27 outbuildings. Many of these date to the era of the original building. Some of the more outstanding examples are the orangerie, the smoke house, the ice house and the stables, where carriages are exhibited. As seen on only a few Maryland plantations, the slave quarters sit beside the farmhouse that served as the family's first home, giving a clear impression of the small society of the plantation. The out-buildings sit in grounds with more than 200 species of trees, imported by the family in the early 19th century.

The gardens, planned and tended by the family throughout the 19th century, are among the finest in the United States. The great terrace in front was planted with magnificent trees in 1800 in a seemingly casual, but highly effective plan. Victorian-era touches, such as garden ornaments and arbors hung with wisteria, are used sparingly as accents. An opening in the trees overlooks a series of terraced parterre gardens, with geometric patterns outlined by boxwood and filled with colorful massed plantings of flowers highlighted by white stone walks. The delight of these gardens is not only their design, but the element of surprise that the design gives to the viewer. Seasonal plantings ensure that the gardens are complete throughout the year. The gardens also include a kitchen herb garden featuring plants that would have been grown for household use in medicine, cooking and fragrance. The greenhouses and orangerie shelter delicate plants raised for food, bedding plants for the gardens and flowers that decorated the rooms

MORRIS MEADOWS
1523 Freeland Road, Freeland
☎ 410-329-6636

This is a privately run museum and one to savor slowly. Five generations of Morrises have lived here since the family acquired the property in 1793, and visitors are likely to be guided by Clyde Morris, its current owner. A large sprawling farm from the beginning, hardly a thing that any Morris ever acquired has been thrown away. This, of course, provides the fertile ground for countless family stories, each associated with some item or place on the property.

The collection here ranges from rare old farm equipment, such as a horse-powered "merry-go-round" threshing machine, to the small everyday things that people have around their homes. As you go around from alcove to alcove, don't be surprised to be offered popcorn fresh from the old black popper on the woodstove or to see someone pumping a tune out of the old player piano. Getting to see how some of these fascinating old machines worked is part of the fun here. Have you ever seen a wagon that converts to a sled in the winter? They have one.

Among the collections are newspapers, photographs and memorabilia that record local contributions to the national defense, beginning in 1812 when one of the Morris ancestors walked to Baltimore to enlist. A journal kept near the player piano is maintained as a place where present day veterans can record their own recollections. Don't miss the chance to read some of these vignettes of the American experience and add your own if you are a veteran. Morris Meadows is open weekends year-round, or by appointment.

TIP

The Morris Meadows Museum is fully wheelchair accessible; several wheelchairs are provided for guests and there are ramps for transferring from both buses and cars.

From I-83, take Exit 36; turn right at the "T" onto Route 439. At Route 45, turn right (north). After about 1.3 miles turn left onto Freeland Road (Route 409), which winds about 3½ miles to the museum, on the left.

TAWES DRIVE COVERED BRIDGE

Tawes Road, Fair Hill

When the bridge was built in 1860, Tawes Road was the main route between Baltimore and Philadelphia. The Tawes family, for whom the bridge is named, has a long and distinguished history of public service to the state. In the northern section of Fair Hill Natural Resources Management Area, north of Elkton, the bridge is a link to the more quiet and rustic pace of centuries past. Close to the bridge are the buildings of the former DuPont Hunting Lodge and its barns, which now store hay for the horses stabled at Fair Hill NRMA. From Route 213 in Fair Hill take Route 273 east to Tawes Road.

Havre de Grace

CONCORD POINT LIGHTHOUSE

Concord and Lafayette Streets, at the end of the boardwalk from Tydings Park
Free

The lighthouse was built in 1827 of granite quarried upriver in Port Deposit and is the oldest continuously operating in the state. Lt. John O'Neil, who had single-handedly tried to defend the town during the War of 1812, was named its first keeper. Look for a cannon used in the War of 1812 on the water side of the lighthouse. Originally lighted by nine whale oil lamps, the light is now electrified with a fifth-order Fresnel lens. Across the street, the stone house that originally served as the keeper's house is now under restoration. The lighthouse is open from April through October, weekends and holidays, 1-5 pm.

Chesapeake City Area

MOUNT HARMON PLANTATION
Grove Neck Road
Earleville
☎ 410-275-8819
Admission: $5

The original name for this splendid property was Worlds End, and the name was well chosen. It is almost surrounded by the tributaries of the Sassafras River. Its brick gates lead to a long tree-lined lane; the cloister-like passageway created by the arching trees heightens the sense of solitude. The three-story Georgian manor house dates from 1730, and is furnished with American and British antiques from the late 18th and early 19th centuries.

Even when the house is closed, you can visit the gardens, with their boxwood terraced parterre and wisteria vines twined along the ornamental iron railings and a serpentine brick wall. Magnolias overhang the garden, and the walkway leading into it is flanked by a pair of English yews with trunks more than three feet in diameter. The terraces overlook the marshlands along the river bank. Tours of the plantation are given Tuesday and Thursday, 10-3; and Sunday, 1-4.

Chestertown

GEDDES-PIPER HOUSE
101 Church Alley
☎ 410-778-3499

The restored 1780s Philadelphia-style row house sits in a town that, if it weren't for all the 21st-century activity, could be mistaken for a historic re-creation like Williamsburg. As headquarters of the local historical society, the house is the place to learn about walking tours of the historic section, both guided and self-guided. If you haven't time for a street-by-street tour, you might want to see at least a few of the more significant examples. **Widehall**, on the corner of Water and High Streets, next to the landing, is one of the most elaborate town homes, built about 1770 by the wealthiest merchant. Chestertown had its own Tea Party at this landing. The building opposite was the Customs House. **Queen Street** is lined by 18th- and early 19th-century tradesmen's homes as well as a few owned by wealthy merchants, including the **Nicholson House** at 111 Queen Street. The **Palmer House**, at 532 High Street (north of Kent Street) is one of Chestertown's most unusual homes from the 1700s, built entirely of oddly shaped stones. The Geddes-Piper House is open for tours on weekends, May through October, 1-4 pm.

Gardens & Parks

Just Outside Baltimore

LADEW TOPIARY GARDENS
3535 Jarretsville Pike, Monkton
☎ 410-557-9570
Admission: for the gardens only, adults, $8; seniors and students, $7; children under 12, $2. For the gar-

dens and house tours, adults, $12; seniors and students, $11; children, $4.

These gardens have some of the most extraordinary topiaries you'll see anywhere. The theme of one garden is a fox hunt (a favorite pastime of its socialite creator, Harvey Ladew) and a fleeing green fox is seen outdistancing yew hounds bounding across the lawn. The leafy hunter is caught freeze-frame in mid-jump over a white fence. Figures of arbor vitae and yew are carved and trained into improbable shapes. Sculptured swans swim along a waving hedge and other creation range from fanciful birds and animals to a Buddha.

Topiary isn't the only attraction here; you can stroll into a Victorian garden or one of several color-themed gardens, a rose garden and a water lily garden. Each is beautifully conceived and often marked by a touch of whimsy or surprise.

A 1½-mile nature walk passes a quarry pond, fields, forest and marshlands. Habitats are discussed in interpretive signs and in a booklet. Along with the birds – Canada geese, wood ducks, mallards, woodpeckers, bluebirds, swallows, indigo buntings – you may also spot painted and snapping turtles, frogs, salamanders and several varieties of butterfly and moth along the nature walk.

The house itself is open and it has some nice pieces of furniture, but its decorations and style mostly reflect the horse-and-hunt passions of its original owner. Of particular interest is the library, an elegant oval room that was created especially to showcase a Chippendale partners' desk. Royalty followers will want to see the room where the Duke and Duchess of Windsor stayed during their visits.

The house and gardens are open from mid-April to October, Monday-Friday, 10-4; weekends, 10-5. From June to August the gardens are open until 8 pm on Thursdays. Flowers are at their height of bloom in May. From I-695, head north from Exit 27-B on Route 146. From I-95, follow Route 152 north from Exit 74 to Route 146.

Chesapeake City Area

PLUMPTON PARK ZOO
1416 Telegraph Road, off US-1
Rising Sun
☎ 410-658-6850
Admission: $6,50, adults; $5.50, seniors; $3,25, children two-12; free, under age two

In this family-friendly park you can meet deer, zebra, camel, gibbon and monkeys, or a giraffe that may lean down to nibble on your hat. About 250 well-tended animals live in the park – even an alligator, although you can't pat him. Other facilities such as nature trails and a picnic area make this low cost park good for a day's outing with children. The zoo is open daily, 10-5.

Recreation

Just Outside Baltimore

CHAKRA CYCLES
1235 Paper Mill Road
Cockeysville
☎ 410-527-0593

Cockeysville is a pleasant area for biking, and Chakra is a one-stop center for cycling needs, with repairs, sales and rentals of road and mountain bikes, baby seats, children's carts and helmets. You can rent by the hour, the half-day or full day.

OREGON RIDGE NATURE CENTER
13555 Beaver Dam Road
Cockeysville
☎ 410-887-1815
Open Tuesday-Sunday 9-5.

The park is readily accessible to Baltimore via I-83 and it provides nice walking and hiking opportunities. Among the features to look for as you walk here are rock outcrops, iron-ore pits, marble quarries, forests, meadows, swamps and streams. The quarry is the source of the stone used in the building of the Washington Monuments in Washington DC and in Baltimore. Ivy Hill Pond, on the trail system and bordered by hemlock trees, is cool even in the summer. You can expect a few short but steep climbs in places. The park is a habitat for wildflowers and bird life you don't expect to see so close to a major city. Trail maps and interpretive displays are available at the headquarters; the trail system begins across the bridge that spans the ravine.

NORTHERN CENTRAL RAILROAD TRAIL

Hereford

The rail trail was part of the Northern Central Railroad, and stretches more than 20 miles from the Pennsylvania state line south to Ashland, near Cokeysville. It follows the Gunpowder Falls River, crossing it several times. Access points are reached from Route 45, which runs parallel to I-83. Several roads cross the trail, but not all of them provide parking. For access to the northern section in Gunpowder Falls State Park, take I-83 to Exit 27 and go east on Route 137. You'll quickly come to Route 45 in the village of Hereford. Go south (right) on Route 145, then almost immediately turn east (left) onto Route 138. The trail starts about three miles from there, on the left, at the restored railway station. The southern access to the trail is off Paper Mill Road (accessed off I-83 from Exit 20), near the trail's terminus in Ashland. But we like the northern reaches of the trail best.

GUNPOWDER FALLS STATE PARK

Park Headquarters
10815 Harford Road
Glen Arm
☎ 410-592-2897

The park follows the tributaries and main Gunpowder Falls River to its mouth. In the upper reaches where icy waters flow out of the Prettyboy dam, is some of the best catch-and-release trout fishing in Maryland, with an astonishing trout-count. You must park on Falls Road and reach the river by a walk of less than half a mile along the Highland Trail. You can reach this from I-83 Exit 31, about 5 miles south of the Pennsylvania border. **Dundee Creek Marina**, in the lower section of Gunpowder

Falls State Park, has boat rentals, a bait-and-tackle shop and a launch ramp (fee $5). For current information on tides, weather and what's biting, call ☎ 410-335-9390.

CONOWINGO DAM
US-1, Darlington

The dam blocks the progress of the Susquehanna River, creating a 14-mile impoundment that is popular with anglers year-round. The area below the dam is an artificial environment which often teems with fish unable to pass the dam on spawning runs or which are attracted to the aerated waters. This is not a place to fish in solitude; it's well known and very popular but also very good. Even when the rest of the waters are ice-bound, water going through the turbines warms enough to create open patches.

SUSQUEHANNA STATE PARK
Along the Susquehanna River, below the Conowingo Dam, off Route 161 between Darlington and Webster.
☎ 410-557-7994

A level three-mile trail borders the west bank of the Susquehanna where, in spring, the high river banks are literally covered in a carpet of spring bloom. It is doubtful that you will ever see as many trillium as you will find growing here along the Susquehanna Gorge. In April, Dutchman's breeches, violets and Virginia bluebells are also here in profusion. Birds are plentiful from May throughout the summer.

Eastern Shore

STARRK MOON KAYAKS
500 Warren Street
Havre de Grace
☎ 410-939-9500 or 877-KAYAKS-1
www.starrkmoon.com

In addition to kayak rentals, Starrk Moon offers lessons at all levels and a complete line of kayaks and equipment for sale. They sponsor a number of events and special programs, including fall and winter kayaking and new product festivals where you can try out gear. Their small classes are strong on personal instruction, from beginning introductory classes to courses on whitewater paddling. Guided full- and half-day trips on the bay are available.

BAYSAIL
Tidewater Marina, Bourbon Street
Havre de Grace
☎ 410-939-3779
www.baysail.net

The upper reaches of the Chesapeake Bay are the ideal place to sail and BaySail can teach you how. Lessons are in the protected harbor and are offered at all skill levels. They are certified by the American Sailing Association. In addition to its sailing school, BaySail has recent-model Catalina and Hunter yachts, which you can charter on a bareboat, captained or instructional cruise basis.

TRAIL RIDES AT FAIR HILL
Route 273
Fair Hill
☎ 410-620-3883

This stable offers rides over countryside trails in the Fair Hill Natural Resource Management Area. They will accept guests eight years old and older, and you must reserve in advance. The fees are $25 per hour.

ELK NECK STATE PARK
Route 272
9 miles south of North East
☎ 410-287-5333

A high point of land known as Turkey Point separates the Elk River from the mouth of the Northeast River which, along with the Susquehanna, forms the upper reaches of the Chesapeake Bay. **Turkey Point Lighthouse** is at the southernmost tip, an active light powered with solar panels. The main channel to the C&D Canal is to the left of the lighthouse, a good place to watch ships and barges.Follow the walkway to the edge to see the pit for the foghorn that once sounded there. The long stretch of shallow water makes the beach here popular for those with small children.

KAYAK ADVENTURES
Skipjack Cove Marina
Fredericktown
☎ 800-BOATSLIP (262-8154)

Skipjack Cove Marina is on the west side of Route 213 just uphill from the bridge over the Sassafras River in Fredericktown. They rent kayaks and also give guided tours of the Sassafras, which was first explored by Captain John Smith in 1607. Our guide was not only an excellent kayaker, but a good ecologist and historian as well. He regaled us with great tales all the way up river.

Tours

On Land

WALKING TOURS

The streets of Havre de Grace, especially Union Street, are lined with fine Victorian mansions. Pick up a copy of the excellent street map and the **Self-Guided Tour** brochure at your inn or at the Chamber of Commerce, 220 North Washington Street. The tour descriptions put all the fine examples of architecture here into their historical perspective.

A TOURS
Havre de Grace
☎ 410-939-1133

Havre de Grace was a center of both pro- and anti-slavery sentiment before and during the Civil War. This tour company conducts Underground Railroad tours featuring sites and history of the pre-Civil War era. Tours are given Tuesday through Sunday, by appointment only.

On Water

SKIPJACK *MARTHA LEWIS*
Congress Avenue
Havre de Grace
☎ 302-777-5488 or 800-406-0766

The Chesapeake Heritage Conservancy operates this boat, one of the few working oyster boats left that dredges under sail. The two-sailed 50-foot skipjack has discovery programs for schools and for the public. These focus on the environment, weather, celestial navigation, oysters, birds and marine life of the Susquehanna Flats and the Chesapeake Bay. On weekends, at two hour intervals between noon and 6 pm, and at 6 pm Thursday evenings, April through October, the boat offers 90-minute public trips, exploring the Susquehanna Flats.

APPLEGARTH
Mooring at Tydings Park
Havre de Grace
2524 Ady Road, Forest Hill
☎ 410-879-6941

A smaller version of the skipjack was also part of the history of Bay watermen, used for oystering, crabbing and fishing. This boat is one of the few remaining of its type. *Applegarth* was used in the Paramount movie *IQ* and was later restored as a charter and tour boat. They operate cruises by charter, from one hour ($80) to 12 hours ($200), for up to six passengers (on holidays or during festivals the *Applegarth* may be available for harbor cruises on a first-come-first-served basis). Make your reservations early. Cruises are available from May through October.

MISS CLARE
Chesapeake City
☎ 410-885-5088

Cruise on the canal, the Bohemia River and on the bay on board this boat, for a close-up look at some of the working transport ships that ply the canal. One-hour cruises head south along the Elk River, and two-hour trips go all the way to Turkey Point Light, where the river meets the bay. Prices are $10 per hour for adults, less for children.

Wineries

BOORDY VINEYARDS
12820 Long Green Pike
Hydes
☎ 410-592-5015
Free

Maryland's oldest vineyard was established in 1945, on property around the restored fieldstone barn dating from the 1800s. The winery lies north of Baltimore, between Routes 146 and 147, just west of Baldwin Falls State Park. It is about 10 miles from I-695, and can be reached from either Exit 29 or 31. The vineyards are open year round, Monday to Saturday, 10-5; Sunday, 1-5. Tours are given on the hour, daily, 1-4.

FIORE WINERY
3026 Whiteford Road (Route 136)
Pylesville
☎ 410-836-7605

With a name like Fiore, they almost have to make traditional Italian wines – and they do. Visitors are invited to picnic by the vineyards in addition to taking tours and sampling the product. Pylesville is in the northern part of Harford County, about 40 miles from I-695, not far south of the Pennsylvania line, off US-1 to Route 136. Call for exact directions. Fiore is open Wednesday-Sunday, from noon-6 in summer; noon-5 in winter.

Shop Till You Drop

Just Outside Baltimore

VINCENTI DECOYS
303 West Lane
Churchville
☎ 410-734-6238
www.vincentidecoys.com

The decoys of artists Pat and Jeannie have been featured in the Smithsonian, and in several books about the craft. You can buy examples of this wholly American art form at prices beginning at about $65.

Eastern Shore

THE AVENUE AT WHITE MARSH
8133 Honeygo Boulevard
White Marsh

The Avenue at White Marsh, off I-95, northeast of Baltimore just beyond the Beltway, is a shopping center built to re-create a Main Street feel. Its creators get points for their successful efforts at making this mall less generic and far more attractive than most. Facing rows of shops along a street of angle-parked cars are connected by a square bordered with the outdoor tables of the two flanking restaurants (see *After Dark* and *Best Places to Eat* for listings). To reach The Avenue, take I-95 to Exit 67-B.

BOMBOY'S
322 Market Street
Havre de Grace
☎ 410-939-4970
www.bomboys-candy.com

Bomboy's will ship their chocolates.

Handmade chocolates are created here fresh daily. The wide variety in their shop includes centers such as peanut butter soufflé, lemon cream, Irish Cream truffle and marzipan, as well as nut combinations. Bomboy's is open Tuesday through Saturday, 10-6; Sunday, noon-5.

ANTIQUES ROW
Saint John Street
Havre de Grace

The street has acquired its nickname because of the large number of shops located there and on North Washington Street, Franklin Street and North Union Avenue, which run off Saint John. Pick up a map at any one of these shops, which will show you the names and locations of the other shops.

After Dark

Music & Performing Arts

BAYOU BLUES CAFE
The Avenue at White Marsh
8133 Honeygo Boulevard
White Marsh
☎ 410-931-2583
www.BayouBluesCafe.com

Live blues and jazz fill the air every night. Bayou Blues Café is open daily until 11 pm; until midnight on weekends. The bar is open until 2 am. Take I-95 to Exit 67-B.

CECIL COMMUNITY COLLEGE CULTURAL CENTER
Route 272
North East
☎ 410-287-1037

This is a community cultural center that produces shows in theater, dance, voice and instrumental arts throughout the year. Their theater company produces two musical shows and one drama annually. The cultural center is just north of town.

Best Places to Stay

ACCOMMODATIONS PRICE SCALE	
Inexpensive	under $100
Moderate	$100-$200
Expensive	$201-$300
Deluxe	more than $300

Havre de Grace

CURRIER HOUSE BED & BREAKFAST
800 South Market Street
☎ 410-939-7886 or 800-827-2889
www.currier-bb.com
Inexpensive to moderate

Several of the guest rooms at the Currier House have Currier & Ives prints and original paintings.

The central section of this historic 1790s home was among the few structures to survive an attack by the British during the War of 1812. The dining room wall exhibits the Currier family tree (Jane, your host, is a Currier). A decoy collection, old photographs and memorabilia decorate the common and guest rooms, which are furnished with a mix of family antiques and newer pieces. Two rooms have a lighthouse view and one has a small upstairs porch of its own. All rooms have private baths. They serve a hearty waterman's breakfast and, if you ask, you may get a few family stories of Havre de Grace's livery stable, thoroughbred track and hunt clubs that were on land now owned by the Aberdeen Proving Ground.

VANDIVER INN
301 South Union Avenue
☎ 410-939-5200 or 800-245-1655
www.vandiverinn.com
Inexpensive to moderate

The inn is in a National Historic Register-listed three-story mansion built in 1886. Guests can enjoy a tree-shaded streetscape of other fine Victorian homes from a rocker on its wide front porch. Fine Victorian furniture decorates guest and public rooms, creating an atmosphere of elegance, but a very comfortable one. Stunning tiles decorate the fireplaces of some rooms, and each room has its own unique architectural details. Floor-to-ceiling step-out windows in the breakfast room open onto the front porch.

SPENCER-SILVER MANSION
200 Union Street
☎ 410-939-1097 or 800-780-1485.
Inexpensive to moderate

This imposing and beautifully maintained stone Victorian mansion has excellent painted medallions on the exterior and a two-storied wide front porch with a gazebo corner. There are myriad other Victorian details such as stained-glass windows, a patterned slate roof and a third-floor cupola among its other architectural features. The guest rooms in the main house and carriage shed are furnished in Victorian antiques. Some of the baths have clawfoot tubs, others whirlpool baths.

THE CRAZY SWEDE
400 North Union Avenue at Franklin Street
☎ 410-939-8020
Moderate

Guest suites at the Crazy Swede are available with one or two bedrooms. Discount on meals are offered to guests who eat lunch or dinner in their restaurant (see page 265), where a complimentary continental breakfast is served.

Chesapeake City Area

THE BLUE MAX
300 South Bohemia Avenue
Chesapeake City
☎ 410-885-2781, fax 410-885-2809
Moderate

The Blue Max was named by former owner Jack Hunter, author of the book of the same title, a best-seller that was made into a movie starring George Peppard. This is a charming inn within easy walking distance of everything in town. It has large well-decorated rooms, each with a private bath. A common sitting room is on the third floor and a refrigerator stocked with complimentary juices and soft drinks is on the second. Breakfast is served on the sun porch, where light filters through the trees and the view up the street is through white porch columns to a line of similarly colonnaded porches. We suggest the full breakfast (included with room).

CRYSTAL INN
1 Center Drive
North East
☎ 410-287-7100 or 800-631-3803, fax 410-287-7109
Moderate

This is a convenient, reliable lodging with an indoor pool and hot tub. It has a 24-hour restaurant and complimentary buffet breakfast. All rooms have microwaves, refrigerators and hair dryers. It is at the intersection of Lums Road and Route 272. Take Exit 100 from I-95.

GARDEN COTTAGE AT SINKING SPRINGS FARM
234 Blair Shore Road
Elkton
☎ 410-398-5566
Moderate

At Christmas, the owners of the Garden Cottage offer house tours by candlelight, bringing to life the centuries of history that linger here.

Lodging here is limited to a rustic cottage, really a small log cabin, with antique linens and a cozy warm air. The attraction of the cottage, which sleeps two people, is not luxury, but the charm of the simple country atmosphere. The cabin is filled with good reading material and the quiet makes sleeping easy. Breakfast is served in the dining room of the 1740s farmhouse, and features herbal delicacies and hearty dishes that get your day off to a good start.

Georgetown

KITTY KNIGHT HOUSE
Route 213
☎ 410-648-5777 or 800-404-8712, fax 410-648-5729
Inexpensive to moderate

Just south of the bridge over the Sassafras River, the Inn sits high above the water with views of marinas on this bay-like section of the river. The rooms are pleasant but vary greatly in size; all have private baths. Suites have plenty of space for families. Rates include breakfast.

KITTY KNIGHT

Kitty Knight was as courageous as she was pretty, and when the British came to torch the inn, she met them at the door and convinced them to spare not only the inn, but the home of an old man next door. Her original rocking chair is in one of the rooms and, if you rock in it, her ghost might come to sit in it during the night. Or so they tell.

If you are interested in historic building methods, ask to see the booklets about the White Swan Tavern's archaeology and restoration.

Chestertown

WHITE SWAN TAVERN
231 High Street (opposite the park)
☎ 410-778-2300, fax 410-778-4543
Moderate

Built in 1733, the inn at one time served as a tavern and during its restoration, an archaeological dig of the property yielded a large deposit of 18th-century artifacts. The inn has four rooms and two suites, all with private baths and the handsomely restored original interior is furnished in period antiques. The most unique guest room is the original kitchen on the first floor overlooking the terrace, with a huge walk-in fireplace. Rates include a continental breakfast and afternoon tea.

THE PARKER HOUSE
108 Spring Avenue
☎ 410-778-9041, fax 410-778-7318
www.chestertown.com/parker
Inexpensive to moderate

Attractively furnished and decorated with antiques, the inn is an easy walk from the center of the historic downtown. The good-sized guest rooms feature Victorian bedsteads and other antiques and each has a private bath. The comfortable public rooms are furnished in antiques and reproductions. Credit cards are not accepted.

GREAT OAK MANOR
10568 Cliff Road
☎ 410-778-5943, fax same or 800-504-3098
Moderate

Rooms in this stately brick plantation house are tastefully furnished. Some have working fireplaces and all have private baths and telephones. The house overlooks Chesapeake Bay, near Great Oak Landing, where guests have free access to a golf course and tennis courts. The Inn has a private beach reserved for guests and they can stroll its 12 acres of gardens and lawns. Rates include a continental-plus breakfast. The Inn is west of Melitota, about eight miles west of Chestertown.

Best Places to Eat

DINING PRICE SCALE	
Inexpensive	Entrées are $10 or less
Moderate	Entrées are $11-$20
Expensive	Entrées are $21-$30

Save your receipt from the Bay Bridge for a refund at some of the restaurants on the Eastern Shore.

On the Eastern Shore, there will be no shortage of places to eat, but most will feature deep-fried seafood, with a smattering of other items. We think the restaurants listed below are good places to start. It's a selection of varying styles from shore-side to upscale.

White Marsh

BAYOU BLUES CAFE
The Avenue at White Marsh
8133 Honeygo Boulevard
☎ 410-931-2583
Inexpensive to moderate

The bar at Bayou Blues Café stays open until 2 am.

The menu here is lively and includes well-prepared Jambalaya, gumbo, seafood Creole, pan-blackened fish and Cajun ribs – even an appetizer of alligator tail – along with rack of lamb, trout stuffed with andouille sausage in a bourbon sauce, blackened chicken pasta and several vegetarian choices, such as Cajun vegetarian jambalaya. The upscale "main street" style shopping mall location has outdoor seating in the summer, live blues and jazz every night. Expect a high noise level. Bayou Blues is open daily, 11-11, and until midnight on weekends. To reach The Avenue, take I-95 to Exit 67-B.

RED BRICK STATION
The Avenue at White Marsh
8133 Honeygo Boulevard
☎ 410-931-7827
Inexpensive to moderate

Across the plaza from Bayou Blues, the brew-pub atmosphere here is lively, but more conducive to conversation. Ales, bitters and stouts are brewed and served here. Steaks, ribs, crab cakes, blackened chicken served with blue-cheese Alfredo sauce, several pasta combo dishes are on the menu and they offer a number of daily specials such as thick mahi-mahi served with Yukon Gold potatoes. The British chef also insists that they offer traditional pub favorites – shepherd's pie, fish & chips, roast beef with Yorkshire pudding, bangers and mash. A long sandwich list is also on the menu. To reach The Avenue, take I-95 to Exit 67-B.

Havre de Grace

THE CRAZY SWEDE
400 North Union Avenue
☎ 410-939-8020
Moderate

The chef isn't too crazy, because he comes up with great variations on some old standard seafood dishes. Take, for example, his veal Havre de Grace, which isn't your standard veal Oscar. In this dish, he pairs veal with jumbo shrimp and lump crabmeat in a creamy sherry sauce. For those who don't like seafood, they offer more choices than most other local restaurants, with chicken, pasta, beef and veal dishes. The Crazy Swede Restaurant also has guest suites with one or two bedrooms; they offer a discount on meals in the restaurant to overnight guests and serve a complimentary continental breakfast. The Crazy Swede is on the corner of Franklin Street. They are open Monday through Thursday, 11-10; Friday and Saturday, 11-11; Sunday, 10-10, in season. They have shorter hours in the winter.

McGREGOR'S
31 Saint John Street
☎ 410-939-3003 or 800-300-6319
Moderate

Quesadillas, sandwiches and calamari are the type of light fare offered at this popular local spot on the waterfront. Begin your dinner with fried oysters wrapped in bacon, crab fritters or scallops in puff pastry. For an entrée chose crab cakes, crab-stuffed flounder, baby back ribs, apricot-glazed salmon or veal scallopini with asparagus and smoked portobellos. Follow Franklin Street to the water.

PRICE'S SEAFOOD
654 Water Street
☎ 410-939-2782

At Price's, ask for help if you don't know how to attack a crab.

This is a traditional crab house, unchanged since the 1940s and a popular place for a favorite Chesapeake Bay pastime – attacking hardshell crabs with wooden mallets. Along with mounds of hardshell crabs or succulent softies, you can get other seasonal seafoods. Definitely a casual dress activity. Price's is located between the boat ramp and the Lock House Museum.

TIDEWATER GRILLE
300 Franklin Street
☎ 410-939-3313
Moderate

This charming dining room is right on the bay with a water view from every table. Seafood is the specialty of the house, with choices of fried or broiled crab cakes, shellfish and linguine Alfredo, or shrimp and scallops joined in shallot butter. Non-seafood dishes don't take a back seat, however, and might include a mixed grill of chicken and fillet with andouille sausage. The lunch menu includes crab cakes, crab melt and a crab-and-ham croissant sandwich, along with burgers and salads.

Chesapeake City Area

BAYARD HOUSE RESTAURANT
11 Bohemia Avenue
Chesapeake City
☎ 410-885-5040
Expensive

From a window table overlooking the canal, you're sure to see large ships passing by during dinner. The view across the water combined with the food and professional service make this a very pleasant dining experience. Maryland crab soup, a softly spicy tomato base with chunks of crab, potato, onion, carrot, peppers and celery, is famed throughout the area. Look for surprising – but successful – combinations, such as Anaheim peppers stuffed with lobster, shrimp and crab. Monkfish is crusted in cashews and finished with mango chili. The dessert list tempts with lemon mousse, chocolate torte, Key lime pie or a chocolate chip cookie pie with pecans.

Delicious appetizers at Bayard House include oysters baked with backfin crab cake and warm brie in puff pastry.

CHESAPEAKE INN RESTAURANT
605 Second Street
Chesapeake City
☎ 410-885-2040
Moderate

Also overlooking the canal, this dining room is decorated with ship models, which you can buy. The experienced waitstaff is well informed and genuinely helpful in guiding patrons to entrée and wine choices. The frequently changing menu may include veal marsala with shiitake mushrooms, seared tuna medallions topped with crab imperial, or a splendid veal Oscar, made with lightly sautéed veal, generous lump crab and a hollandaise just barely tart. Vegetables here are treated as a dish worthy of attention, each served with its own identity intact. During warm weather they have a deck with its own menu of sandwiches, soft crab or crab cake, pasta entrées and creative pizzas. Another blessing is that they tell patrons the prices of specials when describing them. Desserts include tiramisu, crunchy chocolate torte, lemon chiffon cake, sorbets of mandarin, lemon, peach or cantaloupe, served in fruit. Friday and Saturday evenings bring piano or other live music.

FAIR HILL INN
Intersection of Routes 213 and 273
Elkton
☎ 410-398-4187
Moderate to expensive

The Colonial Room, in the oldest part of the Fair Hill Inn, has a huge stone fireplace.

Dating from the 1600s, the inn is an impressive stone building at the entrance to the Fair Hill Management Area. Each of its several dining rooms has a slightly different atmosphere. The Hunt Room has a brick floor and fireplace, while the two fireplaces of the Mitchell Room date from the 1760s. Veal saltimbocca, roast duck with orange, and lamb chops with mint jelly are examples of the updated continental cuisine featured on the menu. Lunch at the Fair Hill Inn is served Tuesday-Friday, 11:30-2:30; dinner, Tuesday-Sunday, 4-9.

WOODY'S CRAB HOUSE
29 Main Street
North East
☎ 410-287-3541

Woody's is a very popular traditional crab house, where you can find hardshell crabs in the rough or more genteel dishes that require less effort. It's open March through December.

Georgetown

KITTY KNIGHT HOUSE
Route 213
☎ 410-648-5777 or 800-404-8712, fax 410-648-5729
Moderate to expensive

Sitting high above the Sassafras River bridge, the house was the home of a brave Maryland woman who held off the British army. Now its large restaurant offers fine views and dishes such as blackened tuna with shrimp, cashew-crusted chicken breast, tomato-basil crab crêpes, or a complete shore dinner. Dine in small dining rooms or in the large one overlooking the river.

Chestertown

BLUE HERON CAFE
Cannon Street
Just south of Cross Street
☎ 410-778-0188
Inexpensive to moderate

The innovative New American menu features regional ingredients and the setting is just as appealing. Blue Heron is open for lunch and dinner, Tuesday through Sunday.

PLAY IT AGAIN SAM
108 South Cross Street
☎ 410-778-2688.
Inexpensive

For a change, have your lunch to the sound of classical music in a café/cultural center where the staff is laid-back and pleasant and the sandwiches are *so* good. Fresh croissants are layered with thick-sliced ham or piled with creamy white-meat chicken salad for only $4. Pies and cakes, good coffees, ice cream and milkshakes are served, and you can browse here for local art and used CDs. Sam's is open Monday-Saturday 7-5:30, Sunday 9-4.

WHITE SWAN TAVERN
231 High Street
☎ 410-778-2300, fax 410-778-4543

This is the place to go for afternoon tea from 3 to 5 every day except Wednesday, or when the inn is booked for a special event. During the winter they serve hot cider, and in summer hot or iced tea or lemonade with accompanying goodies. The price is a reasonable $4 and is complimentary for inn guests.

It's wise to call ahead if you are traveling some distance. The White Swan is opposite the park.

Rock Hall

BAY WOLF RESTAURANT
21270 Rock Hall Avenue (Route 20 South)
☎ 410-778-6855
Inexpensive to moderate

This popular restaurant, set in an old converted church, is known for its continental/regional menu and for the favorite Bavarian dishes of the German-born chef. These show up as his specials on Monday evenings in the winter. Some of these, such as Wiener schnitzel and roast pork with dumplings, stay on the menu from mid-September through April. Pastries here are excellent – as one would expect from a Salzburg-trained chef.

The Lower Eastern Shore

Orientation

From the area around the eastern end of the William Preston Lane Memorial Bridge (locally called simply the Bay Bridge) to the tiny piece of Virginia at the end, the lower part of Maryland's Eastern Shore offers a little bit of everything, from a rich tradition of plantation farming to people whose families have depended upon the fruits of the Bay for their survival. Vast parcels of tilled land still cover the gentle countryside; the miles of rivers, bays and inlets that line the bay side are still peopled by **watermen**.

WHO ARE THE WATERMEN?

In other coastal areas, people who earn their living from the sea are called fishermen, but not here. The primary yields of the Chesapeake Bay are oysters and crabs, and the people who harvest them are called watermen (even if they happen to be women).

The Lower Eastern Shore is a world apart from the City of Baltimore. The only population centers of any appreciable size are **Easton** and **Cambridge** (both on the western side), **Salisbury** (in the mid-

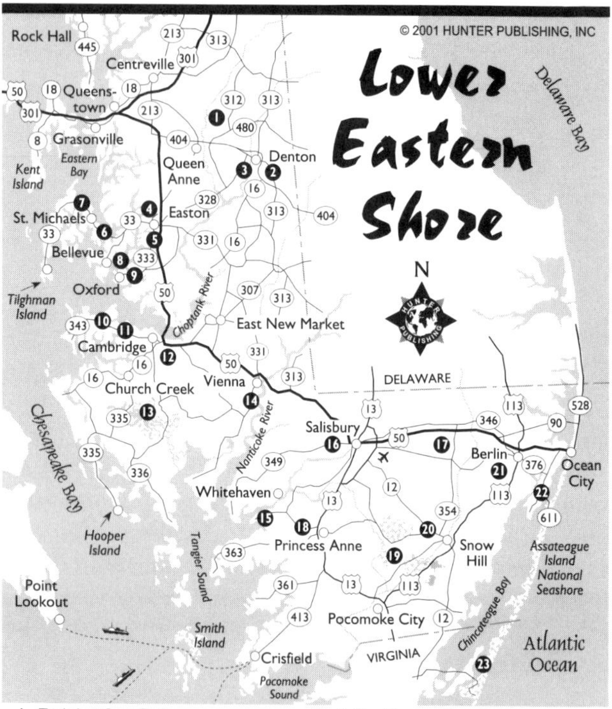

1. Tuckahoe State Park
2. Museum of Rural Life
3. Martinak State Park
4. Historical Society of Talbot County
5. Third Haven Friends Meeting House
6. Chesapeake Bay Maritime Museum
7. St. Mary's Square Museum
8. Oxford-Bellevue Ferry
9. Oxford Museum
10. Sopcot Windmill
11. Dorchester Heritage Museum
12. Dorchester County Historical Society; Richardson Museum; Brannock Museum
13. Blackwater National Wildlife Refuge
14. Adkins Museum Complex
15. Whitehaven Ferry
16. Salisbury Zoo; Ward Museum of Wildfowl Art; Salisbury Pewter
17. Wicomico State Forest
18. Teackle Mansion
19. Pocomoke State Forest
20. Nassawango Iron Furnace; Furnace Town; Byrd Park
21. Merry Sherwood Plantation; Globe Theatre; Taylor House Museum
22. Assateague Island Visitors Center; Verrazano Bridge
23. Chincoteague Island & Chincoteague National Wildlife Refuge

dle) and **Ocean City**, which is built on a sand spit on the edge of the Atlantic Ocean. For the people who live here, and for visitors, the Chesapeake Bay is the attraction. The many arms of its waters and tributary rivers reach deeply into the land, setting the stage for the unique maritime culture that has developed here since the 17th century.

In Easton and St. Michaels, the tone is more upscale than elsewhere, with trendy shops and boutiques. Oxford is a town of quiet streets filled with old homes that are less showy than St. Michaels' and with a feeling of refined long-term settlement. This is a place for watersports and waterfowl enthusiasts, especially those who enjoy genteel lodgings and the small dining spots they'll find in these three towns.

It is to this small section of the Eastern Shore, and to its well-known beaches on the Atlantic coast, that most visitors head. Most miss entirely the many attractions of the area in between and to the south – towns rich in maritime history, long lazy rivers bordered in cypress trees, salt marshes alive with birds and villages inhabited by warm, friendly people.

History

The whole Eastern Shore is rich in history. Settled in the middle 1600s, there were several active ports by the time of the Revolution. Revolutionary leader **Robert Morris**, known as the man who financed the war, was from Oxford, and Washington's aide-de-camp **Tench Tilghman**, also from the Eastern Shore, carried the news of Cornwallis's surrender to the Continental Congress in Philadelphia.

> **DID YOU KNOW?**
>
> **Salisbury**, even though it is inland, is the second-largest port in Maryland. It's linked to the Bay by the Wicomico River and much of the oil and other supplies for the region arrive by ship.

Getting Here

By Air

Salisbury Airport is served by US Airways, which offers about 14 flights daily from Baltimore, Philadelphia and Washington.

By Car

From Baltimore, take **I-97** south (it passes close to Baltimore-Washington International Airport) to **US-50** east. An alternative is to take **Route 2** south to US-50 at Annapolis. Take US-50 east over the Bay Bridge, following it south (to the right) when US-301 splits off to the north.

Getting Around

By Car

US-50 takes you through the heart of the lower Eastern Shore, skirting the ends of bays and rivers, into Cambridge. From this point it runs inland southeasterly to Salisbury and then on to Ocean City. From Salisbury, **Route 13** drops through the center of Somerset County with **Route 413** leading from it south to Crisfield and **Route 113** turning north through Snow Hill and connecting with US-50 again near Ocean City. The driving distance from Annapolis to Salisbury is about 90 miles.

By Ferry

OXFORD-BELLEVUE FERRY
☎ 410-745-9023
One-way fare: $5 car and driver plus 50¢ per passenger. Walk-on $1; bicycles $2.

This is the oldest privately owned ferry in the United States: it was established in 1683. It crosses the Tred Avon River between Bellevue (off Route 329) and Oxford (Route 333), saving many miles of driving between Oxford and St. Michaels. The ferry can accommodate RVs and trailers as well as cars, bicyclists and pedestrians.

From June through August, hours of operation are 7 am to 9 pm on weekdays, 9 am to 9 pm on weekends. From Labor Day through November and from March through May, hours are 7 am to sunset on weekdays and 9 am to sunset on weekends. Crossings are at 20-minute intervals. The ferry does not operate December through February.

> **TIP**
>
> Southwest of Salisbury, the only way to get across the Wicomico River is by ferry. One crossing is at Upper Ferry (close to Salisbury), and another runs between Whitehaven and Mount Vernon, connecting routes 352 and 362. The ferries are free and frequent, and the Upper Ferry is available well into the evening. During times of unusually high tides, they close for the hour when water is the highest.

Information Sources

Talbot County Visitors Center, Tred Avon Plaza, off US 50; ☎ 410-822-4606 or 888-BAY-STAY, www.talbotchamber.org. The Center is also a ticket sales and information center for the Waterfowl Festival (see *Festivals & Events*, page 24).

Shuttle buses leave on a regular schedule from the Talbot County Visitors Center parking lot during the Waterfowl Festival.

Dorchester County Visitors Center, Sailwinds Park, Cambridge 21613; ☎ 410-228-1000 or 800-522-TOUR, www.tourdorchester.org. There is an interpretive display on the culture of the local area.

Caroline County Visitor Center, 16 North 2nd Street, Denton; ☎ 410-479-2055. They are open Friday and Saturday, 10-3; Sunday, noon-4.

Wicomico County Convention & Visitors Bureau, 8480 Ocean Hwy (US 13) Delmar, ☎ 410-548-4914, 800-332-8687, www.wicomicotourism.org. The office is handicapped-accessible. Direct lines to area lodgings are available. The center is open 8:30-6, Memorial Day to Labor Day; 9-5 Labor Day to Memorial Day. Closed for major holidays.

Ocean City Maryland Chamber of Commerce, 12320 Ocean Gateway, Ocean City 21842, ☎ 410-213-0552, 800-626-3386, www.oceancity.org.

Sunup to Sundown

The pleasures of the Eastern Shore are quiet ones – apart from the razzle-dazzle atmosphere of Ocean City, whose high-rise buildings seem far more akin to the overbuilt beach towns of Delaware and New Jersey than to Maryland's Eastern Shore. Historic sites abound, and even very small towns have interesting historical houses and museums to see. Tree-lined rivers and tidal marshes invite kayakers and canoeists to paddle among their wildlife, and quiet country roads are good for cycling.

Highlights for those interested in the bay and its boats are the **Richardson Museum** in Cambridge and the **Maritime Museum** in St. Michaels. Several boats take passengers on excursions in the bay and up the rivers, a pleasant way to spend a warm afternoon. Even if you don't normally seek out zoos, you will want to stroll through the free park-like **Salisbury Zoo**, where you can see a surprising number of rare animals as well as the local and visiting birds that stop by for a free lunch in the pond.

If, like us, you eschew the crowded sands and noisy streets of beach resorts, you will find a sandy haven on the long barrier-island beaches of **Assateague**, where wild horses roam amid the dunes.

How you divide your time on the Eastern Shore – and how much time you spend here – will depend on your personal interests. Those seeking historical sites will want to spend time in the Easton-Oxford-St. Michaels area and in Princess Anne, with a stop in Salisbury to explore the streets of Newtown. Those who love nature and outdoor sports could spend several days paddling the many tidal rivers and exploring the dunes of Assateague. You can explore the entire area from a single base, but it makes more sense to divide your stay between the Easton-Oxford area and the Princess Anne-Snow Hill section, each of which has good lodgings to offer. Either area makes a good weekend trip out of Baltimore or Annapolis.

The sites described below are in general north-to-south order, and grouped by town or area.

Museums

Denton

MUSEUM OF RURAL LIFE
16 North 2nd Street
☎ 410-479-2055

At the Caroline County Visitors Center, this small museum has salvaged the homes of families in four different social and economic levels, dating from

1790 to 1840. The museum is open Friday- Saturday, 10-3; Sunday, noon-4.

Easton

HISTORICAL SOCIETY OF TALBOT COUNTY
25 South Washington Street
☎ 410-822-0773
Admission: $3, adults; $2, ages six-12. Tour of houses $3; combination $5.

The museum, along with its changing historical exhibits, maintains three homes facing its Federal-style gardens. The James Neall House is a fine example of Federal architecture, a restored 1810 brick home of a Quaker cabinetmaker. Joseph's Cottage was built in 1795 and the building "Ending of Controversie" is a reconstruction of a 17th-century house. Scheduled tours are given from April to November, Tuesday-Saturday, 10-4; Sunday, 10-3. Hours are shorter in the winter. Gardens are open Monday to Saturday, 10-4.

St. Michaels

CHESAPEAKE BAY MARITIME MUSEUM
On the Community Wharf
☎ 410-745-2916
www.cbmm.org
Admission: $7.50, adults; $6.50, over age 61; $3, ages six-17; $18, family admission

This fine museum celebrates the history and the culture of the entire bay. The 1879 Hooper Straight screw-pile lighthouse is the centerpiece of the multi-building complex, restored and furnished as the keeper's cottage it once was. There are dozens of historic boats on display, and the exhibits include decoys and their makers; fishing since the time of the Native Americans; shipbuilding and maintenance; steamboating; and the skills of watermen. Hands-on experiences encourage visitors to try their hand at crabbing and examine a tank full of shedding soft-shell crabs up close. They are open daily, 9-6 in summer; 9-5 in spring & fall; 9-4 in winter.

ST. MARY'S SQUARE MUSEUM
St. Mary's Square
☎ 410-745-9561

This museum examines the land side of the development of the community of St Michaels. St. Mary's Square Museum is open weekends, 10-4, from May-October, or by appointment.

☛ DID YOU KNOW?

During the War of 1812 the British decided to attack St. Michaels and destroy its port. Local residents darkened the town and hung lanterns at the tops of ship masts and in treetops. Using these lights as guides, the British fired harmlessly over the tops of the buildings and ships, leaving the town relatively unscathed.

Oxford

OXFORD MUSEUM
Morris and Market Streets
No phone

The historically minded will enjoy these carefully collected local artifacts. These are the expression of a community's being. They are open Friday-Sunday, 2-5, from mid-April to mid-October.

Cambridge

RICHARDSON MUSEUM
401 High Street
☎ 410-221-1871
Free; donations welcome

The Richardson celebrates and records the city's rich maritime heritage. A mural shows the waterfront on the wide Choptank River as it was in the harbor's glory days. Several landmarks in the mural can still be spotted along its banks. The museum is named for Jim Richardson, the larger-than-life local skipjack builder. He felt very strongly about preserving and passing down the unique skills of generations of shipbuilders. The museum has a waterman's boat shop with all the tools needed for trade, from basket-like eel pots and crab nets to oyster scrapers and clam rakes. Model boats include a freight transport ship built there in World War II called the *Pride of Baltimore*, and a ¾-scale model of the *Nathan of Dorchester*, launched here in 1993, whose construction is also recorded in photographs. The Richardson is open Wednesday, Saturday & Sunday, 1-4 pm, from April to October.

> ☛ **DID YOU KNOW?**
>
> There were two types of ships used by watermen in the Chesapeake, the **bugeye** and the **skipjack**. The bugeye was a two-masted boat with a more rounded bottom than a skipjack. A skipjack had a single mast with a tall, powerful sail and fairly flat, V-shaped bottom that allowed it to better navigate the shallow waters of the rivers. About a dozen of these are left today, most on Tilghman Island.

BRANNOCK MUSEUM
215 Glenburn Avenue
☎ 410-228-6938
Free; donations welcome

The museum is dedicated to the preservation of local, regional and national maritime artifacts. In addition to its models and artifacts, it has an extensive historical research library of old ships' logs and shipping records and more than 7,000 photographs. People who have sailed with the Maine-based windjammer fleet will be interested to find records on the *Edwin and Maud*, built in the area as a working ship and now sailing the Maine coast as the windjammer *Victory Chimes*. They are open weekends, 1-4:30, or by appointment.

DORCHESTER HERITAGE MUSEUM

Horne Point Road, off Route 343,west of Cambridge
☎ 410-228-5530
Free

The museum was founded by a group of high school students. Housed in the airplane hangar of a former Dupont estate, it has displays on archaeology, shellfish harvesting, farming, and vintage toys and clothing. The Dorchester is open weekends, 1-4:30, from mid-April to October.

DORCHESTER COUNTY HISTORICAL SOCIETY

LaGrange Avenue (off Crusader Road)
☎ 410-228-7953

This is a collection of restored homes maintained by the society. The **Meredith House** was built in 1760 and "modernized" in the 1850s. It is furnished in fine antiques, and features a collection of antique dolls and toys. The **Neild Museum** is dedicated to preserving the rural and agricultural heritage of the region, with agricultural and household tools, equipment from the various maritime trades, and a collection of Native American artifacts. The **Goldsborough Stable** contains a collection of early vehicles and tools of those trades that created them: blacksmith, wheelwright and harnessmaker. An **Herb Garden** re-creates a typical Colonial garden to show the horticulture and uses of herbs. The Historical Society is open for tours all year, Thursday-Saturday, 10-4.

Vienna

ADKINS HISTORICAL AND MUSEUM COMPLEX

Main Street, Mardela
☎ 410-749-4871

The complex is a lovingly gathered collection of significant local buildings assembled about 1983. Included are a General Store, Odd Fellows Hall, a one-room schoolhouse and a livery stable that is being developed into a farm museum. The Youngs Purchase farm house on the property was built in 1724. The buildings are open only by appointment, but you can walk around the site on your own. The complex is located just off US-50 east of Vienna, via the Station Street exit.

Salisbury

WARD MUSEUM OF WILDFOWL ART

909 South Schumaker Drive
☎ 410-548-4870
Admission: $7, adults; $5 seniors; $2 children

Lem and Steve Ward were decoy carvers from Crisfield whose work was so fine that they changed the status of waterfowl carving from hunting decoys to fine art. The museum named for them has an exquisite collection of examples from decoys to sculpture and paintings. Housed in an attractive modern building, the museum traces the history of the art form; many of the works in the collection have been winners of prestigious awards. The museum shop sells museum quality waterfowl art.

Berlin

TAYLOR HOUSE MUSEUM
North Main Street at Baker Street
Admission is by donation

This museum combines a classic restoration of a splendid 19th-century house with a gallery that features historic local memorabilia. Of particular note is the restored false graining, a hallmark of that period of architecture. The home is also noted for the butterfly medallions, sunbursts and fluted columns of its main entrance. The house is close to the restored downtown area. Taylor House is open Memorial Day weekend through September, Monday, Wednesday, Friday and Saturday, 1-4 pm.

Princess Anne

THE TEACKLE MANSION
11736 Mansion Street
☎ 410-651-2238
Admission: $3

Now under restoration by an organization of local people who value this historic property, this treasure is a grand five-part American Federal home built at the beginning of the 19th century of Flemish-bond brick (alternating headers and stretchers). Its story is a classic tale of the cycle of wealth and fallen fortunes that prevailed in that century. Bought and sold to relatives three times, the house is a history of the travails of the family, and their stories thread through the narrative given by the excellent guides. The entryway is unusually large, a first taste of Teackle's passion for Georgian symme-

Throughout the Teackle Mansion, look for false doors and windows that maintain the illusion of matching architectural detail.

try. Behind the house the gardens are being restored and some of the boxwood is thought to be original, although much overgrown. The gardens are open even when the house is not; enter on the left-hand side of the house to find the gate. The gift shop is a good place to look for well-chosen reproductions, good pottery and baskets. The mansion is open Wednesday, Saturday & Sunday, 1-3 from April to mid-December; and Sunday, 1-3, from January to March.

Historic Sites

Easton

THIRD HAVEN FRIENDS MEETING HOUSE
405 South Washington Street
☎ 410-822-0293

This is the earliest dated (1684) structure in Maryland, and it may well be the oldest religious building still in use in the United States. The meeting house is significant in the history of the Religious Society of Friends, or Quakers, in America.

Cambridge

SOPCOT WINDMILL
Washington Street (Route 343) west of Cambridge
☎ 410-228-7090

The windmill is a restoration of one built on this site that was destroyed by a blizzard in 1888. Dorchester was one of the last counties on the east coast where windmills were used commercially to grind corn. The windmill operates on special occasions.

Salisbury

PEMBERTON HISTORIC PARK

Route 349
west of Salisbury
Free

The park is the site of Pemberton Manor, a small early 1700s brick home that clearly shows the humble origins of the great plantations of later years. The adjacent Heritage Center is a museum of early local artifacts, some of which were unearthed at an archaeological dig on the site, which has yielded pre-Colonial artifacts, as well as the original docks on the river at Bell Creek Marsh Overlook. The plantation sent its cotton and other crops to market by ship from this pier. The dock area is a .3-mile walk on the History Trail. A **Colonial Fair** on the last Saturday in September brings the plantation to life, with re-enactors demonstrating the evolution of plantation life there with tools and authentic foods. The experiences include a look at the life of Native American and Black members of the plantation community. Visitors can sample venison, roast goat, and oysters cooked as Native Americans prepared them.

The park interprets its wide variety of Eastern Shore eco-systems with regular year-round nature programs, led by the park naturalist and exploring the changing seasons along the Wicomico River. The 4½ miles of walking trails lead through habitats that include tidal and freshwater wetlands, freshwater ponds, a river island, upland pine groves, hardwood forests and meadows, providing habitat for nearly 160 bird species. The Environmental Education Center at Pemberton has regular programs on nature subjects, all open to the public.

Reservations are suggested. Program costs are $2 per person, $5 family. They have a full schedule of seasonal activities, such as a "Haunted Trail" walk, Earth Day observations in the spring, maple sugaring in January, full moon hikes, owl prowls and special programs for toddlers. Pemberton is open from April to November; call the Park Service (☎ 410-548-4870) for hours.

Berlin

GLOBE THEATER

Broad Street

Built in 1910 as a garage, the building was re-created in 1917 as the art deco Hollywood Theater and enjoyed a 50-year life. After a 20-year rest it was recycled as a venue for the arts, with a café, a few shops and a small classic film theater. The old place is also an unofficial community center where bulletin board notices for church bazaars and dance lessons are sure to be found. On the second floor look for the gallery of handcrafts. The shops include a bookstore, gourmet food shop and café.

Snow Hill

FURNACE TOWN HISTORIC SITE

Old Furnace Road
☎ 410-632-2032

The Nassawango Iron Furnace was a thriving iron producer from 1828 to 1850. It prospered because of the coincidence of bog iron from the nearby swamp, oyster and clam shells from the bay and charcoal made from local timber. Around the giant brick furnace there was a village that was dependent upon this iron manufacturing center. The product of the furnace was transported to market by a mile-long canal leading to the river, remnants of which are still visible. The furnace is the focal point for the restoration of the full collection of businesses and services that comprised the short-lived community. Docents demonstrate home and village skills, including weaving and blacksmithing, and a museum in a little gothic cottage shows the entire process of iron-making. This is one of the few places that clearly shows how the process worked, from the gathering of bog iron and other locally available materials to the finished product. From Salisbury, go 16 miles south on Route 12, then take Old Furnace Road to the right.

Recreation

A look at any map of the Eastern Shore will reveal that one of its greatest attractions is the water, a wonderful place for paddling on many of the bays, estuaries and rivers. The shore is heavily indented with deep bay and rivers, each of which has many arms and branches to explore. These rivers and the bay itself provide fishing waters, as well.

Smith Island

AMPHIBIOUS HORIZONS
600 Quiet Waters ParkRoad (in the park)
Annapolis
☎ 410-267-8742 or 888-I-LUV-SUN
www.amphibioushorizons.com

To paddle in the waters of **Smith Island**, part of a group of islands in Tangier Sound, contact this Annapolis outfitter, which runs guided trips and arranges lodging at a B&B in Tylerton. This is a rare chance to experience the unique culture of the island firsthand. Their three-day trips are offered during Memorial Day, July 4 and Labor Day weekends, and cost about $400 per person. Visit their Web site for a more complete list of trips available.

Denton

MARTINAK STATE PARK
Deep Shore Road
Off Route 404, south of Denton
☎ 301-479-1619

This is a good place to put in a canoe or kayak and enjoy the upper reaches of the Choptank River. A boat pier and ramp give access for a pleasant trip along the wooded shore of the river.

Easton

LITTLE BOAT RENTALS
846 Port Street
☎ 410-819-0881 or 800-221-1523

Easton is at the head of the Tred Avon River, a wonderful web of water for paddling. Just across the peninsula is the Miles River with more places to explore. Little Boat rents canoes for about $35/day, $20 half day or $6/hour with a two-hour minimum. With the canoe comes a chart of the river and its feeder creeks.

Tilghman Island

CHESAPEAKE BAY KAYAK
Molowes Wharf Marina, Route 33
Sherwood
☎ 410-745-9744

This enterprising little company not only rents kayaks, they also conduct guided nature tours of the waters around Tilghman Island. This is a perfect way to learn about the ecology of the Bay.

HARRISON'S SPORTFISHING CENTER
Route 33
☎ 410-886-2121, fax 410-886-2109

Fishing packages include dinner, overnight lodging, breakfast and box lunch, in addition to the fishing trip. The cost is $175 per person for the overnighter and $75 per person for fishing only. Bait and tackle are included; fish cleaning and packing are not. Boat charters at Harrison's are $450-$600.

MISS KIM

Dogwood Harbor, south of the drawbridge
☎ 410-886-2176.

Six-hour crabbing trips on board this working boat cost $60 per person, which includes a bushel of crabs. The cost is $30 if you don't keep the crabs. Fishing trips are $50.

Cambridge Area

BLACKWATER NATIONAL WILDLIFE REFUGE

Route 335
Church Creek
☎ 410-228-2677

Bald eagles are a common sight on the tall snags that stick out of the water at Blackwater National Wildlife Refuge.

The park is a vast stretch of tidal marsh and water, where you can drive, walk or cycle to see birds in profusion. This is a spectacular place, especially in the late afternoon. Thousands of geese and ducks float in the water, looking like decoys against the gold marsh grasses. Roads passing the refuge are studies in blue and gold, with nothing except a few stands of pine to break the vista of grass and water.

LADY KATIE

Commerce St., behind Snappers Waterfront Café
Cambridge
☎ 410-228-6400

For a chance to get out onto the Bay in a piece of history, sail on this ship, an historic vessel that is still a working skipjack, dredging oysters during the winter. During the rest of the year, when it is not doing cruises, it is available for fishing charters. Scott Todd, the captain, descends from several generations of skipjack captains, and knows the bay and its fishing grounds well. To find the boat, follow High Street to Commerce Street; you will see the restaurant.

Salisbury

SURVIVAL PRODUCTS
1116 North Salisbury Boulevard
☎ 410-543-1244 or 543-1493, fax 410-543-9146
Canoes rental $40 a day, kayaks $35

This is an equipment outfitter that also gives kayak and canoe lessons. Rentals include tie-down kits for your car. This is a good place to pick up topo maps and information on access point and conditions for paddling in the lower Eastern Shore. They also serve as a clearing house for service outfitters who can provide guided overnight trips or shuttles.

SALISBURY ZOOLOGICAL PARK
South Park Drive
☎ 410-548-3188
Free

The zoo is a small but outstanding community zoo and well worth a visit. It does a good job of introducing both native and exotic wildlife, and is very popular with local children who get to know the animals and see them at all times of year. On its 12 acres live more than 300 animals of 90 species. Native and migratory waterfowl take advantage of the natural setting of the park. One wonderful feature are raised boardwalks that provide good vantage points for watching animals such as buffalos, spider monkeys, prairie dogs, a rare black jaguar, spectacled bears, guanaco and capybaras.

Salisbury Zoological Park also serves as a refuge for injured and orphaned wildlife, as well as a nursery.

The otter house has its own water slide and pool, where you can see the otters play in the early morning and just before closing in the afternoon. The best time to see the slow-moving sloth is in the morning as the zoo opens. A forested enclosure is filled with bright tropical birds, including Amazon parrots. The zoo is open daily, 8-4:30 in winter; until 7:30 in summer.

Snow Hill

POCOMOKE RIVER CANOE COMPANY
312 North Washington Street
☎ 410-632-1700

Kayaks are $5/hour, $30/day; canoes are $7.50/ hour or $35/day. Weekend rentals are $40 kayaks or $50 canoes. Trips $35-$50, two-day trips $75. High-quality canoes and knowledgeable advice on local waters are the stock-in-trade of this center for paddling on the Pocomoke. Rentals include gear and shuttle to up-stream put-ins.

BYRD PARK
From this park and from the bridge in the center of town, you can fish in the Pocomoke River without a sportfishing license, whether you are from Maryland or out of state.

Berlin

ASSATEAGUE ISLAND
NATIONAL SEASHORE VISITORS CENTER
7206 National Seashore Lane (Route 611)
☎ 401-641-1441

The visitors center has a touch tank where adults and kids can play with sea creatures. Information on the famous wild "ponies" (really horses), including an 18-minute film, is plentiful, and other films deal with different aspects of park wildlife. The refuge area is across the Verrazano Bridge and you are better off to park at the visitors center and walk; there is a separate bike and pedestrian bridge. The refuge is adjacent to Assateague Island State Park, which has a boat landing and a picnic area.

For the excellent shore fishing in the park, you need only a Maryland license, but you must check in with both state and federal offices, because each has different season dates and rules. The park visitors center is open 9-5 daily, and can give you details on fishing license requirements.

Ocean City

PUBLIC FISHING PIERS
On the bay side: south of 10th Street
On the ocean side: opposite the end of Wicomico Street, south of the US-50 intersection with Philadelphia Avenue. A fishing license is required.

Atlantic Coast

The boardwalk at Ocean City is fully wheelchair-accessible. Handicapped access points on the boardwalk are well marked from the main streets.

OCEAN CITY BEACH & BOARDWALK

The place to look for beaches is on the ocean side of the peninsula, where the Atlantic washes an almost solid line of sandy barrier islands from Delaware to Virginia.

On the north end of Maryland's Atlantic shore is Ocean City, whose entire existence is due to its long sandy beaches, which shelter Assawoman Bay. At one time, the sandy barrier stretched from Delaware into Virginia, but a hurricane in 1933 created an opening just south of Ocean City.

ATVs and dune buggies are not allowed at Assateague Island National Seashore.

ASSATEAGUE ISLAND NATIONAL SEASHORE

South of Ocean City is another barrier island, Assateague, which is protected as a wildlife refuge. At the north end, Assateague Island National Seashore can be reached from Route 611 South, just before the bridge to Ocean City. The refuge has a state park and beach on a long strip of white sand. The southern end of the barrier island is across the state line in Virginia (by a quirk of government reasoning, the Chincoteague National Wildlife Refuge is on the southern end of Assateague Island, not on Chincoteague Island itself; there is a separate visitors center in Virginia for that section of the island, which cannot be entered from the northern park except on foot).

Tours

On Land

Several Eastern Shore towns have walking tours of their historic areas.

St. Michaels

St. Mary's Square Museum (☎ 410-745-9561) has an excellent map that describes historic sites and buildings and arranges them into a walking tour. These free maps can be found in a number of other places if the museum is closed. Look for the brochure entitled *Explore St. Mary's Square Museum*. Among the interesting things you'll find with this map is a log house hidden beneath Victorian-era siding.

For a guided walking tour of St. Michaels, get the latest schedule from **Dockside Express** (☎ 410-886-2643). Tours operate from mid-April through mid-November and may be of a general historic nature or more specific, such as the Ghostly Tour in the fall.

Easton

Self-guided walking tour maps of the downtown area can be found at the **Historical Society**, at 25 South Washington Street.

Cambridge

Cambridge has the most detailed walking tour map and brochure in the area. The tour takes you past many of the distinguished buildings of the Cambridge waterfront neighborhoods. The free 20-page booklet, *Historic Walking Tour of Cambridge*, is well illustrated and explains not only the history, but the architectural niceties of the buildings it passes. High Street is lined with outstanding examples of Federal, Queen Anne, Second Empire and high Victorian. You can pick up a copy of the booklet at the Dorchester County Visitors Center (see page 278).

East New Market

Established in 1660, East New Market has an architectural heritage so significant that the entire town is listed on the National Register of Historic Places. They have a walking tour map describing the residences of its founders and other citizens of the 18th century. The town is at the intersection of Routes 14 and 16, just off Route 392; ☎ 410-943-8112.

On Water

St. Michaels & Tilghman Island

HM *KRENTZ*
Dogwood Harbor, south of the drawbridge
Tilghman Island
☎ 410-745-6080

The HM *Krentz* is a working skipjack whose captain has been a waterman for 25 years. A two-hour tour ($30 for adults, $15 for ages 12 and under, discounts for groups) gives you the chance to help crew the boat; the *Krentz* is also available for charter.

LADY PATTY
Knapps Narrows Marina
5907 Tilghman Narrows Road
Tilghman Island
☎ 410-886-2215 or 800-690-5080.
Two-hour trips about $30

This 45-foot classic bay ketch sails daily on two-hour trips on the Choptank River and the bay.

REBECCA T. RUARK
Dogwood Harbor, south of the drawbridge
Tilghman Island
☎ 410-886-2176
Two-hour sails, $30 per person

The bay's oldest (and one of its fastest) skipjacks, built in 1886, is a beautiful craft, still a working oyster dredger in the winter. You will sail with a third-generation waterman with a thorough knowledge of the bay, its boats and its history.

ST. MICHAELS LADY
Town Dock Marina
305 Mulberry Street
St. Michaels
☎ 410-745-5776
Cruises $9

A 42-foot Chesapeake workboat is captained by a fourth-generation waterman, whose cruises emphasize the work of the people who harvest fish and shellfish. Cruises on the Miles River offer a chance to see ospreys, ducks, swans, herons, possibly even bald eagles. Four daily one-hour cruises each explore an aspect of the river.

EXPRESS ROYAL
Town Dock Marina
305 Mulberry Street
St. Michaels
☎ 410-886-2643
$20 for adults; $10 for children under 12

Departing every morning on a 90-minute nature cruise, the boat carries a naturalist to point out sights along the shore and describe the waters and their residents. Reservations are needed.

PATRIOT
Maritime Museum Dock
St. Michaels
☎ 410-745-3100
Daily at 11, 12:30, 2:30 and 4, April through October
$9 adult, $5 children

The large tour boat explores the Miles River with a narration that includes local history along with nature and wildlife information.

Cambridge

LADY KATIE
Commerce St., behind Snappers Waterfront Café
☎ 410-228-7277
$20 and up

The only working skipjack sailing from Cambridge is captained by Scott Todd, who is descended from several generations of skipjack captains, and is a full-time waterman himself. His two-hour cruises include watermen's tales and a chance to see how oysters are harvested by these historic boats. Longer cruises, as well as trips on Scott's fiberglass crabbing vessel, are available, too. Reservations are essential.

NATHAN OF DORCHESTER

Waterfront park at the end of Washington Street
☎ 410-228-7141
$10 for a two-hour trip

Built and launched here in 1993, this replica skipjack usually hosts Sunday afternoon cruises, but the schedule is erratic so call for dates. Reservations are essential on this popular boat.

CAMBRIDGE LADY

Corner of Court and Gay Streets, off High Street
☎ 410-221-0776
E-mail clady@shorenet.net

This passenger boat is built in the style of a classic wooden motor yacht. You may opt for a one-hour sunset/cocktail cruise for $6.50, Friday-Sunday evenings; or a 90-minute harbor cruise for $10. Longer river cruises are $15. Full-day "Michener's Chesapeake" cruises are $18, and sail from Cambridge to Oxford, with time ashore there. The narration on this trip quotes passages from the novel as the boat passes sites mentioned in the book. This tour is offered at least once a week. Reservations are recommended for all tours. *Cambridge Lady* sails Friday and Saturday from June through August, and Saturday only in May, September and October. Sunday afternoon cruises run May-October.

Shop Till You Drop

Crafts

ARTISTE LOCALE
112 North Talbott Street
St. Michaels
☎ 410-745-6580

A showcase for local crafts in several media, the shop includes pottery, furniture, baskets, art prints and metal arts. Call the shop for hours.

CAPTAIN DAN VAUGHN
Mission Road
Tilghman Island
☎ 410-886-2083

You'll often find Captain Vaughn in his studio working on a decoy. You can see his past creations and buy one or order a decoy specially made. Waterfowl carving is high art in the Eastern Shore.

CAMBRIDGE ARTS CENTER
High Street
Cambridge
☎ 410-228-7782

The restored Victorian-era hotel has become a crafts venue, showing and selling the work of local artists and craftsmen. They sponsor an arts festival along tree-shaded High Street during the fourth weekend in September. Art, crafts, music and food highlight the weekend. The arts center is open Monday-Saturday, 10-2.

BROOKS BARREL COMPANY
5228 Buckthorne Road
south of US-50, opposite the Airport
Cambridge
☎ 800-398 BROOKS (2766), fax 410-221-1693

One of the last slack cooperages operating in the United States, Brooks creates sturdy barrels and buckets from local pine logs. You can watch these made or buy them at the factory store.

WATERLOO COUNTRY INN
28822 Mount Vernon Road
Princess Anne
☎ 410-651-0883

An inn may seem like a strange place for shopping, but this one has a fine gift shop in a space that once served as a doctor's office. They have a nice collection of unusual ornaments, ceramics, floral art and hand-worked fine cotton lingerie, much of it the work of inn owner Therese Kraemer.

SALISBURY PEWTER
Ocean Highway
Salisbury
☎ 410-546-1188, 800-824-4708

Lead-free pewter crafting is taken to a new level in this studio, where you can see pewter spinners who have perfected their techniques over a lifetime. Each artisan creates his own tools and chucks. The craftsmen here are called upon to create works for the White House, State Department and high-end stores such as Tiffany's. The range of items available runs from Christmas ornaments and jewelry to tableware and exquisite presentation pieces. Prices in the main showroom are at a 20% to 50% discount, and in their seconds showroom you'll find discounts

At Salisbury Pewter, look for the pewter crab, formed in a mold made from the shell of an actual Chesapeake blue crab.

of 50% to 80%. Salisbury Pewter is open weekdays, 9-5; and Saturdays, 10-5.

Antiques

Shops in St. Michaels and Easton tend to be pricey but you will find some fine pieces in their upscale displays. Move inland for better prices, although you're less likely to find museum-quality pieces. Both individual and group dealers are found throughout the area. There are also a number of weekend auctions, where you can still get some real bargains. Check for them in the newspapers.

For a number of shops in one cluster, try those on North Harrison Street in Easton, opposite the Tidewater Inn. More are on South Harrison, Washington and along US-50.

CANTON ROW ANTIQUES
216-C Talbot Street
St. Michaels

More than a dozen dealers show in this group gallery, specializing in high quality pieces.

CONSIGNMENT TREASURES
300 North Talbot Street
St. Michaels

Vintage clothing, jewelry and a miscellany of collectibles fill the retro shop.

CHARITY ANTIQUES SHOW AND SALE
Academy of the Arts
Easton
☎ 410-820-5170

Select dealers are invited to show and sell at this prestigious antiques event in late June each year.

After Dark

Apart from the bars and clubs of Ocean City, there's not much night life on the Eastern Shore. And that's one good reason for going here – to spend a quiet weekend away from the city lights.

Performing Arts

AVALON THEATRE
40 East Dover Street
Easton
☎ 410-822-0345

The theater was built in 1921, in the height of the art deco era, and has recently been restored to its former grandeur as a performance venue. Events include symphonic concerts, children's theater, dance, and classic films. Most events are open to the public.

Sunset Cruises

ST. MICHAELS LADY
Town Dock Marina
305 Mulberry Street
St. Michaels
☎ 410-745-5776
Cruises are $12.

The 42-foot Chesapeake workboat, captained by a fourth-generation waterman, makes 90-minute cruises in the evening, Friday-Sunday, to watch the sunset over Tilghman Point. Narration on these cruises emphasize the work of the people who harvest fish and shellfish in local waters.

EXPRESS ROYAL
Town Dock Marina
305 Mulberry Street
St. Michaels
☎ 410-886-2643
$20 for adults, $10 for children under 12

The boat departs every evening for sunset or moonlight cruises. Reservations are required.

NATHAN OF DORCHESTER
Waterfront Park at the end of Washington Street
Cambridge
☎ 410-228-7141
$15 for a two-hour trip

Follow High Street from the town center to its end at the park; the boat will be on your right.

The replica skipjack usually makes Saturday evening sunset cruises, which include a complimentary drink after the cruise at McGuigan's Pub (see *Best Places to Eat*, page 326).

Best Places to Stay

ACCOMMODATIONS PRICE SCALE	
Inexpensive	under $100
Moderate	$100-$200
Expensive	$201-$300
Deluxe	more than $300

Queenstown

THE QUEENSTOWN INN BED & BREAKFAST
7109 Main Street
☎ 410-827-3396
Moderate

The B&B is in the center of the village yet is very quiet, with no traffic noises. Pleasantly eclectic, a mix of modern and antique furniture decorates large rooms with amply sized modern baths. There are seven guest rooms in the main house and two in a connected house. One room is fully handicapped-accessible with a private entrance from the parking area. The large guest parlor is well stocked with books. The full breakfast may feature apple French toast or another specialty. A public boat landing, giving onto a cove, is a few blocks down the street, at Second Avenue.

MANOR HOUSE AND IRISH HOUSE AT PINTAIL POINT FARM

511 Pintail Point Lane
☎ 410-827-7029
Moderate to expensive

Located on the Pintail Point sporting preserve, the property offers a choice of renting either house in its entirety for a family group or separate rooms on a B&B basis. The smaller house sleeps six in three doubles with two shared baths, at $400 per night for the whole house. Bicycles are provided free of charge.

Kent Island

KENT MANOR INN

500 Kent Manor Drive
☎ 410-643-5757 or 800-820-4511
Moderate

One of the finest dining rooms on the Eastern Shore makes the Kent Manor Inn a good place for a weekend retreat.

The elegant building was constructed in stages, the earliest wing in 1820 and the center section just before the Civil War, and it was lovingly restored and rebuilt when it became an inn. Big, bright and airy rooms and the convenient location near the bay and the Bay Bridge make this a delightful place to stay. It's just south of US-50 on Kent Island within a minute or so of the highway, but set back enough to be away from the noise. The rooms, the menu, and the sunset view are every bit as good as when we first relaxed on the expansive veranda over a glass of wine a decade ago. It's on a 225-acre tidewater farm, with its own docks, walking trails and bicycles for guests' use.

Easton

TIDEWATER INN
101 East Dover Street
☎ 410-822-1300 or 800-237-8775
www.tidewaterinn.com
Moderate

There's an unmistakable Old South hunt club atmosphere in the sedate and elegant hotel that forms the centerpiece of Easton. You may find a pair of hunting dogs lying in front of the fireplace during bird season. The guest rooms and suites are warm and inviting and are furnished in reproduction Colonial furnishings. Make reservations early, especially during the Waterfowl Festival (see *Festivals & Events*, page 24).

ASHBY 1663 BED & BREAKFAST
27448 Ashby Drive
☎ 410-822-4235 or 800-458-3622, fax 410-822-9288, www.ashby1663.com
Expensive-deluxe

The mansion overlooks its own half-mile of riverbank through Palladian-style windows; fine antiques furnish the spacious public rooms. Outside, formal gardens lead to the river, where canoes and paddleboats are moored for guests use. The rooms are extraordinary, most with whirlpool tubs or working fireplaces and half of them with decks or patios. Other facilities include a pool, lighted tennis courts and exercise room.

St. Michaels

VICTORIANA INN
205 Cherry Street
☎ 410-745-3368
Inexpensive to moderate

The mansard-roofed inn is close to the Maritime Museum, a good location for strolling about the town. Its four guest rooms overlook the cove or the inn's garden. Most rooms share baths, except for the first floor room, the most luxurious, with a four-poster canopied bed and a fireplace. Rates include a hearty breakfast.

DR. DODSON HOUSE BED & BREAKFAST
200 Cherry Street
☎ 410-745-3691
Moderate

One of the two guest rooms is in the 1700s part of the house, the other in the 1860 part, and both have working fireplaces. The furnishings are period antiques and the beds are adorned with vintage quilts. Return to a warm fireside or enjoy evenings with wine and snacks in the parlor. You choose from a breakfast menu the night before and they deliver your wake-up coffee and a paper to your room. Guests can explore the town on one of their bicycles.

INN AT PERRY CABIN
308 Watkins Lane
☎ 410-745-2200 or 800-722-2949, fax 410-745-2200, www.perrycabin.com, perrycbn@friend.ly.net
Expensive-deluxe

Built by Commodore Perry's aide-de-camp, the mansion has one wing designed after Perry's cabin on board the USS *Niagara*. It was once owned by the husband of the late Laura Ashley, and the inn has many examples of her designs. As might be expected, the room décor is definitely feminine. Guests in the 41-room inn can enjoy its swimming pool, sauna, snooker room, boats and bicycles. The inn has its own fine-dining restaurant. Rates include afternoon tea and breakfast.

Tilghman Island

BLACK WALNUT POINT INN
☎ 410-886-2452, fax 410-886-2053
www.tilghmanisland.com/blackwalnut
Moderate

Tilghman is itself an isolated place, and Black Walnut Point is a remote part of Tilghman. The inn's grounds fill the private point, surrounded by the Chesapeake Bay. At dusk, guests have an unobstructed view of the setting sun. Rates are higher for the private riverside cottage, which has its own kitchen.

Oxford

THE 1876 HOUSE
110 North Morris Street
☎ 410-226-5496
Moderate

Oxford is a quiet town and the only central B&B we know of is this one. A beautifully restored home furnished in Queen Anne style, this is a good place to stay if you are arriving without a car, since the owners also operate a limousine service and will pick you up at BWI airport quite reasonably.

THE ROBERT MORRIS INN
Morris Street
☎ 410-226-5111, fax 410-226-5744
Moderate to expensive

You can trust the detailed room descriptions the innkeepers at the Robert Morris Inn provide; when rooms are small, they say so.

The inn is well known on the peninsula – and throughout the region, both for its historic rooms and for its excellent dining room. Guest rooms are well cared for and tastefully decorated, some with high, four-poster beds and simple Colonial décor. Views of the Tred Avon River highlight some rooms, which are in two buildings. In general, the best views are from the newer Sandaway Lodge, which has efficiencies in the higher price range. These have private porches over the water. The inn offers discounts for dinner and lodging packages.

Cambridge Area

COMMODORE'S COTTAGES
215 Glenburn Avenue
Cambridge
☎ 410-228-6938 or 800-228-6938
Moderate

This is probably one of the better buys in this whole part of Maryland. In addition to its fine guest quarters in separate cottages, it has its own private museum, also set in its beautiful gardens. A pergola shades benches where you can enjoy the towering trees – pine, crape myrtle, magnolia, walnut, pecan, a giant willow oak and three other oak varieties. The two comfortable guest cottages, reached by garden paths, sleep four and six respectively. The larger

Carriage House has a separate living room, bedroom and full kitchen. Both units are stocked with breakfast makings, and fresh baked goods are brought each evening. Minimum stay is two nights on weekends, three on holiday weekends.

SARKE PLANTATION
6033 Todd Point Road
Cambridge
☎ 410 228-7020 or 800-814-7020
Inexpensive

Off Route 343 (Washington Street) about 10 miles west of Cambridge, these lodgings sit on the Choptank River. A wide porch wraps around the house, with water views. A continental breakfast is included.

LOBLOLLY LANDINGS AND LODGE
2142 Liners Road
south of Church Creek
☎ 410-397-3033
Moderate

A cathedral-ceilinged room welcomes guests with a blazing fireplace set in a giant fieldstone wall. But the overwhelming memories of this combination B&B and retreat for people who enjoy hunting and fishing will revolve around the breakfasts. Designed to carry outdoors enthusiasts through a day of canoeing, fishing or hunting, the dishes are not only hearty and filling, but are beautifully prepared. We still talk about the crab quiche. The property offers an archery course of 17 stations with moving targets. Rooms are newly decorated in a tasteful blend of new and antique furnishings. New comfortable log cabins provide handicapped access, as well as more spacious lodging than the cozy king-bedded rooms in the main house. When booking be sure to get directions. The Lodge is some distance from the town of Church Creek and closer to the Blackwater refuge.

Near Salisbury

WHITEHAVEN B&B
23844 River Street
Whitehaven
☎ 410-873-3294
Inexpensive

The Whitehaven is actually a collection of small homes facing the Wicomico River a few steps from the river ferry. If you are coming from the south, be sure to get to the ferry before 5:15 in the winter, 7:30 in the summer, when it stops running. After that you have to approach from Salisbury. The attractive front rooms look out to the river. This is pretty remote country, but the B&B will arrange dinner at the Green Hill Yacht and Country Club and will take you there on their boat up the Wicomico River, and pick you up afterward. Ask for the key to the neighborhood museum.

Princess Anne

WATERLOO COUNTRY INN
28822 Mount Vernon Road
☎ 410-651-0883
Moderate

One of our favorite places to stay in the state, this brick inn overlooks a peaceful countryside with immediate access to tidal streams. Three canoes are available to guests who want to paddle on meandering water paths that wander through golden fields. There are also four bikes for exploring the surrounding back roads. A stately plantation-style home, the inn has been fully restored, its spaciously elegant and comfortable rooms furnished with fine antiques. The Swiss owners bring an undefinable continental finesse to the inn, which shows in many small ways. A gift shop in a former doctor's office adjoining the inn offers fine linens and handmade lingerie, among other unusual items. The gardens are as elegant as the inn, a wonderful place to relax after a paddle in the tidal estuary.

Breakfast at the Waterloo Country Inn is served on fine china and includes the classic European choice of a cheese plate and breads.

Snow Hill

RIVER HOUSE INN
201 East Market Street
☎ 410-632-2722
Moderate

This beautiful inn, right on the Pocomoke River, has its own dock and landing, making it perfect for paddlers. The rooms are large and nicely decorated, all with private baths. For a moment of relaxation guests have two parlors that are filled with books dealing with the area. The hosts enjoy good food themselves, and will advise guests on the best places to eat, one of which is across the street. They also have a full supply of menus to browse. The River House Inn is a short distance from the Pocomoke River Canoe Company, where guests can rent canoes and kayaks.

The River House Inn is one of a group that welcomes inn-to-inn canoe trippers.

Berlin

ATLANTIC HOTEL
2 North Main Street
☎ 410-641-3589, 800-814-7672
Moderate

Originally built in the 19th century, the gracefully restored hotel fits right into Berlin's classic downtown. Rooms have been beautifully restored to their Victorian splendor, with matching suites of furniture, most marble-topped with oak-leaf cluster pulls, carved or brass beds, claw-foot tubs. We like rooms 10, 11, 12 and 14, which overlook the quiet main street.

MERRY SHERWOOD PLANTATION
Route 113 south of Berlin
☎ 410-641-2112, 800-660-0358, fax 410-641-9528
Moderate

If you've always wanted to make believe that you live on an old plantation, this is the chance. Rescued from decay in the nick of time, this old home has been lovingly restored to its original antebellum splendor. Rooms and common areas are furnished with fine Victorian pieces, many of them unique. The inn is surrounded by a dozen acres of splendid gardens, which include Japanese trained pine and topiary shrubs. In addition to physical appeal, Merry Sherwood offers the sense of calm and repose appropriate to its architecture, with iced tea served in the garden on a hot summer afternoon, breakfast in a grand dining room and a fireplace to socialize around on brisk autumn evenings.

Ocean City

Some rooms at the Commander feature nicely framed enlargements of old postcards showing Ocean City in its heyday.

COMMANDER HOTEL
1404 Baltimore Avenue
☎ 410-289-6166 or 888-289-6166
Expensive

Rather than having only one side face the ocean, as most beach hotels do, these innovative hoteliers rebuilt in 1998 so that rooms on two sides could have ocean and boardwalk views. All rooms are suites with full sized refrigerators, plus microwaves, in-room safes, two double beds and a convertible couch. All of the rooms are handicapped-accessible. You can cook in your room or choose from a full breakfast buffet for $6.95.

INN ON THE OCEAN
1001 Atlantic Avenue
☎ 410-289-8894, 877-466-6662
www.innontheocean.com
Moderate to expensive

This six-room luxury accommodation sits overlooking the beach. Two of the rooms are on the first floor, the others are on the second. Each is tastefully decorated with fine fabrics.

ATLANTIC HOUSE
501 North Baltimore Avenue
☎ 410-289-2333
Inexpensive to moderate

A somewhat larger B&B, this too is an extremely attractive place to settle in for a while. There is an aura of the 1920s, with lots of wood softened with floral fabrics. Touches such as breakfast in their sunroom and a hot tub on the porch add to the B&B's

allure. The 11 rooms are nicely decorated and comfortable.

Best Places to Eat

DINING PRICE SCALE	
Inexpensive	Entrées are $10 or less
Moderate	Entrées are $11-$20
Expensive	Entrées are $21-$30

Grasonville & Kent Island Area

HARRIS CRAB HOUSE
Kent Narrows
Grasonville
☎ 410-824-9500
Moderate

Expect a wait at Harris Crab House, especially on Saturday nights, since locals like this place.

Harris's is best known for their crabs, and for good reason. Brown paper covers the tables and you get paper towels, much better than napkins when you're consuming messy foods like crabs. The dining room isn't fancy, which makes it just about the right atmosphere. A half-dozen impeccably fresh soft crabs with onion rings, coleslaw and a muffin are $15, or a half-pound of boiled shrimp with two sides is $13. Tea, coffee and soft drinks include unlimited refills. There is a small, very crowded, bar upstairs. Harris's opens at 11 am daily.

BLUE CRAB BASICS

- Blue crabs, the Chesapeake specialty, turn red when they are cooked.
- Crabs are meatier and best eaten when the moon is full, before they shed their shell.
- Crab cakes should be made with backfin meat only.
- In winter hibernating crabs burrow in the mud at the bottom of the bay.
- Crab season begins in March, and by April all the crab houses are open and ready for business.
- Saltwater hardens the crab's shell.

HEMINGWAY'S
Foot of the Chesapeake Bay Bridge
☎ 410-643-CRAB
Moderate

This is an upscale seafood restaurant, where the food is well prepared and has more flair than other run-of-the-mill seafood restaurants that line US 50 east of the bridge. Mushroom caps are filled with escargot and crabmeat, crab and artichoke dip is served in a boule of sourdough bread and shrimp are served Spanish-style, sautéed in olive oil and garlic. Entrées may include salmon and portobello mushrooms baked in phyllo, sesame-crusted rockfish, flounder stuffed with shrimp mousse, or grilled catfish with béarnaise. Hemingway's is open year-round, daily, from 11 am.

Hungry? At Hemingway's, the Chesapeake Sampler (crab cake, duck breast, clams and two styles of oysters) is a real plateful.

KENT MANOR INN
500 Kent Manor Drive
☎ 410-643-5757 or 800-820-4511
Moderate to expensive

We found this place when it was just opening and have been sending our Annapolis friends here ever since. It's on Kent Island, a short way from the bridge and south of US-50. Dining rooms are small, nicely decorated and are in the old part of the Inn, a perfect place for a special dinner. For starters, we think that they just might have the best crab cakes around; don't miss the chance to sample them. Entrées are varied and could feature buffalo, roast duck or a magnificent creation filled with local seafood. Lunch and dinner are served daily.

Easton

TIDEWATER INN
101 East Dover Street
☎ 410-822-1300 or 800-237-8775
Moderate to expensive

The dining room of this inn is a legend – and for good reason. It is a warm and inviting place that creates a fitting atmosphere for savoring the chef's outstanding shore specialties. This is definitely on the shortlist of best places to order crab cakes. If you enjoy buffets (we don't), take advantage of their bountiful buffet brunch on weekends.

HANGAR CAFE
Easton Airport
☎ 410-820-6631
Inexpensive

We like to stop for a no-nonsense breakfast at this diner with a view of planes landing and taking off. Breakfast enough to keep you running all day is under $3. The café is open daily 6 am to 3 pm.

If you're going for a plane ride in the World War II-era biplane at the airport, you get a 10% discount at the Hangar Café.

RESTAURANT COLUMBIA
28 South Washington Street
☎ 410-770-5172
Moderate

Elegant dishes – autumn specials might include quail stuffed with wild rice and pecans – are served in a stylishly decorated townhouse setting.

St. Michaels

SUDDENLY LAST SUMMER
106 North Talbot Street
☎ 410-745-5882
Inexpensive to moderate

With fewer than a dozen tables, this cozy and intimate restaurant concentrates on its excellent food. If you are looking for a change from the steady round of traditional Eastern Shore seafood restaurants, this is the place. The Euro-California menu is complemented by a well-chosen wine list. Look for dishes such as rabbit or breast of duck with peppercorns. Sunday brunch is a specialty, and live music is provided by a local guitarist on Friday and Saturday evenings.

Tilghman Island

HARRISON'S
Route 33
☎ 410-886-2123
Moderate

The island has the largest fishing fleet and sportfishing charter fleet on the bay, and Harrison's is possibly the bay's best-known seafood restaurant. People come from all around the bay, often by special excursion boats that bring them from the western shore. They don't come for fancy delicate presentations, but for hearty, often fried dinners of impeccably fresh seafood, served family-style. The Eastern Shore dinner combines traditional Maryland fried chicken with crab cakes or you can order several other combination dinners – all under $20. And, of course, you can attack a tray full of steamed crabs with a wooden mallet here. Dine indoors, or in good weather on the deck overlooking the water where your dinner was recently swimming.

Oxford

LE ZINC
101 Mill Street
☎ 410-226-5776
Moderate

At Le Zinc, Wednesday and Thursday are pasta nights, with several innovative pasta entrées on the menu.

Dark and stylish décor and its constantly changing menu give this small restaurant a European feel. There's no telling what will be on the evening's menu, but it will be varied and each dish will have some out-of-the-ordinary touch: peppered mackerel might be enlivened with fresh horseradish cream, oysters served with scallion-lime tartar sauce or tuna crusted in cracked pepper and served with citrus butter. There are usually about six entrées each day. Le Zinc is open Tuesday through Saturday from 6 pm.

THE ROBERT MORRIS INN
Morris Street
☎ 410-226-5111, fax 410-226-5744
Moderate to expensive

We won't admit how long ago it was that we first sampled the crab cakes at the Robert Morris, but it was long before James Michener proclaimed them the best on the Eastern Shore. The old-fashioned and gracious dining room serves a variety of other dishes, depending heavily, but not exclusively, on local seafood. Breakfast is served daily, as well. Dinner is served daily 6-9, lunch noon-3, April through November; winter hours vary.

PIER STREET
West Pier Street
☎ 410-745-3737
Inexpensive to moderate

Mounds of steamed crabs and the rockfish, fresh from the Tred Avon River, are piled on picnic tables on the deck overlooking the water. You can sail right to the door and use one of their guest slips while you eat lunch or dinner. Pier Street is open only April through October.

Cambridge

SNAPPERS WATERFRONT CAFE
112 Commerce Street
☎ 410-228-0112
Moderate

You can eat Mexican and Cajun-inspired dishes inside or outside. Their deck overlooks the historic skipjack *Lady Katie* (see page 294). Snappers is open Monday through Saturday, 11 am-10 pm; Sunday, 11-9.

McGUIGAN'S PUB
411 Muse Street
☎ 410-228-7110
Inexpensive to moderate

Scottish and traditional English pub food – hearty beef stew, fish & chips – are served in a like atmosphere. Good ales and stout on tap.

PORTSIDE SEAFOOD RESTAURANT
201 Trenton Street
☎ 410-228-9007
Moderate

Boat slips are available for those who arrive at Portside by sea.

Serving local seafood at the foot of Creek Bridge, Portside has curtains to enclose the deck over the water, extending its "outdoor" season. Portside is open Tuesday-Sunday for lunch and dinner.

Hooper Island

OLD SALTY'S
☎ 410-397-3752
Inexpensive to moderate

Located on a barrier island in the Chesapeake Bay, south of the Blackwater National Wildlife Refuge, this place is popular with local residents, serving homestyle dishes – veal patties, chicken and dumplings – as well as a heaping seafood platter (a bargain at $12). Lunch specials offer full meals on a daily schedule that includes ham with cabbage on Saturday. Salty's is open Wednesday through Monday for lunch and dinner.

Salisbury

ENGLISH'S FAMILY RESTAURANT
South Salisbury Boulevard (US-13 South)
No phone
Inexpensive to moderate

English's is known for its sweet potato biscuits – and rightly. These are but one of the Eastern Shore specialties dished up in this original O'Mahoney Diner. The food here is good, plentiful and available to take out; a dozen biscuits costs about $3.

AESOP'S TABLE
124 North Division Street
☎ 410-742-6600
Inexpensive

Aesop's Table is in an antiques shop, which invites browsing while you wait for your sandwich.

A local favorite for breakfast and lunch. The coffee bar serves espresso, café latte and cappuccino (not common on the Eastern Shore) to go with your bagels, muffins or rolls; at lunch they serve beer and wine.

WATERMAN'S COVE
925 Snow Hill Road
☎ 410-456-1400
Inexpensive to moderate

The Eastern Shore is noted for good seafood, and this place is known as among the best. The chef here excels at the delicate art of deciding the exact moment to remove seafood from the heat. Crabs here are served any way you like them: in the shell, soft-shell, or in some of the best crab cakes around. Look here, too, for the other bay specialty – oysters. For the non-seafood types there are prime rib and chicken dishes. For lunch they have a big list of sandwiches, most of which are under $6.

LEGENDS
Downtown Plaza
☎ 410-749-7717
Moderate

Influences from many cuisines fill the menu of the area's most innovative choice for fine dining. The menu of interesting and flavorful New American dishes could include blackened pork chop in onion marmalade or a tuna steak grilled with lemon pepper. The menu will vary with the season, taking advantage of the freshest produce from local farms.

CACTUS TAVERNA

2420 North Salisbury Boulevard
☎ 410-548-1254
Inexpensive-moderate

The Cactus Taverna is owned by the same family that owns English's.

The name tells you what to expect from the food. Try lamb chops served with chipotle sauce or giant shrimp grilled in their shells and served with a raspberry sauce. They have entertainment nightly.

RED ROOST

Clara Road
Whitehaven (southwest of Salisbury)
☎ 410-546-5443, 800-953-5443
Inexpensive

Follow the road from the Whitehaven ferry landing, turn left onto Capitola Road and again onto Clara Road, where you will see signs to the Red Roost. It's in the middle of nowhere.

A crab feast in a former chicken coop sums up the split personality and character of the Eastern Shore. The Roost is a tradition in the area and a favorite place to go for an evening out. Along with the crabs, you'll find ribs, chicken, and corn on the cob on the menu, but blue crab is really king. On Wednesday nights you can join in a sing-along with the Backfin Banjo Band. The Roost is open daily during the summer, weekends in spring and fall, and is closed November through March.

Princess Anne

DAVID'S AT WATERLOO
28822 Mount Vernon Road
At the Waterloo Country Inn
☎ 410-651-0883
Moderate to expensive

The dining room at David's is small and popular, so reservations are recommended.

This is a fine dining experience best enjoyed while staying as a guest at the inn, but if you are not a guest you still should not miss it. The dining room has the refined charm of the 18th century, and the food is first rate. The menu changes with the seasons and the chef focuses on the freshest locally produced ingredients. And the chef puts them together in original and thoughtful ways with particular attention to vegetables. We were very happy with a filet served with crabmeat-stuffed shrimp.

Snow Hill

SNOW HILL INN
East Market Street
☎ 410-632-2102
Moderate

In the very pleasant town of Snow Hill, the inn has an excellent reputation as one of the best places to eat in the region. Some examples of local seafood you might expect to find on the menu are petit filets topped with Maryland crab, crab imperial and scallops with mushrooms and wine. A few land meats are always featured, too; always at least one rendition of the locally grown Delmarva chicken. The restaurant is right in the center of town opposite the

River Inn, very handy for guests staying there. Snow Hill Inn is open for dinner Monday through Saturday evenings.

Berlin

THE ATLANTIC HOTEL
2 North Main Street
☎ 410-641-3589, 800-814-7672
Main dining room, moderate-expensive;
Drummer's, moderate

We love the grace and charm of fine old hotel dining rooms and the restored dining room of this hotel is a beauty. The menu is equally pleasant, with updated versions of continental dishes, well prepared and nicely served. Look for choices such as salmon bouillabaisse, veal medallions or their own take on crab cakes. They have a nice wine list. The other dining room is the **Drummer's Café**, a bit less formal but with good lunch and dinner choices.

Crisfield

CAPTAIN'S GALLEY
1021 Main Street (facing the ferry pier)
☎ 410-968-1636 or 800-CRAB-MIX
Moderate-expensive

Crisfield is located on a point of land in the southwestern portion of Maryland's Eastern Shore, just north of Virginia's Tangier Island, and straddling Tangier and Pocomoke Sounds.

Much of the food here comes right from the docks where watermen unload their catch every day. The crab cakes here are baked, broiled or fried, as you wish. They have other choices for people who don't like seafood, but why go to the Eastern Shore's primary crab port to eat steak? They have an outdoor crab deck in the summer.

Ocean City

PHILLIPS BY THE SEA
Beach Plaza Hotel
Boardwalk at 13th Street
☎ 410-289-9121
Moderate

The Phillips family is from Ocean City, and their restaurants have sprung up in many places, but Ocean City was their first. The specialty is seafood with well prepared versions of some of the classics, such as flounder stuffed with crabmeat, fried oysters (nice and juicy), crab cakes, lump crab au gratin and grilled or blackened tuna. The food is good, the atmosphere nice.

HARRISON'S HARBOR WATCH
On the Inlet
☎ 410-219-5121
Moderate

A huge list of fish can be ordered broiled, baked or grilled, as you like, or you can choose other traditional seafood options. The food is fresh and well prepared; they know how to treat sea critters. Tagalongs who don't do fish will find options such as pasta dishes and vegetarian entrées.

REFLECTIONS
Holiday Inn
Coastal Highway at 6th Street
☎ 410-524-5252
Moderate

One of the better hotel dining rooms, Reflections features a style that combines classic French with New American. Nice food pairings might include grilled salmon topped with artichoke hearts, shrimp and béarnaise, or pork tenderloin served over fried leeks in a sauce of green peppercorn and shallot. They also have a few flambéed items for dining room drama.

WINDOWS ON THE BAY
61st Street
☎ 410-723-3463
Moderate to expensive

Seafood with a different touch is the key to the menu here. Choices such as shrimp marsala and flounder à l'orange separate Windows from the rest of the seafood restaurants. The non-seafood side is also interesting, with options that might include roast duckling with peaches and port, or Wiener schnitzel. The restaurant overlooks the bay, as you might have guessed.

KITTY HAWK GRILL
Bayside at 46th Street
☎ 410-723-5966
Moderate

Nouvelle creations integrate Chesapeake Bay foods and vegetables into a cohesive dining experience. A cuisine influenced by Asia and California shines with shrimp and artichoke over linguine or marinated breast of chicken served with steamed veggies and black bean salsa.

West to the Mountains

Orientation

This section is west and northwest of Baltimore. If you have tired of the bay and all those crab dinners, you'll appreciate the rolling farmlands that rise to Maryland's share of the Appalachian mountains, just west of Frederick. If you thought that all Maryland was like the corridor between Baltimore and Washington, you have a surprise waiting for you in the large areas of open fields and meadows, forests and wild-running streams. There is considerable farming still in this area that once fed the Baltimore-Washington area with enough surplus to ship off to the Northeast and Europe.

The closer one gets to the Appalachians the steeper and more rugged the hills. The famed **Appalachian Trail** passes through Maryland from Highfield, Pennsylvania, to a point close to Harpers Ferry, in West Virginia.

History

Some of the first surges of the westward expansion took place here, with settlements in the fertile inland farmlands. These lands began to supply food and products needed by the new and growing United

States. Demand for these items eventually led to the construction of the **Chesapeake and Ohio Canal**. This waterway – the concept was George Washington's – was built early in the 19th century to bring coal and produce from more western regions to East Coast markets. It was also the age of **railroads**, and the Baltimore and Ohio finally beat out the canal for the right to carry western produce.

This region figured prominently in the **Civil War**. The Confederacy saw it as a route to bring the war into the north and to capture the city of Washington DC. At several times military thrusts from the area around Harpers Ferry sallied deep into the north. The **Battle of Antietam** (Sharpsburg) took place here, and the grand march of General Lee to Gettysburg moved through the city of Frederick and the area around it. Southeast of Frederick, the **Battle of Monocacy** saved the city of Washington from capture.

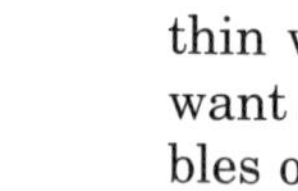

Getting Here & Getting Around

I-70 will carry you all the way from Baltimore to the thin waistline of Maryland at Hancock, but if you want a slower paced road, take **Route 26**, which ambles out of Baltimore just north of I-70 and goes to Frederick. **Frederick** is a nice combination of big and small town with a good share of attractions, but a leisurely pace. From Frederick, **US-15** heads north to **Thurmont**, through the Catoctin area, the locale of the Presidential retreat at Camp David. From **Emmitsburg**, just south of the Pennsylvania bor-

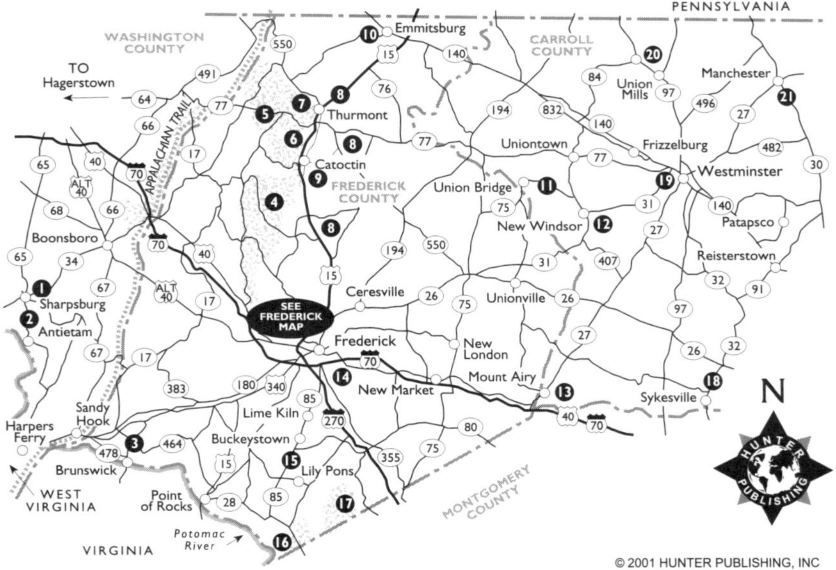

West to the Mountains

1. Antietam National Battlefield
2. John Brown Museum; Restoration Museum; Black Voices Museum
3. Brunswick Railroad Museum
4. Cunningham Falls State Park
5. Cunningham Falls
6. Catoctin Wildlife Preserve & Zoo;
7. Catoctin Mountain National Park
8 Covered Bridges (three locations)
9. Catoctin Iron Furnace
10. Shrine of Saint Elizabeth Ann Seton
11. Western Maryland Railway Museum
12. Robert Strawbridge House
13. Linganore Winecellars
14. Monocacy Battlefield
15. Lilypons Water Garden
16. Monocacy Aqueduct
17. Sugarloaf Mountain Natural Area
18. Sykesville Gate House Museum of History; Sykesville Railroad Station
19. Carroll County Court House; Old Jail; Carroll County Farm Museum
20. Union Mills Homestead
21. Cygnus Wine Cellars

der, **Route 140** travels southeast to **Westminster**, one of the most attractive and pleasant towns in the state.

To reach Westminster, take Route 140 from the northwest corner of Baltimore. It's also called Reisterstown Road. An alternative is to pick up the Beltway on the west side of Baltimore and then take **I-795** north past Reisterstown, following **Route 140** when the highway ends.

For trips to the Frederick area , take **I-70** from Baltimore. You can reach it from **Franklin Street**, near the harbor. Franklin Street will become Edmonston Avenue, and signs will direct you to I-70.

Information Sources

The Tourism Council of Frederick County, 19 East Church Street, Frederick, ☎ 301-228-2888 or 800-999-3613; www.visitfrederick.org.

Carroll County Visitors Center, 210 East Main Street, Westminster, ☎ 410-848-1388 or 800-272-1933; www.carr.org/tourism.

> ★ **TIP**
>
> The handy annual calendar of events from the Carroll County Visitor Center includes church and firehouse suppers, craft fairs, concerts, herb festivals, musical performances and holiday events.

Sunup to Sundown

From Baltimore, take scenic Route 26, which runs through the gently rolling countryside, coming into **Frederick** from the north. Take the faster I-70 to Frederick if time is a problem. Two or three days in Frederick allows for a day-trip down US 340 to **Harpers Ferry** and back up through **Sharpsburg** to Frederick. An extra day allows for a two-day trip on this route, adding the **Monocacy Battlefield**, **Lilypons Water Gardens** and the attractions along the C&O Canal east of Harpers Ferry. From Frederick, go north on US-15, stopping at **Catoctin Park**, the nearby **zoo** and **iron furnace**, and at Cunningham Falls. In Emmitsburg, see the **Basilica of the National Shrine of Saint Elizabeth Ann Seton**. From there, travel southeast on Route 140 to **Westminster**. Enjoy Westminster before continuing down Route 140 to Baltimore.

Museums

Just Outside Baltimore

SYKESVILLE GATE HOUSE MUSEUM OF HISTORY
7283 Cooper Drive
Sykesville
☎ 410-549-5150

The museum has a collection of materials, including historic photographs, related to the town's past and the Baltimore & Ohio Railroad. The Historic District Commission operates the museum in the recently restored gatehouse to the State Hospital. Stop at the Sykesville Railroad Station (now Baldwin's Station Restaurant; see *Best Places to Eat*) in the center of town to inspect the progress of their locomotive restoration. They are open Wednesday and Sunday, 1-6.

Frederick

DELAPLAINE VISUAL ARTS CENTER
40 South Carroll Street
☎ 301-698-0656
www.delaplaine.org

Situated at the head of Carroll Creek Linear Park, the Visual Arts Center is central to the city's renovation plan. The rehabilitated old factory building, with its high ceilings and rough textures is a perfect setting for the works exhibited here. The exhibit space features changing shows of quality art, mostly contemporary and by local artists. This also serves as the headquarters of the Frederick County Art Association which has a number of art related programs.

NATIONAL MUSEUM OF CIVIL WAR MEDICINE
48 East Patrick Street
☎ 301-695-1864, fax 301-695-6823
www.civilwarmed.org
Admission: $6.50, adults; $6, seniors; $4.50, children 10-16; under 10, free

The story told here is the tale of the men and women of both sides of the Civil War who struggled to save the lives of the wounded and dying. This part of Maryland was at the center of the war for most of its

Frederick

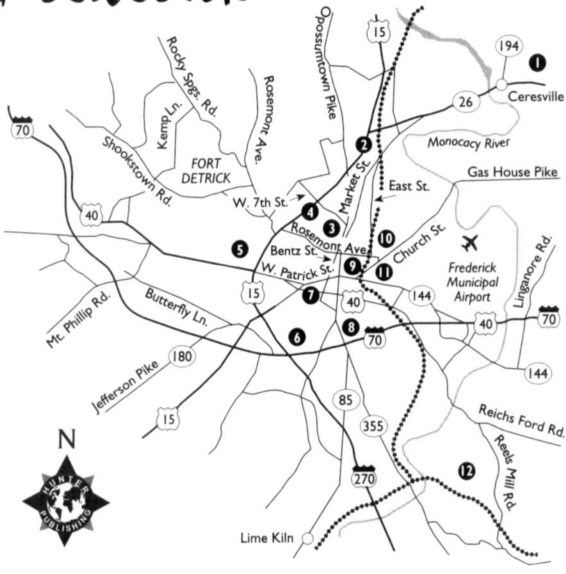

1. Beatty Cramer Architectural Museum
2. Rose Hill Manor
3. Roger Brooke Taney House; Francis Scott Key Museum
4. Baker Park
5. Schifferstadt Architectural Museum
6. Carrollton Park
7. Barbara Fritchie House
8. Hessian Barracks
9. Wineburg Center for the Arts; Linear Park; Delaplaine Visual Arts Center
10. Historical Society of Frederick County
11. National Museum of Civil War Medicine
12. Monocacy National Battlefield

duration – Frederick itself was the scene of several engagements. The tales of surgeons, doctors, nurses, hospitals and medical stewards are told through their words, photographs and the tools they used. On Saturday and Sunday afternoons or evenings, special programs are presented on topics such as the role of nurses, the caregivers, the battlefield embalmer or camp life. Outside the museum's headquarters on East Patrick Street, re-enactors often stage live-action re-creations of an actual battle that took place on this street. Museum hours are Monday through Saturday, 10-5; Sunday, 11-5; they are closed on major holidays.

BARBARA FRITCHIE HOUSE
154 West Patrick Street
☎ 301-698-0630
Admission: $2, adults; $1.50, children and seniors

When Stonewall Jackson entered Frederick, 90-year-old Barbara Fritchie defied him by proudly flying the Union flag. Her challenge to him made her a heroine of the Union cause and his respectful treatment of her made him a symbol of Southern honor. It's rare indeed that two adversaries in a war each emerges from a confrontation looking so good. Although the original brick house was destroyed years ago in a flood, the present structure is a faithful reconstruction. The house is open April through September only, on Mondays and Thursday-Saturday, 10-4; Sunday, 1-4 (last tour at 3:30).

ROGER BROOKE TANEY HOUSE AND FRANCIS SCOTT KEY MUSEUM
121 South Bentz Street
☎ 301-663-8687

Roger Taney is best remembered as the Supreme Court Justice who wrote the Dred Scott decision in 1857.

Roger Taney was Chief Justice of the US Supreme Court and his brother-in-law and law partner was Francis Scott Key. The museum is devoted to the lives of both of these historic figures. There is an elaborate century-old statue of Francis Scott Key at Mount Olivet Cemetery, 515 South Market Street in Frederick, where both he and Barbara Fritchie are buried. The museum is open April through October, by appointment only.

THE HISTORICAL SOCIETY OF FREDERICK COUNTY
24 East Church Street
☎ 301-663-1188
www.fwp.net/hsfc

The Society has its headquarters in a fine old 1820s home. The building is decorated with period furniture, paintings, tapestries and pottery as well as other items from their collections of local history. They are open Monday through Saturday, 10-4; Sunday, 1-4; closed during the first two weeks of January and on major holidays.

SCHIFFERSTADT ARCHITECTURAL MUSEUM
1110 Rosemont Avenue
☎ 301-663-3885
Donations requested for tours

Noted as a classic example of German Colonial architecture, this fine old two-story sandstone home was built by Joseph Brunner in 1756. Its thick stone walls, unusual eaves, a built-in German iron stove, wishbone chimneys and other unusual features make it particularly interesting, and quite unlike other old homes in the area. The Schifferstadt is open mid-April to mid-December, Tuesday through Saturday, 10-4.

BEATTY CRAMER ARCHITECTURAL MUSEUM
Route 26, east of Ceresville
☎ 301-293-2215

This museum is in the only building in Frederick County that dates as far back as 1748, when it was built. Among other unique attributes, the museum has a well house and smokehouse on the property. The museum is located just past the bridge over Israel's Creek, on the left. It is open April to November, Saturday only, 10-4.

Brunswick

BRUNSWICK RAILROAD MUSEUM
40 West Potomac Street
☎ 301-834-7100
www.bhs.edu/rrmus.rrmus

Brunswick was a center for both the railroad and C&O Canal in its heyday. The museum captures those times in three floors of exhibits. The history of the railroad and its effect on the town are shown through little details – tools, soot-stained clothing, period rooms, china from a dining car. Brunswick once had a 33-mile-long classification yard and a 16-bay roundhouse; it was such a busy rail center that trains passed through town every five minutes during World War II. An HO-gauge model railroad with landmarks from the '50s and '60s re-creates the railroad from Brunswick to Union Station in Washington. Visitors can change switches, work lights and move trains in the authentically re-created landscape. The third floor of this appealing museum separates the kids of all ages – those who stop and play with the trains – from the grown-ups. Count us with the kids. The Railroad Museum is open weekends, year-round, and Tuesday-Saturday, from June-October. Hours vary; call before you visit.

Westminster Area

Westminster's tree-shaded streets are lined with fine homes, mostly in the vernacular styles common to this part of northern Maryland and eastern Pennsylvania. The earlier homes in the center of town have simple square lines; later ones show the influence of the Pennsylvania Germans, with rounded windows. The Flemish bond brickwork is typical of the Georgian style, as it was interpreted in Pennsylvania.

Parking in downtown Westminster is free on weekends and after 3 pm on weekdays.

CARROLL COUNTY FARM MUSEUM
500 South Center Street
☎ 410-876-2667, 848-7775 or 800-654-4645
Admission: $3, adults; $2, seniors and children; under six, free

Located in the restored former county poor farm, this is a fine museum filled with the artifacts of rural Maryland life. Its collections of 19th- and early 20th-century agricultural techniques and technology are outstanding, housed in the brick residence, fine barns and outbuildings. The almshouse serves as the Living History Center. The tinsmith and blacksmith shops have demonstrations of techniques, and upstairs in the barn is a large collection of horse-drawn vehicles. Docents demonstrate activities from baking and needlework to animal husbandry and planting. Museum hours are noon-5, Saturdays and Sundays, from May through October, and Tuesdays through Fridays, 10-4, in July and August.

WESTERN MARYLAND RAILWAY MUSEUM
Union Bridge (Route 75)
west of Westminster
☎ 410-775-0150

In the center of town, it's hard to miss the old depot, which in 1902 was the headquarters of the of the Western Maryland Railroad. Inside is a wide collection of railroad memorabilia and artifacts, including Callers Boards and an N-scale model railroad showing parts of the Western Maryland route. The Museum is operated by the Western Maryland Railway Historical Society; it is open Sundays, 1-4.

Historic Sites

Frederick Area

ROSE HILL MANOR
1611 North Market Street
☎ 301-694-1646

The large 18th-century plantation house was the home of Thomas Johnson, Maryland's first elected governor. The Farm Museum shows the tools and implements of early agriculture with special events and children's programs. Rose Hill is open Monday-Saturday, 10-4; and Sunday, 1-4, from April through October; and weekends only in November.

MONOCACY NATIONAL BATTLEFIELD

Route 355, off I-70
southeast of Frederick
☎ 301-662-3515
Free

Confederate troops numbering 16,000, under General Jubal Early, marched on Washington in 1864 after collecting a ransom for not burning Frederick. Three miles outside of town they met up with 5,800 Union troops under the command of General Lew Wallace. While the battle was lost by the Union forces, their effort stopped the attempt to capture Washington DC. An orientation program at the Visitors Center provides the history; self-guided tour maps help you explore the battlefield. The battlefield is open daily, 8-4:30, from April 1 through October 31; until 5:30 on weekends from Memorial Day to Labor Day; and 8-4:30, Wednesday through Sunday only, from November through March.

Potomac River Area

ANTIETAM NATIONAL BATTLEFIELD

Route 65
Sharpsburg
☎ 301-432-5124
Admission: $4

The bloodiest single day of battle during the Civil War took place in this peaceful spot along Antietam Creek. Deaths on both sides totaled 22,000 men. The battlefield is now rolling, open countryside, but plans call for the restoration of the fields and forests to their 1862 appearance. The primary features are the **Dunker Church**, site of the first clashes in the early hours, the **Sunken Road** where the next phase of battle occurred, and **Burnside Bridge,** where Union troops finally crossed after several attempts, and forced Robert E. Lee to withdraw to Sharpsburg. From the heights overlooking the stone bridge it is easy to imagine the pandemonium as Union troops repeatedly tried to cross under fire from the banking above.

The visitors center has a film, orientation talk and an eight-mile self-guided tour. There is also a guided two-hour caravan tour free with park entrance. Battlefield Walks cover subjects ranging from Civil War flags to artillery. The small museum in the visitors center displays uniforms, equipment, personal items and a searchable archive of those who fought here. In summer the museum is open daily, 8:30-6; in winter, daily, 8:30-5; closed on major holidays.

HARPERS FERRY NATIONAL HISTORIC PARK

Across the Potomac, in West Virginia
☎ 304-535-6223
Admission: $5 per vehicle

The lower part of this town, overlooking the confluence of the Potomac and Shenandoah Rivers is entirely in the hands of the National Park Service. Visitors park in lots at the edge of town and are bused to the main street of the restored area (there is no public parking within the town of Harpers Ferry).

DID YOU KNOW?

Known for the role it played in the Civil War, Harpers Ferry is where John Brown and his party stood off the United States Army for two days in 1859, after raiding the military arsenal there.

A reconstruction of the armory where John Brown's famous standoff occurred is open. Other buildings contain exhibits on the general store, the ecology of the river, and a chronology of John Brown's raid. Most exhibits are done in pictures and educational signboards; artifacts are few and live interpretation scarce, but we found two exhibits of particular merit. The **Restoration Museum** shows methods used by archaeologists to date and learn about the history of buildings. The second is the **Black Voices Museum**, which brings life to the people who once lived here. Interactive displays use readings from letters, reminiscences and contemporary descriptions to chronicle the life of blacks, both slave and free. The park is open daily, 8-5; the admission is paid at the visitors center at the parking lot outside of the town of Harpers Ferry, and it includes the bus fare into town.

THE KENNEDY FARM
2406 Chestnut Grove Road
Sharpsburg
www.johnbrown.org; e-mail captain@johnbrown.org
Free admission

The Kennedy Farm is the small, unpretentious place where John Brown met and plotted with his followers. The farm is outside the village of Sandy Hook off

US-340, approximately five miles north of Harpers Ferry, and is well signposted from town. It is on the Maryland side of the Potomac. A rough sandstone monument records the fate of the members of the group that assembled here with him during the summer of 1859. The farmhouse, like others nearby, is built of chinked log above a first floor of stacked fieldstone. The grounds are open to the public.

Thurmont Area

CATOCTIN IRON FURNACE
Cunningham Falls State Park
14039 Catoctin Hollow Road (Route 806)
☎ 301-271-7574

This historic and well-preserved iron furnace was built and put into operation in 1776. During the American Revolution it provided needed cannonballs and other iron products. After the war it made tools and household goods for farmers and households thereafter until it finally closed in 1903. The ironworks provided 100 tons of shells for use at Yorktown alone, and one of the furnaces produced 3,300 tons of pig iron annually. These huge furnaces are in surprisingly good repair. The ruins of the ironmaster's house with brick and stone fireplaces intact are nearby.

COVERED BRIDGES
Three of the five covered bridges remaining in Maryland are in the Thurmont area, two of them close to Catoctin. Traveling north from Frederick on US-15, look for **Roddy Road Covered Bridge** on Roddy Road, which turns off US-15 about four miles north of the Catoctin Iron Furnace. The **King Post Truss**

Bridge crosses Owens Creek, less than a half-mile east from the main road. Off Route 77 to the east of Thurmont there is another covered bridge. Its road is marked by a "Red Dot #19" sign. It has a picnic area and playground alongside the creek.

Emmitsburg

BASILICA OF THE NATIONAL SHRINE OF SAINT ELIZABETH ANN SETON

333 South Seton Avenue
☎ 301-447-6606
www.setonshrine.org

The first American Roman Catholic to be canonized was Elizabeth Ann Seton. Known as Mother Seton, she founded the Sisters of Charity of Saint Joseph in 1809 and was noted for the many good works performed during her lifetime. The Basilica was built in 1965 in anticipation of her canonization and was designated a minor basilica in 1991 by Pope John Paul II.

Westminster Area

THE EPISCOPAL CHURCH OF THE ASCENSION

The church, opposite the courthouse in Westminster, was built in 1854. Its needlepoint-covered kneelers were designed by the same artist as those in the National Cathedral in Washington DC. Francis Scott Key contributed to the construction of the church, and taught America's first Sunday School for Blacks here. Adjacent to the church is its atmospheric churchyard with the split stone tomb of Legh Master, the subject of several local ghost stories. Nearby, under a tree, is the tomb of Lt. William Murray, who was killed in Jeb Stuart's raid. The church is open dawn to dusk.

THE STORY OF LEGH MASTER

In the mid-18th century, an Englishman, Legh Master, abandoned his family and settled in Westminster. A man of wealth, greed and avarice, he had an iron furnace and an estate with 50 slaves. Master attempted to seduce a slave, and when she refused he beat her. When her fellow slave and lover tried to protect her, Master had him thrown into the iron furnace, and, it was rumored, had the woman bricked into an old chimney of his mansion. After a fire in the house in the 1930s, a brick wall was opened, revealing the skeleton of a Black female inside. Legh Master was buried on his plantation, but after his coffin repeatedly rose to the surface it was moved to the churchyard of Ascension Episcopal Church in Westminster. Within weeks of his re-burial the heavy stone tablet on his tomb split in half, further fanning the rumors of his ghostly escapades. His house, Avondale, is privately owned, but our local relatives tell us the family still has a difficult time getting babysitters.

THE CARROLL COUNTY COURT HOUSE

The court house, a stately brick building in the Georgian style, has what has been called one of the 10 most beautiful courtrooms in America. It contains the original clerk's desk and the jurors chairs, with arms carved by local farmers. Ask at the Tourist Office for guided weekend tours. A block behind the courthouse is the Old Jail, unmistakable among the finer residences that surround it. The Sheriff lived on the top floor, prisoners in the basement.

ROBERT STRAWBRIDGE HOUSE
2650 Strawbridge Lane
New Windsor
☎ 410-635-2600
Donations welcome

New Windsor, west of Westminster, is considered to be the home of American Methodism. The four buildings are all closely associated with the pioneering ministry of Robert Strawbridge, who was an early founder of American Methodism. The Strawbridge house and farm, the John Evans House – home of the first American convert to Methodism, a replica of the log meetinghouse and the Asbury Smith Visitor Center are all close to one another. A map is available at the visitors center showing the location of other related historic buildings and sites in the area. Tours are given from April to October; the buildings are open year-round.

UNION MILLS HOMESTEAD
3311 Littlestown Pike, Union Mills (on Route 97, north of Westminster)
☎ 410-848-2288
Admission: $2.50, adults; $1.50, ages six-12

This fascinating old home was built in 1797 by Andrew and David Shriver, who also erected a grist mill and a sawmill. Adding a tannery to their holdings later, they and their descendants continued to add to the house until it grew from six to 23 rooms. The house contains the furnishings and personal belongings of over 200 years of Shrivers, one of whom served in the John F. Kennedy administration. Union Mills is open Tuesday-Friday, 10-4; Saturday-Sunday, noon-4, from June 1 through September 1.

UNIONTOWN

Nearby Uniontown, west of Westminster, has a nice main street lined with buildings representing the entire 19th century. You will find brick, wood, log, Dutch stepped gables and an interesting example of a quoined house. The settlement of **Frizzellburg**, on Route 823, has more fine old homes and two antiques shops at its crossroads center.

Gardens & Parks

Frederick Area

LILYPONS WATER GARDENS
6800 Lilypons Road, Route 85
Buckeystown

The gardens, named for the famed petite French opera diva of the mid-20th-century, grow and sell an amazing array of aquatic plants. The ponds along the Monocacy River bank are dotted with water lilies, in shades from white through yellows, pinks and brilliant reds. The display garden, with pools and stone paths around a gazebo, is handsomely landscaped to show settings for water plants. Visitors can wander past the raising ponds, where all the varieties are labeled, and perhaps admire a great blue heron as it wades or rises into the air. The gardens also sell brightly colored carp for backyard ponds, which you can see in tanks behind the shop. The shop has a good selection of books on water plants and decorative fish. Lilypons is open Monday-Saturday, 9:30-4:30, from October through February; and Monday through Saturday, 9:30-5:30, and Sunday, 11-5:30, the rest of the year.

Thurmont

CATOCTIN WILDLIFE PRESERVE AND ZOO
13019 Catoctin Furnace Road
☎ 301-271-3180
www.CWPZoo.com
Admission: $9.95, adults; $7, seniors (over 60); $6.75, children

This 26-acre park has not only exotic animals – such as a golden tiger, a rare black jaguar, monkeys, grizzly bear, alligator and a huge Seychelles giant tortoise – but a petting area where kids can get close to goats, rabbits, ducks, geese and other farm animals. It is well designed for families, with an emphasis on learning about the animals. There are special programs, such as the 2 pm daily talk with the grizzly bear's keeper. When it's appropriate, signs encourage further interaction, telling, for example, that the 575-pound tortoise enjoys having his head scratched. The preserve is open daily, 9-6, from May through September; daily, 10-5, in April and October; and weekends, 10-4, in March and November.

Recreation

Frederick Area

CARROLL CREEK LINEAR PARK

Between East and West Patrick Streets and All Saints Street
Frederick

The canalized creek runs through the center of Frederick, and a very attractive promenade along its banks makes a pleasant and easy 1.15-mile stroll. You can follow it from the Delaplaine Visual Arts Center on South Carroll Street, across Bentz Street, to the 44-acre Baker Park. Benches invite you to stop and watch the antics of skateboarders or listen to a summer concert.

The carillon tower in Baker Park has concerts on Sunday afternoons.

Potomac River Area

RIVER AND TRAIL OUTFITTERS

604 Valley Road (off US-340)
across the river from Harpers Ferry
Knoxville
☎ 301-695-5177
www.rivertrail.com

For those not interested in canoeing, River and Trail Outfitters rents tubes on the historic Antietam Creek.

These outfitters offer rafting trips on the Shenandoah River and on Antietam Creek in the spring. Canoe and kayak trips explore both the Potomac and the Shenandoah and beginner canoe trips are of varying length on the Potomac.

Their rates are $50 per day ($90 for a weekend), including two paddles, vests and shuttle within 25 miles. River and Trail will also provide shuttle service for your own canoe.

BLUE RIDGE OUTFITTERS
PO Box 750, Harpers Ferry WV 25425
☎304-725-3444
www.broraft.com

You can rent mountain bikes from Blue Ridge in Harpers Ferry or join them for a guided trip along the C&O Canal. Rentals and trips include bike, helmet, maps, shuttle and water bottle. Rates are $20 per day for rentals; special packages and trips vary. Reserve ahead for either and they will give you rental pick-up information.

C&O CANAL NATIONAL HISTORIC PARK
Parallel to the Potomac River
Southwest of Frederick

One of the primary routes for supplies and provisions for the westward migration, the canal runs along the entire western side of this area, following the route of the Potomac River, which is too shallow for navigation much of the year. The railroad and canal companies raced to control commerce with the new settlements in the west, and the railroad finally won. But the canal builders have left us some of the most remarkable architecture of America's industrial age. These are some of the highlights, going northwest along the route of the canal.

The **Monocacy Aqueduct**, near Dickerson, was built between 1828 and 1833 and is 536 feet long.It has become one of the icons of the canal and, in fact, of transportation history. Carrying the canal across the Monocacy River, the aqueduct is made entirely of stone, most of it red quartzite mined from nearby

Sites along the C&O canal are all shown on the excellent free map distributed by the National Park Service and readily available throughout the area.

Sugarloaf Mountain. The stone was carried to the canal by a specially built tramway and by boat down the Monocacy River. Sugarloaf Mountain is visible from the marker in the center of the aqueduct. The Confederacy tried several times to destroy the Monocacy Aqueduct but could never blow it up. The aqueduct is now shored up in a harness, awaiting restoration, but you can walk or cycle across it.

A few miles west of Point of Rocks is the last arch remaining from the **Catoctin Aqueduct**. A series of locks at Harpers Ferry took the canal around rapids on the Potomac. A short distance upstream is **Antietam Creek Aqueduct**, one of the nicest remaining on the canal.

You can reach these canal landmarks by following Route 28 from I-270 in Rockville. From Frederick, take Route 85 to Route 28, near Nolands Ferry, and travel a short distance south. Signs for the Monocacy Aqueduct are on Route 28. To reach other canal sites, follow Route 28 west and look for signs. Harpers Ferry is connected directly to Frederick by US 340.

Thurmont Area

CUNNINGHAM FALLS STATE PARK
Route 77 (Catoctin Hollow Road)
Southwest of Thurmont
☎ 301-271-7574
Day-use fee, $2 per car; weekends, $1 per person.

Cunningham Falls State Park, named for one of the tallest falls in the state, is a major outdoor recreational area. The cascading falls drop more than 78 feet, in a series of small connected falls. Try to go the first sunny day after a rainy period to see the falls at their best. A 1½-mile walk over a good trail (although it has a lot of uphill sections) takes you to the falls from the parking lot. This park is popular with school groups, and it may be busy on weekdays. Access to the park and to the trail to the falls is well marked. Both fishing and boating in Hunting Creek Lake, a 43-acre body of water, make the park a favorite. Visitors can rent canoes at the lake. The park offers outdoor programs such as orienteering, wildflower identification and others, as well as picnic areas and playgrounds. The park is divided into the William Houck and Manor areas (look for signs on Catoctin Hollow Road for these and for the beach parking area for lake access).

CATOCTIN MOUNTAIN PARK
Route 77
☎ 301-663-9330
Free

Hiking, climbing and walking trails are the prime draw of this mountainside park that protects a section of the spine of the Appalachian Mountain Range, as it passes through Maryland on its way from Maine to Georgia. One trail leads from the visitors center to the remains of a mountain whiskey still, where illegal moonshine was once made.

Tours

Frederick Area

THE TOURISM COUNCIL OF FREDERICK COUNTY
19 East Church Street
☎ 301-663-8687 or 800-999-3613
Admission: $4.50, adults; $3.50, seniors; children under 12, free

Ninety-minute guided walking tours begin at the Council office; you can also get a brochure with a self-guided walking tour map of the city of Frederick, which leads you to most of the historic sites and significant buildings. The brochure has photos and short descriptions of sites. The map is marked to allow you to decide how long a walk you want. Tours are given Saturdays, Sundays and most holiday Mondays at 1:30 pm from April through December.

LINGANORE WINECELLARS
13601 Glissans Mill Road (off Route 75)
Mount Airy
☎ 410-795-6432
www.linganore-wine.com

In addition to wines produced from grapes, Linganore has a selection of berry and fruit wines.

Linganore started producing wines in 1976 on their family-owned farm. The winery hosts tastings and tours and holds an outdoor festival the first weekend of June and the third weekends of July, August and September. Picnic tables and grills are available near their pond, making this a good place for a picnic. The last weekend of February brings wreath making, using their discarded vines. Linganore is open 10-5 weekdays, 10-6, Saturday and noon-6 Sunday, except major holidays.

FREDERICK CARRIAGE COMPANY

☎ 301-694-7433
Cost: about $40 for a 30-minute ride or $65 for a 60-minute ride for up to four people

Tour Frederick in the style of its founders, by horse-drawn carriage. The cost of the trip will depend on the size of the vehicle, but a family of four (or up to six if most are small children) can ride in a charming vis-à-vis carriage quite reasonably. Reservations are required; call the carriage company directly or reserve through the Tourism Council of Frederick County (page 338), ☎ 301-663-8687 or 800-999-3613.

Westminster Area

CARROLL COUNTY VISITORS CENTER

210 East Main Street
☎ 410-848-1388, 800-272-1933

Local historians not only take you to see the sights, but tell interesting stories that include subjects from architecture to ghosts. To tour any time on your own, look in the tourist office for the free guide and map called *A Walking Tour of Carroll County – Westward Expansion*. The 90-minute walk takes you past 31 historic properties built between 1800 and 1915. The Center also offers a Ghost Walk brochure and map that leads past eight haunted sites; among these is the split tombstone of Legh Master (see *The Story of Legh Master*, page 352) in the churchyard of Ascension Church. Another tour visits the site of Corbit's Charge, an in-town battlefield where Captain Charles Corbit and a small troop of Union soldiers held off the cavalry of Jeb Stuart. The walking tour brochure describes the battle, in which the outnumbered Yanks held Stuart off long enough to delay his arrival at Gettysburg.

Also available at the information center in Westminster is *A Walking Tour of Courthouse Square*, which gives you details of a tour of the days of growth and prosperity when Westminster became a shire town. The buildings date from 1800 through 1900, but most were erected by 1840. The map and brochure describe each of the buildings. Guided tours are available; call the visitors center for information.

J-MAR-B
Smith Hill Farm
343 Springdale Road
New Windsor
☎ 410-848-9015

Smith Hill Farm offers covered wagon rides over back country roads that surround the farm. When snow is more than four inches deep, they do sleigh rides. Either vehicle is pulled by a team of registered Percherons, a breed of work horses seldom seen today. They have a collection of antique carriages and wagons used for special events. If you're interested, they teach the art of driving horse-drawn vehicles, too.

CYGNUS WINE CELLARS
3130 Long Lane, intersection of Routes 30 and 27, Manchester
☎ 410-374-6395

This small and growing winery has been open for business only since the mid 1990s but has already made a name for its reds, whites and sparkling wines. Cygnus is open Saturday and Sunday noon-5, otherwise by appointment.

Shop Till You Drop

Crafts

Frederick

CATOCTIN POTTERY
Lewis Mill, Poffenberger Road
Jefferson (west of Frederick on Route 180)
☎ 301-371-4274

Susan Hanson's fine pottery, which includes lamps, tableware and art pieces, is contemporary in style and colorfully glazed; the work is shown in the setting of a handsome old mill. The pottery is open Monday through Saturday, 10-5.

Antiques

Frederick

The city of Frederick alone has more than 20 antiques shops, most of which are along **East Patrick Street**, **Carroll Street** and around the intersection of **2nd** and **East Streets**. **Antique Station**, at 194 Johnson Drive, has 200 dealers in 35,000 square feet of showroom. The shops in Frederick have everything from furniture to china, pottery, glass and art. **New Market**, off I-70 east of Frederick, is also known for its antiques, with more than 16 shops lining Main Street and more on the adjoining streets.

Frederick County is one of the best areas of the state for antiques shopping.

Farmers Markets

Frederick

EVEREDY SQUARE AND SHAB ROW
Downtown Frederick

Several cafés and carry-out counters make Everedy Square a pleasant place to spend a rainy afternoon.

The Shab Row Farmers Market is open on Thursdays, June to October, 3-6 pm. This Market was created from several 19th-century buildings that were saved from demolition, restored, and converted into 30-plus shops selling everything from Irish clothing and crafts to antiques. Look here for such diverse items as stuffed animals, fine British antique furniture, pottery you can paint yourself, garden accessories, jewelry, housewares and home décor items and fudge.

After Dark

Performing Arts

Frederick

BALTIMORE SYMPHONY ORCHESTRA IN FREDERICK
PO Box 453, Frederick MD 21701
Call Sound Source ☎ 301-695-2633, code 6358, or 301-620-1798

The Baltimore Symphony has an annual season in Frederick that includes concerts in October, December, February and May at the Governor Thomas Johnson High School. The events feature rising guest conductors and soloists with programs of varied classical works. Tickets are about $25 for adults and under $10 for students.

WINEBURG CENTER FOR THE ARTS
20 West Patrick Street
☎ 301-228-2828

This performing arts center has a variety of music, theater and other arts events from October to May, as well as community events through the summer.

WAY OFF BROADWAY DINNER THEATRE
5 Willowdale Drive
☎ 301-662-6600
Admission: $29, Sunday; $30, Friday; $31, Saturday

Look for spirited renditions of works such as Neil Simon's *The Odd Couple* (maybe in its updated female version) performed in an intimate dinner theater setting. Dinner performances are Friday and Saturday evenings; there are also brunch performances on Sunday.

Westminster

THEATER ON THE HILL
Western Maryland College
☎ 410-857-2448

Each summer's program includes a children's musical, Broadway musicals and drama. Performances are held from June through August in the Dorothy Elderdice Theater, named for the costume designer, who lived in Westminster.

CARROLL PLAYERS
Various locations
☎ 410-876-2220

This lively theater company performs three or four shows a year, but has no permanent stage venue. Call them for a schedule of what, when and where.

Live Music

BALDWIN'S STATION
7618 Main Street
Sykesville
☎ 410-795-1041

The restaurant in the old railroad station offers live music performances featuring folk, traditional and contemporary blues several times a month. Reservations are a good idea, especially on weekends.

Bars & Discos

BREWER'S ALLEY AT FREDERICK BREWING COMPANY
124 North Market Street
Frederick
☎ 301-631-0089 (301-694-7899 for brewery tours)

Lively, noisy – and very crowded on weekend evenings – brew-pub atmosphere in a chic, sleek setting that spills out onto the terrace in warm weather.

DOWN UNDER NITE CLUB & GRILL
4 West Main Street
Westminster
☎ 410-876-0320

Literally down under, this lively bar and club is underneath Johanssons restaurant, with DJ music and occasional live performances.

Best Places to Stay

ACCOMMODATIONS PRICE SCALE	
Inexpensive	under $100
Moderate	$100-$200
Expensive	$201-$300
Deluxe	more than $300

Frederick

McCLEARY'S FLAT
121 East Patrick Street
☎ 301-620-2433 or 800-774-7926
www.fwp.net/mcclearysflat
Moderate

The elegant and hospitable B&B occupies a lovingly restored 1876 Second Empire mansion in the heart of the antiques district, within walking distance of just about everything. We haven't seen a room we didn't like here, but our favorite is the Caroline McCleary Suite on the second floor. Warm and cheerful hosts serve a wonderful breakfast in their dining room, or on the patio. Parking is in a nearby public parking deck.

TYLER SPITE HOUSE
112 West Church Street
☎ 301-831-4455
Expensive

Around 1810, the owner of the land where the house sits disagreed with the town's plan to build a street. In order to prevent the building of the street he built this house, giving rise to the appellation "spite house." This inn is downtown in the historic district and is furnished with fine old antiques.

Thurmont

COZY COUNTRY INN
103 Frederick Road (Route 806)
☎ 301-271-4301, cozyville@aol.com
www.cozyvillage.com
Inexpensive to moderate

The Cozy is a long-time family operation that has served as temporary home to many of the well-known visitors to the nearby Presidential Retreat at Camp David. Journalists, media celebrities, domestic and foreign government officials and others without the pull to get into Camp David stay here – and enjoy it, as do plenty of other travelers. The clean and attractive rooms are themed to the administrations of the past eight Presidents, and one is dedicated to Winston Churchill, who ate here during the 1940s (see *Best Places to Eat*, page 374).

Westminster Area

WINCHESTER COUNTRY INN
111 Stoner Avenue
☎ 410-848-9343, 800-887-3950, fax 410-848-7409
Inexpensive

This fully restored 1760s period home is furnished with antiques of its period. The charming small B&B is the oldest house in the county and was the home of William Winchester, founder of Westminster. The B&B serves a full country breakfast and afternoon tea is available. It is opposite the entrance to the Farm Museum.

WOOD'S GAIN BED AND BREAKFAST
421 McKinstry's Mill Road
Linwood
☎ 410-775-0308
www.woodsgainbnb.com
Inexpensive to moderate

Ask your hosts at Wood's Gain about the Civil War history of the B&B and the neighboring main house.

This beautiful small B&B is one of our favorite places to stay in the area. Not only are the rooms beautifully done, but the hosts couldn't be nicer or more helpful. It's just a short distance out of Westminster on Route 75 between Union Bridge and Route 84. Rooms in the main house are furnished in family antiques, each with a private bath, but our favorite room is the Summer Kitchen, a two-story separate building that forms a two-room suite, furnished in country antiques and with the feel of your own private home. Breakfasts are splendid, served in the elegant family dining room. The first-floor guest room is fully handicapped-accessible.

BOWLING BROOK COUNTRY INN
6000 Middleburg Road
Middleburg
☎ 410-876-2893
Moderate

This quiet B&B is only 12 miles west of Westminster in the countryside. The farm was once the breeding and training ground of five consecutive Preakness winners (1878-82). It won't be a surprise, therefore, to find out that the six beautifully appointed guest rooms are named for race horses and race tracks. Guests enjoy a full country breakfast. A suite is available in a separate building. Middleburg is off Route 84 from Uniontown or off Route 194 from Keymar.

Best Places to Eat

DINING PRICE SCALE	
Inexpensive	Entrées are $10 or less
Moderate	Entrées are $11-$20
Expensive	Entrées are $21-$30

Just Outside Baltimore

BALDWIN'S STATION
7618 Main Street
Sykesville
☎ 410-795-1041
Moderate

Baldwin's really is a station, its dining rooms in an old railroad station, with summer dining on the old platform. Begin dinner with a nice selection of breads and a tasty tapenade as you decide between entrées such as grouper in an orange marmalade sauce, Louisiana-style fried chicken or rack of lamb. Dinner finishes off with nicely prepared chocolate pâté with crème anglaise, or perhaps strawberry shortcake of fresh berries over an almond biscuit. On the down side, we found the wines a bit pricey, and on our last visit the service was uneven. Live music performances several times a month feature folk, traditional and contemporary blues. Reservations are a good idea, especially on weekends.

Frederick

BREWER'S ALLEY AT FREDERICK BREWING COMPANY

124 North Market Street
☎ 301-631-0089 (301-694-7899 for brewery tours)
Inexpensive to moderate

Far from pub fare, the brewery serves unusual and well-prepared dishes such as Louisiana boudin with jumbo shrimp, chipotle-garlic grilled strip steak, or a pasta with Thai grilled chicken. They even have alligator on the menu as a delicious appetizer. The brewery produced its first batch of beer in 1993 and now brews and sells a golden, amber and red ale as well as a porter and a wheat beer. Seasonal special beers and their own birch beer soda are also available. Brewer's Alley is usually busy and noisy, attracting a young crowd on weekends.

THE PROVINCE RESTAURANT

129 North Market Street
☎ 301-663-1441
Moderate

The Province is well known for its desserts.

This downtown bistro presents imaginative American dishes, such as a seafood combo with herbed butter; veal Amontillado with almonds; pasta parmesan with shiitake mushrooms; veal piccata; or lamb chops seasoned with dill, Dijon mustard and garlic. Parisian Poulet is a delectable chicken scallopini in sherry, layered with brie. Prix-fixe dinners are offered Tuesday through Thursday, and on weekends brunch is available. The Province is open Tuesday-Sunday (except holidays) for lunch and dinner.

Index

Index

B

C

D

G

H

M

O

P

Q

R

S

Index

T

U

Z